GERMANY'S MASTER PLAN

The Story of Industrial Offensive

JOSEPH BORKIN and CHARLES A. WELSH

with an Introduction by THURMAN ARNOLD

DUELL, SLOAN AND PEARCE

NEW YORK

TO L. H.

A mighty maze, but not without a plan.

—Pope

ACKNOWLEDGMENTS

TO the Antitrust Division of the Department of Justice, the Office of Price Administration, the Board of Economic Warfare, the Alien Property Custodian, and the Foreign Funds Control of the Treasury Department, which, despite the many obstacles and the brilliant planning of the enemy, have done so much to fight successfully the economic war, and to the members of these agencies who helped in the growth of this book, our profoundest thanks.

To Walton Hale Hamilton, Professor of Law, Yale University, to Edward Levi, Chief of the Economic Warfare Unit of the Antitrust Division, to Ernest Meyers, Special Assistant to the Attorney General, to Myron Webster Watkins, Head of the Department of Economics, University College, New York University, and to William B. Ziff, author of *The Coming Battle of Germany*, our thanks for reading and criticizing the manuscript.

To Nathan B. Lenvin, of the Office of the Alien Property Custodian, and to Helen Frank, of the Antitrust Division, our thanks for their research assistance.

Thanks are due to Irene S. Driver and to Mary D. Waldron for their assistance in typing the manuscript, and to Mary Saunders, whom the authors helped to write this book, and whose editing and faith account for its completion.

It should be understood that this acknowledgment in no way constitutes an endorsement of the views expressed herein, by either the agencies or the individuals concerned. The authors assume sole responsibility for the views contained in this work.

Because of the official position of the authors, it should also be stated that this book does not necessarily constitute the views of the Department of Justice or the Office of Price Administration.

Our thanks also to the various publishers who have permitted us to quote from the following works:

"Winged Warfare," Major General H. H. Arnold and Colonel Ira C. Eaker, Harper & Brothers.

"The Day of the Saxon," Homer Lea, Harper & Brothers.

"Social and Economic History of Germany," W. F. Bruck, Oxford University Press.

"Behemoth, The Structure and Practice of National Socialism," F. Neumann, Oxford University Press.

"An American Doctor's Odyssey," Dr. Victor Heiser, W. W. Norton & Company, Inc.

"Merchants of Death," H. C. Engelbrecht and F. C. Hanighen, Dodd, Mead & Company, Inc.

"Cartels, Concerns and Trusts," R. Liefmann, E. P. Dutton & Co.

"The World Crisis," R. Hon. Winston Churchill, Charles Scribner & Sons.

"Memoirs of a Spy," N. Snowden, Charles Scribner & Sons.

"Geopolitics," B. Strausz-Hupé, G. P. Putnam & Sons.

"What Price Progress," Hugh Farrell, G. P. Putnam & Sons.

"Bottlenecks of Business," Thurman Arnold, Reynal & Hitchcock, Inc.

"Dyes and Dyeing," C. E. Pellew, Robert M. McBride & Company.

INTRODUCTION

THIS book is a brilliant and arresting exposition of the results of the disease of cartelization. In all commercial civilization great industries rise out of initiative and superior efficiency. At a certain stage in their growth, hardening of the arteries takes place. Industrial leaders believe that the time has come to rationalize and stabilize production. Restricted production, high cost, and low turnover become the order of the day. To maintain that order, new industry must be kept out of production and old industry must not produce too much because, according to this order of ideas, too much goods is not wealth but distress goods and an undesirable surplus. Prices and production become fixed at levels which will pay dividends on an existing capital structure. Industrial progress becomes sluggish and then stops. The productive capacity of the nation is curtailed. It is an order of ideas that can produce neither wealth in peace nor strength in war.

There is no short way of defining a cartel. For present purposes we may describe it briefly as a small ring of producers or distributors who have acquired control of domestic or foreign markets. That control is justified as a rationalization of industry management for the purpose of expert economic planning. It is used, however, to crush new enterprise and to prevent maximum production.

The first symptom of cartelization is an unbalanced exchange between organized industry which is restricting production and unorganized farmers and small businessmen who are unable to restrict production. The farmer becomes unable to buy enough industrial goods to keep factories running. Labor is laid off, thus restricting purchasing power still further. Goods pile up in domestic markets because they cannot be distributed at the artificial levels maintained by the cartel. People begin to talk about over-production, even in the face of scarcity in terms of actual need.

The next symptom is the attempt of the domestic cartels to control foreign markets so that the nation can get rid of this so-called over-production, this inconvenient wealth that threatens an artificial price structure. International cartels are formed, dominated by private groups without public responsibility, who control the foreign economic policy in the interests of international scarcity. With the growth of these international cartels democracy becomes a shell which conceals the power of private groups. Political freedom cannot exist except when it is founded upon industrial freedom. If a private group controls a man's livelihood it can control both his actions and his philosophy.

And so with the progression of the disease of cartelization. A new political philosophy arises justifying centralized planning of production and distribution. The
competitive race for efficiency which is symptomatic of
a young and vigorous commercial organization is de-
nounced as waste.

Socialists eagerly advocate this new order. Their only
quarrel with industrialists is in the selection of those
who will manage the brave new world. Socialists want
to recruit the managers from the ranks of the academic
thinkers sympathetic with the underdog. Industrialists
want to choose them from the cartel leaders. Both
groups are ready to abandon industrial democracy. Thus
a culture that is willing to embrace a political dictator-
ship spreads over the thinking of the Nation.

In the first stage of this struggle between socialists
and cartel managers the industrialists win because they
start out in the seats of power. They fail to maintain that
power, however, because their policy of stabilizing prices
at home prevents the distribution of goods—creating
idle capital and idle labor—want in the midst of plenty.
Before Hitler's rise to power, Germany had reached a
stage under private cartel domination when agricultural
products, though scarce, sold at ruinously low prices.
Industrial products, though plentiful, could not be distributed in Germany. The wheels of industry stopped.
There was an irreducible minimum of 7,000,000 unem-
ployed.

When private industry fails to distribute goods, Government is compelled to step in. Deficit financing, subsidies, and huge relief rolls grow with alarming rapidity. In this stage the writers and thinkers of a socialistic tinge flood into Government with dreams of a new world arising out of the collapse of capitalism. But, unfortunately, for socialistic dreamers the techniques of acquiring and holding power in times of economic chaos require individuals of a tougher and less humanitarian mould. In other words, only a Hitler had the ruthlessness and cold cruel realism to consolidate a position of power out of the collapse of the German economic structure which the cartels had brought about.

And thus the vast centralized cartel organization of Germany became a tool in the hands of a dictator who no longer operated for private profit but solely to serve a ruthless ambition. The cartels of the democracy were easy dupes. Hitler was able to aid them in restricting their own production, while Germany's production went ahead by leaps and bounds.

The soft and opulent business organizations of England and America were intent on the pursuits of their short-run policies of restricted production, high costs and low turnover. They saw in German cartels an ally, not an enemy.

To such international cartels we owe the peace of Munich. To our own cartels we owe the failure to expand American industry prior to Pearl Harbor. To the interests of these cartels in stabilizing prices and restricting production we owe our present scarcity in all basic materials.

To a large extent our present industrial unpreparedness of this war is due to the fact that Germany through international cartels built up its own production and assisted the democracies in restricting their production in electrical equipment, in drugs, in chemicals, in basic war materials such as magnesium and aluminum. International cartels with the active assistance of American interests have operated to deprive us of markets in our own hemisphere by giving them away to Germany.

We are now faced with the necessity of making our industrial democracies so efficient that we can win this war, which is essentially a war of industrial production. Our cartel structure has weakened us spiritually by introducing an alien philosophy which leads us to distrust our own economic traditions. It has weakened us materially by making us afraid of full production because it creates surpluses which cannot be distributed after the war.

We must, if we are to fight this war with enthusiasm for our own way of life, destroy both the philosophy and the private power of domestic and international cartels over foreign and domestic economic policy. At such a time this book should be read by everyone interested in the economic future of America.

No other book that I know of analyzes in such vivid

detail the growth and activities of international cartels. The writers have studied the cartel problem not only from books but from first-hand information and observation. Mr. Joseph Borkin has been for many years Economic Advisor to the Antitrust Division, Department of Justice, particularly in relation to foreign international cartels. The fact that the public is now aware of the international cartel structure is in a large measure due to his work. Mr. Welsh is an authority on international trade and finance, and is a cartel expert for the Office of Price Administration. Both of them have shown exceptional ability in this particular field.

While of necessity the emphasis of this book is upon the war problem, I would suggest that the reader consider it in the light of the long-run economic policy for America. We cannot turn over our future economic policy to private groups without public responsibility as we have done in the past. We not only must win the war but the peace which follows. We cannot win the peace if the cartel problem remains unsolved.

I must conclude this introduction with a caveat because of my official position. The research and conclusions of the writers of this book have been done outside of their official duties in the Government. They have not been checked or approved in any official way.

THURMAN W. ARNOLD.

CONTENTS

xvii

GERMANY'S MASTER PLAN

1. THE GRAND ILLUSION

THIS Global War is fought in the twilight of a military and economic age. Had Germany waited for the dawn of the coming era to launch its onslaught the fate of the world would have been sealed.

The tragic consequences of too little and too late which plague the United Nations have an ironic compensation. Germany struck too soon.

For this one reason have we been granted a brief hour of respite. In this short interval of time we must exploit our chance or perish.

Because Germany precipitated war before the master plan for conquest was completed, her armies at the end of 1942 were spread from the Barents Sea to the Mediterranean, from the Channel Islands to the Caucasus,—conquerors, but not victorious. The most comprehensive blueprint for empire which the world has known was meticulously drafted over a period of twenty years by German militarists. But, like Imperial Germany in 1914, the Third Reich made a fundamental and irrevocable error in the execution of its designs. How this master plan was created, and why it was mistimed, are

3

questions which the world must ask and answer now,
lest Germany regain its impetus sufficiently to win, in
this or in another Global War.

To wage a war in modern times is to weld into a
gigantic machine the resources of our technological arts.
Petroleum, rubber, and a host of chemicals are the fuel
of War, light and heavy metals its armor. Without
aluminum, magnesium, tin, tungsten, molybdenum,
quinine, those who would fight a Global War cannot
long survive. The buttress of our strategy rested secure
in the knowledge that we, not they, commanded these
resources. The aluminum, the tin, the manganese, the
nickel, the quinine, the oil, and the rubber are drawn
from the bowels of an earth which was our preserve.
The seven seas were the private lakes on which our ships
patrolled, and which the guns of our battle-wagons ruled
without a rival. Any nation who would challenge this
supremacy was doomed to failure.

On this grand illusion we gazed unperturbed as Germany marched into the Rhineland, effected Anschluss
with Austria, and negotiated Munich. These were paper
victories. We still controlled the reservoirs of power,
and Germany could not tap them. Prophets of victory
predicted German collapse from every conceivable point
of view. The few voices that were raised in question
were shouted down or shrugged aside. Thus were the
books of judgment reckoned.

Those who saw in airpower the horizon of a new

world were execrated for suggesting that a battleship could be jettisoned by a flying artillery platform. Not since gunpowder erased the bloom of chivalry and made the armor of knighthood a museum piece had there been an equal convulsion in military relationships. As gunpowder had given war a greater range, so airpower opened up a new dimension. In this new relativity of space, the battleship became a quarry. Norway, Pearl Harbor, and Singapore are tragic memorials to the vision of the Cassandras who foretold the doom of ships.

For seventy years the grand strategy of Great Britain in her struggle with the growing might of Germany has been embodied in the British fleet. Blockade—enforced by British dreadnaughts and supported by the naval power of the United States—has been the basic element of Britain's hope to thwart the German menace. This policy has been traditional—fixed and rooted in the economic and military structure of the Empire. In 1914, as in 1939, Great Britain and her Allies pivoted their plan to beat back the German thrust on a policy of containment. Simple in its grandeur and apparent impregnability, this barricade of the sea lanes had the semblance of a wall which the mailed fist could never breach. Winston Churchill with dramatic eloquence etched the articles of British faith on the eve of Germany's first lunge: "Consider these ships, so vast in themselves, yet so small, so easily lost to sight on the surface of the waters. . . . They were all we had. On them, as we conceived, floated the might, majesty, dominion and power of the British Empire."

Germany has always understood the fixed and rigid strategy which Britain must pursue. What other course was open to the Island State? Obsessed with the necessity of expansion, Germany tirelessly probed the seams and joints in the British dike. The test tubes glowed and sputtered in German laboratories, and Britain's bulwark slowly began to rot.

In 1912 explosives for Krupp's cannon were still in hostage to the nitrate beds of Chile. The long haul across the seas dominated by Great Britain was the leash which bound Germany to peace. In 1913 Germany cut the knot by making nitrates out of air. In 1914 Germany went to war.

The von Schlieffen Plan called for a swift and irresistible march to Paris, to end the war with a paralyzing blow which would numb the will of her opponents to resist. Because von Schlieffen was not diligently obeyed, the war lasted longer than had been expected, and hence was lost.

The tourniquet of ships remorselessly constricted the German arteries of supply. Nitrates alone could not stave off the rusting of the German mechanism. Forced at last to retire, Germany studied the imprisoning cordon with even greater care. Britain and the United States relaxed, more sure than ever that the barrier held firm. But they reckoned without the cunning of German

militancy. As technology went forward and German industry became more integrated, its dependence on the
outer world increased. With every addition to the myriad of materials not found within the Reich, it seemed
to Britain that the German threat diminished. Germany
had no oil; a new war would require fathomless re-
serves. Great Britain and the United States controlled
the wells of more than half the globe; the United Nations controlled them all. Germany had no rubber; Britain doled it from Malaya to the world. It was impossible for Germany ever to escape this strangulation in
another war.

Britain was not alone in her assurance. The United
States withdrew in haughty isolation. Even if the have-
not power on the Continent should, in desperation,
chance another reckless try, Britain and our eastern sea-
board were secure.

The sweep of German aims in German history has
had one all-embracing theme: world conquest. The
scope and scale of Germany's long-range plan is measured by its grasp of Allied limitations. The principles
of this scheme have been made plain by the sequence of
events. The conquest of the Continent could never yield
enough to be a recompense for the wealth beyond the
sea. To nullify blockade and remove the function of the
British fleet, Germany strove for decades to become a
fortress of self-sufficiency. Cartels became the unit of
German business, and industry was geared to the engine

of the war machine. Once started, the "wheels ran truly," and with increasing speed ground out the where-withal for war.

The German military effort is epitomized in blitz-krieg. But fundamental to the choice of weapons was the desire to end forever Britain's mandate of the seas. Unable to meet the British fleet on an equal plane, Germany failed in the World War to undermine it by the submarine. Now navies could be overwhelmed from above. Heinkels, Messerschmitts, and Focke-Wulfs were the synthesis of firepower on land and sea.

Light metals, high octane aviation gas, synthetic rubber—products of German wizardry—all were marshalled for the coming blow. Air transport was to be the hub from which, in any direction, Germany might capitalize its interior position. Cold logic prescribed the merger of economic and air command. Hence, the warlords tied all planning to the growth of the Luftwaffe.

The execution of these designs hinged on the evolution of technology. The harbingers of scientific change were visible in 1918. Implacable in its devotion to conquest, Germany strained to hasten the new industrial revolution to a point where its optimum force could be turned against the world. In this broad pattern the cartels were more than centers of research and business. They took their place as an integral part in the projection of Germany's program.

Armed with patents, the German cartels laid siege

to the economies of prospective antagonists. How perfectly these tactics interlocked in the design is evident in the succession of maneuvers which made up German policy during the 1920's. A planned inflation liquidated the cost of the first World War. From the day that Hjalmar Schacht stabilized the mark, Germany extended an alluring invitation to foreign capital. The victors, not the vanquished, paid for German reconstruction and rearmament.

Suddenly in 1926 Germany made known a portentous discovery: oil could be obtained from coal, and rubber could be obtained from oil. The obstructions on the road to Armageddon were being cleared. War became a certainty. Only time and timing were in doubt.

It was as though at a given signal the seacocks of the British fleet were opened and the proud ships sank in futile dignity. The whole world strategy of the English-speaking nations had slipped its anchor and drifted aimlessly toward oblivion. It would seem incredible that in the halls of state in which the future of the English-speaking peoples was solemnly discussed there should not have been detected the direst omens of catastrophe. The chain was broken, and Germany was free once more to test the mettle of democracy. Casually, in obscure items in the journals of chemistry and commerce, hints appeared of German economic plans. Clouded in a fog of polysyllables, these notices caused no alarm to those who shaped our policies of State.

Within the realm of industry, however, clamorous conferences were held. Hurried visits to Germany by captains of finance testified to their concern. Contracts were made, interests protected, stability insured. Everywhere there was a feeling of relief. With workmanlike precision, Germany drew together in a grandiose plan of conquest the fears of businessmen, the indolence of politicians, the apathy of democratic peoples, and fashioned in her factories the weapons which would shatter Allied strategy.

Germany struck too soon. Confident that her new technology had given her the implements of certain victory, Germany made—for us—a fortunate miscalculation. Her new machine was not quite ready: it could demolish a decadent France, but could not leap the Channel; it could provide all German needs if victory came fast; it could not touch Detroit.

Whether this forced haste only delays German victory or deals it a mortal blow is for us to decide. We now can grasp the industrial initiative. A few more years might have been enough for the full fruition of the new technology, and Germany would have been unconquerably stronger. Would this postponement have found the democracies armed for the new era? If history is any guide, the same smugness which greeted Germany's development of oil from coal and the rising might of Germany's airpower would have continued to prevail.

Nothing less than Dunkirk could disturb the peaceful slumbers of democracy.

These new scientific forces may yet reach their zenith during the present war. We are in a race in which technology is the decisive, telling factor. In the words of Lieutenant-General H. H. Arnold, chief of our own Air Force, "It may be that the next national determination will be that the nation which produces one thousand 10,000-mile bombers first will be able to conquer or save the world." [1]

2. THE INDUSTRIAL OFFENSIVE

EVERY junkheap of scrap rubber, every pile of aluminum pots and pans which Americans build in public squares is an unwitting tribute to the efficiency of German cartel warfare. As the war progresses, the true significance of shortage becomes clearer. Because of cartels,* critical military goods are either unobtainable or must be carefully rationed to the Army, the Navy, and the Air Force.

The sound and fury of Global War assail our minds. In the tumult of blitzkrieg and terror, we overlook the industrial offensive which Germany began long before the zero hour.

The United Nations were not prepared for the storm

---

* Like the term "pool" or "trust," the term "cartel" is subject to various interpretations. As used herein a cartel means a combination or agreement, national or international in scope, in which the members, whether corporations or governments, seek to control one or more phases of the production, pricing, and distribution of a commodity. Most cartels of the modern type are trusts which govern whole fields of technology through patents, know-how, or control of facilities. World industries dependent upon localized raw materials are cartellized by similar methods. Cartels in democratic countries are formed for two purposes: to eliminate competition and to offset the hazards to vested interests which derive from technological change. In totalitarian states cartels are instruments of national policy, and in a warlike country, such as Germany or Japan, cartels take their place in the scheme of warfare.

12

of propaganda or the lightning thrusts of Axis arms. Surprise attacks wrought havoc in our defenses, and the strategy of terror demoralized whole nations. We have recovered from the initial shock and pain inflicted on us. But because we disregarded the industrial war which Germany waged through cartels, we fight today distracted by the gaps in the fabric of our economy left by cartels.

Wherever there was a cartel before, in 1942 there was a military shortage. The Army and Navy petitioned civilians to turn in binoculars and lenses. The Baruch Committee reported that if we do not solve the synthetic rubber problem, we face a "civilian and military collapse." The gallant stand of MacArthur's men on Bataan became more desperate because they found themselves without quinine. The growing priority lists of chemicals and plastics were an inventory of cartels. When we tried to tool up our new factories, with every second of passing time working against us, the lack of tungsten carbide blunted the edge of our effort. This roster of scarce materials and the absence of substitutes have a common cause.

These shortages speak volumes for the brilliant planning of the German offensive. The first "Report to the Nation," issued January 14, 1942, by the Office of Facts and Figures, says:

> [The enemy] has worked for many years to weaken our military potential. Through patent controls and

cartel agreements he succeeded in limiting American production and export of many vital materials. He kept the prices of these materials up and the output down. He was waging war, and he did his work well, decoying important American companies into agreements, the purpose of which they did not sense. Our businessmen were peaceful traders. The enemy's businessmen were and are all over the world agents of aggression.

The list of materials affected is long—beryllium, optical instruments, magnesium, tungsten carbide, pharmaceuticals, hormones, dyes, and many more. When you match each product with its military use, the significance of the attack becomes clear. Beryllium is a vital element for alloys that make shell springs; magnesium makes airplanes and incendiary bombs; tungsten carbide is essential for precision machine tools.

Concealed behind dummy corporations, the enemy went unchecked for years, *using our own legal machinery to hamstring us.* [Italics added]

During the past twenty years, this cartel device has been the first line of German assault. Not all cartels were controlled by German concerns. Yet, because restriction in other countries served the interests of Germany, every Dutch, English, or American monopolist who signed a contract or instituted a policy limiting his output added to German power.

In the years immediately preceding war, the com-

parative production figures of the United States and
Germany for those materials on which twentieth-century
military efficiency most depends were all in Germany's
favor. In 1939, Germany's plants were capable of turning out 100,000 tons of synthetic rubber. Our plants
were still experimental, making none for commercial
use. In 1938, Germany produced 175,000 tons of
aluminum. The United States made only 130,000 tons.
Germany's magnesium plants poured forth over 16,000
tons of this new metal. We made 3,000 tons. Germany
produced and used in its machine tools and armaments
from twelve to twenty times more tungsten carbide than
the United States.

The effects of Axis victories, in Europe and in the
Pacific, give them an advantage which we will spend
many thousands of lives to overcome. This reversal of
position is starkly evident in the following figures on
some of the major resources:

PERCENTAGE OF AXIS CONTROL OF WORLD PRODUCTION [1]

	1938	*1942*
Rubber	0	91.1
Cement	33.7	51.6
Coal and Lignite	32	45.4
Iron Ore	7.3	44.6
Manganese Ore	10	34.9
Tin Ore	9.4	73.2
Bauxite	25.2	65.8

These figures have sombre implications for the United Nations. The unused capacity of each industrial plant which was left idle because of cartel agreements increased Germany's lead. Our control of many raw materials has been wrested from us. But we lost as much or more by wilful and willing restriction of output and capacity. Stupidity multiplied by cupidity, the desire for "business as usual," was the mark of the cartel mind. Germany counted on such behavior, and was aided at every turn by its results.

Germany has long understood this strategy of total war. Karl von Clausewitz,* the father of modern German militarism, set out its major premise when he said, "War is no independent thing; the main lineaments of all great strategic plans are of a political nature, the more so the more they include the totality of War and the State." To von Clausewitz, peace was a continuation of war by other means. In effect, he said to Germany, "Disarm your enemy in peace by diplomacy and trade if you would conquer him more readily on the field of battle." This philosophy of war-in-peace became the keynote of Germany's political and economic intercourse with other nations. These tenets explain why, twice within a generation, we have entered war not only facing the might of German armies, but shackled by economic bondage to German industry.

* 1780-1831.

German-controlled cartels were at all times the servants of German interest. That their loyalty to Germany was undivided explains the uniformity of the agreements which they made. Germany's industrial attack had as its cardinal purpose the reversal of blockade. Patents and secret "know-how" were used to bar our access to our own technology.

The first World War should have taught democratic nations that Germany used international cartels as the spearheads of aggression. Neither before 1914 nor before 1939 would the industrialists and financiers of the democracies learn the destructive meaning of this outlook. To businessmen in the United States, England, and France, international cartels were an efficient means of guaranteeing monopoly. Industrialists outside of Germany thought in terms of low output, high prices, and maximum profits. They regarded divisions of both territory and fields of production as comfortable and easily policed methods by which they could free themselves from competition and create spheres of monopoly.

The softest impeachment that can be made of those American, British, and French industrialists who consorted with German interests is that they knew not what they did. This is an alarming commentary on the profound political astigmatism of the proud management groups responsible for our industrial welfare. That our loss of the industrial initiative and the rupturing of our

military potential have not had more serious consequences can be credited, not to any foresight of monopolists or of government, but to the inherent flexibility
of democracy. Despite its many weaknesses, democracy
does have "grace under pressure."

3. I.G.—THE VIALS OF WRATH

NO better insight into the German strategy of economic war could be contrived than the history of Interessen Gemeinschaft Farbenindustrie Aktiengesellschaft, commonly known as I.G.*

The record of I.G. in the twentieth century is a recital of Germany's attempt to use scientific achievements to control the world. I.G.'s commercial peacetime monopolies have been the support for its services to German militarism. I.G. has never foregone an opportunity to turn a pretty penny in a business sense, however, if Germany's interest permitted. Time after time financial profit has been subordinated by I.G. to nationalistic aims. While I.G. may prefer to gain its own ends and enhance the power and wealth of Germany by economic means, it has consistently abetted and given force to purely military plans. The audit of I.G.'s contributions to Germany's martial designs is long.

The antecedents of I.G. reach far back into the industrial revolution of the nineteenth century, specifically into those developments which resulted in the establish-

* Community of Interest of Dye Industries, Incorporated.

19

ment of the coal tar chemical industry. The history of coal tar chemicals is in itself one of the most fascinating phases of nineteenth-century industrial development.

In 1856 in the course of his experiments with coal tar, theretofore regarded as an interesting but essentially useless material, a young English chemist, William Henry Perkin, found that it could be transformed into a synthetic aniline dye. This discovery was to bring Perkin (later Sir William) world-wide acclaim. The glory of a major scientific contribution belongs to Perkin and to England, but Germany usurped the gain. At the time of his discovery Perkin was only 18, still a student of the famous Professor Hofmann at the Royal College in London. Perkin had started out, strangely enough, to prepare artificial quinine. He wound up with a delicate purple solution called mauveine, which was to give name to the Mauve Decade, and to color the future military and industrial history of the world.

Perkin himself understood the profound and revolutionary nature of his findings, but the mentally stuffy industrialists of Victorian England failed to grasp their significance. Exhibiting a complacency which would repeatedly imperil the British Empire as the future unfolded, neither the Government nor British capital supported Perkin's struggles to found a coal tar industry. In time this lack of insight so exasperated Perkin that he reproached them for the dalliance and lack of imagination which cost them the industry.[1] Had Perkin's genius and patriotism been given the recognition it merited, England could have become the leader of the organic chemical industry. What is more, there might have been no I.G., and without I.G. Germany could not, twice within a generation, have filled the vials of wrath and hurled their Prussic acid in the face of the world. What might have been was not to be. Perkin's brilliance could not compensate for the dilettante attitude of the universities toward chemical research or the dullness of official and financial minds.

If England was not sufficiently prompt and alert to change, Germany immediately seized on Perkin's discovery. Within a few short years the parent firms of I. G. Farben had been established, and their grip on the dyestuffs industry made secure. German chemists entered upon a perfect frenzy of research. Perkin's own teacher, Hofmann, returned to Germany and helped found the new laboratories. When Perkin's next contribution to the industry, the preparation of an equivalent for natural red dye (madder), was announced and patented, he found that Dr. Caro of the Badische Anilin Works had been before him. Perkin's patent was dated June 26, 1869, Caro's had been issued June 25. The processes were somewhat different, but the Germans had won a major research victory symbolizing their capture of the initiative in the field, which they never lost.

Because of Germany's "patent" system in those early years, there were no barriers to the foundation of the industry. The well-financed organizations formed between 1856 and 1880 expended huge sums on research and chemical facilities. As early as the end of the Franco-Prussian War, the ancestors of I. G. Farben were all strong "going" concerns. Once under way, the establishment of the German patent system of 1877 placed in their hands a shield and a spear. German patents in the hands of German industry have been a branch of German arms since that time.

The names of the firms which were eventually to become the I.G. are worth noting, for their trademarks have carried the banner of German economic imperialism to every land. These firms are:

1. Badische Anilin & Soda Fabrik, of Ludwigshafen;
2. Farbenfabriken vorm. Friedrich Bayer & Co., of Leverkusen;
3. Farbwerke vorm. Meister Lucius and Bruening, of Hoechst am Main;
4. Aktiengesellschaft für Anilinfabrikaten, of Berlin;
5. Leopold Cassela & Co., m.b.H., of Frankfurt;
6. Kalle & Co., A. G., of Biebrick.*

These concerns in time became known as the "Big Six" and were from their inception primarily responsible for the amazing growth of the German chemical industry. Germany's economic might was "built out of a sandbox" by her chemical and metallurgical industries,

* See Appendix.

and the Big Six were the principal artificers of the gigantic structure. The methodical but almost frenetic determination which inspired German research did not observe any scruples in "borrowing" inventions from other countries. As Perkin told the story to Lord Exmouth:

> He went so far as to say that, for years before he left the business, he and other English chemists had entirely abandoned attempts to patent their discoveries in Berlin. He had found, by sad experience, that whenever he sent over an application for a patent on a new dyestuff, or new chemical compound of importance, the German Patent Office would at once call in, for consultation, the leading German chemists who were interested in that line of work. He would get request after request for more and more detailed information about every part of the process; and then, when they had got from him every bit of information that they could, they would grant the patent to some one of his German competitors. . . .[2]

The attitude taken by the German chemical concerns toward the industries of other nations reflected the same chauvinistic inspiration that underlay her political and military views: an overweening ambition to acquire a "place in the sun," driven by a transcendental assumption of the predestined supremacy of German *Kultur*. While this psychological motivation may have been mystical and even irrational, the commercial relations of the Big Six exhibit a completely realistic "trading philosophy" in the course of their transactions with other countries and in the adaptability of their management to domestic political and social changes.

Rapid growth, increasing economic power, and a tendency to carry industrial integration both vertically and horizontally to its limits favored the Big Six in their single-minded pursuit of world-monopoly in the organic chemical field. After it was too late, England realized that it had lost the coal tar industry. The British Government became aware that the German economic offensive had been mounted, and that the citadel of England's historic industrial leadership had been surrounded. That the tactics of I.G. today are an extension of the early practices of its forebears is witnessed by the statements of Joseph Chamberlain in 1883 and Lloyd George in 1907. Chamberlain, speaking in support of the proposed compulsory licensing of patents in Great Britain, said:

It has been pointed out especially in an interesting memorial presented on behalf of the chemical industry that under the present law it would have been possible, for instance, for the German inventor of the hot blast furnace, if he had chosen to refuse a license in England, to have destroyed almost the whole iron industry of this country and to carry the business bodily over to Germany. Although that did not happen in the case of the hot blast industry, it had actually happened in the manufacture of artificial colors connected with the coal products, and the whole of that had gone to Germany because the patentees would not grant a license in this country.[3]

In commenting on this, Lawrence Langner, a well-known authority on International Patent Law, says:

In other words, the first British compulsory license law was directed against the practice of the Germans in taking out patents on the chemical industry in England and using those patents to kill the British chemical industry.[4]

Lloyd George reiterated Chamberlain's view in 1907, in discussing prospective revision of British patent law, stating that:

Big foreign syndicates have one very effective way of destroying British industry. They first of all apply for patents on a very considerable scale. They suggest every possible combination, for instance, in chemicals, which human ingenuity can possibly think of. These combinations the syndicates have not tried themselves. They are not in operation, say, in Germany or elsewhere, but the syndicates put them in their patents in obscure and vague terms so as to cover any possible invention that may be discovered afterward in this country.[5]

In 1904 one of the decisive events of modern economic history transpired almost unnoticed. Dr. Carl Duisberg, one of Germany's foremost chemists, later Chairman of the Board of I. G. Farben, prepared a special report in which he proposed the complete unification of the Big Six into an Interessengemeinschaft.

The three largest firms, Badische, Bayer, and Berlin, immediately entered into the first I.G. in 1904. Shortly afterward, Hoechst, Kalle, and Cassela formed a separate cartel. Mutual competition was eliminated, and technical experience and resources were pooled, with the result that the German twins had attained an almost absolute monopoly in the organic dyestuffs, pharmaceutical, explosive, and synthetic chemical industries of the world. Within a few years the two groups were fully united, and in 1916, when the Weiler ter Meer and the Griesheim Elektron companies were brought in, I. G. Farben's internal integration was complete.

From 1904 to 1914, I.G. made every effort to overcome Germany's dependence on foreign sources of supply. The preparation for the first "Chemists' War" in those ten years was carried on with characteristic Teutonic thoroughness. The chemical industry was welded into a huge arsenal. The economic structures of the countries which stood in Germany's way were corroded by systematic infiltration of I.G.'s chemical patents. Germany in 1904 was dependent on Chilean deposits for the nitrates used in fertilizers and explosives. The outbreak of the war was delayed several years until I.G. had perfected the Haber process for artificially fixing nitrogen. Literally, I.G. plucked enough nitrates from the air to feed German farms and cannon.

No sooner had war begun than the High Command cast about for a new and secret weapon with which to surprise the Allies. I.G. placed in the hands of the Kaiser's legions one of the most terrible of all implements of war: poison gas, the use of which was suggested by the same Professor Haber who had solved the nitrate problem.

Major Victor Lefebure, British Liaison Officer between Britain and its Allies on Chemical Warfare, reported on the preliminary research on gas at the Kaiser Wilhelm Institute as follows:

. . . There is evidence that the Kaiser Wilhelm Institute and the physico-chemical institute near by were employed for this purpose as early as August, 1914. Reliable authority exists for the statement that soon after this date they were working with cacodyl oxide and phosgene, both well known before the war for their very poisonous nature, for use, it was believed, in hand grenades. Our quotations are from a statement by a neutral then working at the Institute. "We could hear the tests that Professor Haber was carrying out at the back of the Institute, with the military authorities, who in their steel-grey cars came to Haber's Institute every morning." "The work was pushed day and night, and many times I saw activity in the building at eleven o'clock in the evening. It was common knowledge that Haber was pushing these men as hard as he could." Sachur was Professor Haber's assistant. "One morning there was a violent explosion in the room in which most of this war work was carried out. The room was instantly filled with dense clouds of arsenic oxide." "The janitors began to clear the room by a hose and discovered Professor Sachur." He was very badly hurt and died soon after. "After that accident I believe the work on cacodyl oxide and phosgene was suspended and I believe that work was carried out on chlorine or chlorine compounds." "There were seven or eight men working in the Institute on these problems, but we heard nothing more until Haber went to the Battle of Ypres." [6]

It should be pointed out that the dyestuff plants required no "conversion" either to the manufacture of gases or explosives. The basic and intermediate dyes are in themselves the direct sources of numerous military products.

These efforts by I.G. were not so widely advertised as those of Krupp, but were even more important, for without them Krupp's cannon would have been useless. Ludendorff, Chief of the German General Staff:

> . . . supplements our information by telling us how he discussed the supply of war material with Herr Duisberg and Herr Krupp von Bohlen in Halbach, "whom I had asked to join the train" in the autumn of 1916. The former was the Chairman of the I.G., the great dye combine.[7]

Even today we do not know exactly when I.G. produced the new type of T.N.T. which was used in German shells. Germany lacked aluminum for metal alloys and thermite bombs. I.G. brought forth magnesium. If Germany finally succumbed, it was not for want of anything that I.G. could do.

The force which I.G. added to the German drive was given even greater impetus by the economic weakness of the Allies. Not only had I.G. fortified Germany against blockade, but I.G.'s control of patents and "know-how" made it almost impossible for England or the United States to build and operate the chemical plants they needed so desperately in the World War. In common with other German international concerns, I.G. representatives had for many years conducted the most complete industrial intelligence service then extant. The invaluable knowledge thus accumulated was analyzed both by the German Government and by a central industrial bureau. This mass of data, which included geographic surveys, plant blueprints, working methods, and every conceivable fact which might be relevant, was the original basis of geopolitical science. The I.G. Sekretariat in Berlin has been, since its formation, a clearing house for the observations of its representatives, and undoubtedly possesses a quantity of such data existing nowhere else on earth.

The value of I.G. to Germany in 1914-18 is summarized by Major Lefebure in "The Riddle of the Rhine" in prophetic language:

On broad lines, the pre-war and war activities of the I.G. produced the same result as an attempt to

strangle the economic life of possible opponents, en-
feebling their resistance to the subsequent delivery
of a hammer blow designed to take maximum advantage of the situation thus created. Twenty years or
more under the regime of a forceful economic policy,
not without its sinister aspects, prepared the ground
by weakening us in the concentrated chemical warfare
which ensued. The success of this policy maneuvered
us into such a position that we barely escaped defeat
under the hammer blows of German chemical aggression. This in fact appears to have been the German
conception of modern war in its relation to industry. . . .[8]

*   *   *

German sources tell us very little of the war activities and future significance of the I.G. A veil of se-
crecy seems to be cast over the whole matter, but behind this veil must exist an acute realisation of the
value of the I.G. as a trump card for the future.
Krupp is uncovered, the whole world was alarmed
at its meaning for war, but heard with a comfortable
sense of security how Krupp was exchanging the
sword for the plough. But the gigantic I.G. controls
in its great hand a sword or plough for war or peace
at will.[9]

Germany lost the war, but neither by this loss nor
during the period of social unrest and inflation which
followed was the strength of the chemical combine viti-
ated. I.G. was stronger at the end of the World War
than at its beginning, because the war increased the

tempo of its production. While it ostensibly passed through a critical period of reorganization, it actually lost no time in surveying its future possible courses of conduct, and reforming its network of commercial contracts with the markets of the victors.

The failure of the Allies to recognize that I.G. was not disarmed was not only criticized by Lefebure but by all who had directly suffered from the war activities of I.G. This oversight, whether due to the political myopia of the Allies themselves or to the astute dissemblance of the guiding interests in I. G. Farben, had repercussions in the war to come. I.G. concealed from prying eyes what it could of its real operations. The British Chemical Mission in March 1920 reported that:

. . . the German manufacturers, consisting of the powerful I.G. combination, were careful to do all in their power to hinder the work of inspection.[10]

An American observer, Lieutenant McConnel of the United States Navy, states:

. . . Upon arrival at the plant the Germans displayed a polite but sullen attitude. They seemed willing to afford the opportunity of a cursory inspection, but strongly objected to a detailed examination. On the third day of the visit the writer was informed that his presence had become a source of serious objection and that if his examination were prolonged a formal complaint would be submitted to the Peace Conference.[11]

A foreign representative of the duPont company in 1920 said:

> . . . Disarmament is a farce while Germany retains organic chemical monopolies.[12]

Late in 1925, the present I. G. Farbenindustrie was organized, including in its framework the preponderant bulk of German chemical companies. At the time of its renaissance, I.G. was capitalized at well over a billion marks and became, by virtue of its enormous plant, working force, and interests, one of the greatest industrial combinations in history. The reborn I.G. launched at once upon a massive program to unify control of the German economy. Krupp, Metallgesellschaft (the metal trust, partly government-owned) and Siemens-Halske became willing brothers-in-arms, under the aegis of I.G.

I.G. was now in position to begin its penetration of the chemical, pharmaceutical, and metallurgical industries and markets of the world. In particular, I.G. sought to form connections with the industries of the United States, Great Britain, and other industrial powers, at the same time that it extended its own distributing outposts around the globe. As stated before the Temporary National Economic Committee, the "colossal ramifications" of I.G.'s interests cannot be exhaustively indicated. It is probable that even after the protracted investigations by students and by government which have been undertaken in recent years, not all of I.G.'s links to American industry or to South American markets have been brought to light. It is even more certain that all of its relationships outside this hemisphere have not been disclosed. Yet we know enough of them to state that I.G. at the outbreak of war in 1939 surpassed any single industrial group in the world in its scope of influence, in the diversity and range of its interests, and in the magnitude and comprehensiveness of its affiliations.

I.G. was and is by all standards of measurement the largest corporation in Europe, and one of the largest in the world, ranking below only the insurance and utility companies, and the colossal Standard Oil (N. J.). As an industrial combine, however, it is certain that I.G. is among the handful of truly world-wide international industrial concerns.

The terms "monopoly" and "cartel" are inadequate when applied to I.G. It is an agglomeration of monopolies and an aggregation of cartels. Beyond German borders I.G. is an international monopolist and, by reason of the number and size of international cartels in which it is a leading, if not in all cases a dominant member, there is justification for adding to the descriptions commonly employed to indicate the scope of I.G.'s interests. It is estimated that I.G. is a party to or the actual promoter of several hundred international cartels. Consequently there is sufficient excuse for coining a term which conveys a more accurate impression than monopoly or cartel. Perhaps by compounding the idea of universality and absolute control a term such as "panopoly" would be more fitting. In any case, I.G. represents the acme of pan-Germanism in the economic sphere.

I.G. in 1926 was the greatest combine ever formed in Germany, and its destiny of larger significance than that of any predecessor. The thrice-reincarnated I.G. was to become the chief advance agent of the Third Reich in the latter's pre-war machinations, not only for the purpose of hewing out the ultimate features of the autarchy so long sought by Germany, but to sap the economic structure of the chosen opponents. In the Four Years' Plan promulgated in 1936, it was announced that "powerful factories will be built according to their urgency. We shall begin with those for armament purposes; that is most urgent. Then come factories which are in other ways needed to make the Four Years' Plan a reality. . . . In a world governed by reason this would not be necessary, but the world is insane." Need it be said that the only world governed by reason, in the view of the authors of this plan, would be ruled by Germany, which has never quite comprehended why other countries were so "insane" as to be unwilling to accept such rule?

Even before the "plan" was announced, I.G. stood at attention, with six decades of service on its record, its hosts already deployed, the terrain in its arena of action already surveyed, its lines established. Werner Bruck in 1938 said, "The trust [I.G.] is a cornerstone in Ger-

many's plan for self-sufficiency as well as for armament." [13] He might well have added that its drive for
world-rationalization of the industries in which it was
interested fitted neatly into the new schemes of world-
domination nursed by German militarism.

As the story of I.G.'s cartel agreements with American, British, and other national monopolies progresses,
there is a certain awesomeness in the sheer scale of its
operations. The boldness and orderliness of its management, combined with a refined subtlety and political
sophistication in business negotiations, command admir-
ation for their artistic and scientific perfection. At the
same time, it is clear that I.G.'s chief reliance was placed
on the political density and financial greed of those with
whom it dealt. The keenest business instincts, when not
modified by industrial wisdom, can become a weakness,
and on this weakness I.G. counted in nearly all of its
transactions. Canny traders of the American type were to
prove almost naïve when matched against the acuity and
perspicacity of the exponents of I.G.'s economic philosophy.

It is not too much to say that the direction of I.G.'s
policies in the years 1926-1939 was the work of genius,
not burdened with ethical conscience. The coupling of
economic and political insight in I.G.'s policies is clearly
traceable in the fabric of cartel agreements which I.G.
wove in American industry. The web of contracts in the
dyestuffs industry, the pharmaceutical industry, the oil

industry, the synthetic rubber industry, the magnesium industry, and others, all promoted by I.G. with leading American concerns, affected the military preparedness and economic independence of the United States. Even today, they force us to do without materials, processes, and industries which in the normal course of competition would have been fully established at the outbreak of the war.

An outline of the actual corporate, physical, and capital structure of I.G. will indicate the basis upon which its power is erected. Each of the Big Six companies and the other major concerns included in I.G.'s first unification in 1904, or in its reorganizations in 1916, 1919, and 1925, was in itself a merger of many, in some cases scores, of smaller companies. Each of the Big Six was in its own right a cartel which represented not only the vertical integration of its particular phase of the chemical or metallurgical industries, but a horizontal association of smaller concerns operating in the same or closely related fields. Consequently, when we speak of I.G. it must be kept in mind that I.G. is at the same time a national cartel in its broadest sense as well as the greatest of all international cartels.

The Armistice had hardly been signed before this multiple trust undertook to expand its capital and plant. A dispatch in the New York *Times* of December 1, 1919, from its Berlin correspondent, stated:

The firms composing the German dye trust have decided to increase their capital to an extent without parallel, I believe, in the history of German industry. The trust, which consists of three great and four minor concerns in the industry, valued at, roughly, 15,000,000,000 marks, is extending for two reasons: It is determined to reassert German supremacy in the dye industry; in the second place, there is the question of nitrate, so important for the agricultural life of the country.

The trust is aiming at making the fatherland independent of foreign supplies and to increase production so that it will be able to export large quantities.

*   *   *

With this vastly increased capital the trust will at the earliest moment begin a vigorous onslaught in the markets of the world.

The value of the mark at the time of this dispatch, while still theoretically at its pre-war level, was perhaps equal to about 3¢ in American money. On this basis, a value of 15,000,000,000 marks would be roughly equivalent to $750,000,000. In 1926 the nominal capitalization of the new I.G. was placed at some 800,000,000 marks, and in 1929, I.G.'s annual report estimated its capitalization at more than 1,000,000,000 marks. These figures in themselves would not entitle I.G. to the status and prestige which it occupies among the financial titans of industry. There is, however, a major qualification to such estimates. It is customary among German cartels to underestimate, rather than overestimate, capital assets in order to conceal their real size. It is probable that the real capital assets of I.G. as they stood at the outbreak of war in 1939 were only slightly below those of Standard Oil, and were certainly greater than the resources of any other concern in the same industry.*

Within Germany, the plants and properties of I.G. are scattered from one end of the country to the other. I.G.'s plants are located in those very cities which have been among the primary bombing objectives of the Royal Air Force, and in all probability provide the specific targets for such raids. The names of many of the towns in which the principal I.G. plants are located will therefore strike a familiar note to those who follow the headlines.† Although there is a good deal of geographic concentration of the I.G. plants, they are sufficiently decentralized from both an economic and military standpoint to make the job of bombing them difficult and dangerous.

I.G.'s holdings in German and European industry have, of course, been enormously increased by military conquest, and by the unctuously legal means to which they have adhered in absorbing conquered industry. An accurate, complete catalog of I.G.'s wholly and partially owned subsidiaries cannot be given, because only

---

* Liefmann in "Cartels, Concerns, and Trusts," places I.G.'s assets ahead of the Royal Dutch Shell Oil interests.

† See list in Appendix.

the I.G. Sekretariat could provide such a list. Various experts have called the roll, but never with final assurance. With similar reservations, the firms which I.G. is known to own, or control, are set forth in the notes below. In scanning this list, it becomes clear that I.G. is the industrial ruler of Germany. Its non-German interests bulk almost as large.

The fields of operation of I. G. Farben are so broad, the array of its products so vast, that the best-qualified investigators cannot name them all. "Dye Industry" is a misnomer. It is true, of course, that I.G. grew out of the dye industry, but in a larger sense, its functions are as unlimited as the scientific application of physics and chemistry to raw materials. In each of the broad areas designated as a field of production there are nearly always a large number of separate products and processes involved. In some cases, such as that of coal tar dye-stuffs, there are tens of thousands of different crude, intermediate, and finished materials which fall within the general class.

There is a quality of Faustian alchemy in the rapidity with which any development in one branch of the chemical or metallurgical industries transforms or affects all other aspects of the field. I.G. has not only taken advantage of the illimitable permutations of the chemical industry itself, but has used the forces of science to build what is probably the world's greatest system of industrial domination. Even if I.G. were confined exclusively to the chemical industry, which it is not, the enormous possibilities within that sphere would kindle the fantasy of any writer of weird tales or horror stories. More important, however, is the fact that throughout its entire domain I.G. always has the power of choice to make products or to use processes which can benefit or injure mankind. This duality of the industry is graphically illustrated in the testimony given by Captain O. E. Roberts, Chief of the Industrial Relations Section, Chemical Warfare Service, United States Army, before the Judiciary Committee of the United States Senate in 1922. Speaking of the chemical industry in general, Captain Roberts said:

> It is a revelation to most people to see the variety of products which this industry produces, and the fact that we may make a delightful violet perfume, or a wonderful dye, or an extremely effective medicine from such a deadly war gas as phosgene, always stirs one's imagination.
>
> The possibilities of this industry, which may include any of the several hundred thousand known organic chemicals or of the millions which are figured as possibilities, are enough to stir anyone's imagination.

In a speech on July 9, 1921, before the House of Representatives, Honorable Caleb R. Layton of Delaware, describing the development of the chemical industry with regard to the increasing dependence of medicine on chemotherapy, said:

I venture the prophecy at this point that the time will come, and is not far distant, when the physician will be enabled to select out of a single large group of synthetical medicines possessing substantially one chief characteristic for his therapeutical use with the same meticulous facility that the essayist employs who chooses the proper synonym for the expression of his thought.

When it is recalled that I.G. produces synthetic medicines, vitamins, hormones, serums, and specifics, some of which are not even known in other countries, it is understandable that its success in opening up new markets throughout the world and in penetrating the markets of others is in part attributable to its consistent policy of trying to lead the field. Knowledge, to I.G., means power.

I.G.'s physical plant includes mines, its own railroads which connect with the state-owned lines, and large tracts of property around its plants and in various German cities. The total number of employees of I.G. and its direct subsidiaries is estimated at about 350,000. It is worth recording that I.G.'s labor policies are paternalistic and, for the most part, predicated upon the native docility and tractability of the German worker. Many of I.G.'s employees live in what, in the United States, would be called "company towns," and historically, it has been part of I.G.'s policy to adopt the type of "social reform" initiated by Bismarck. When the National Socialist Workers' Party seized the government and incorporated all German labor into an enormous company union with the state as ultimate employer, I.G.'s workers were, of course, included. In fact, I.G. personnel made up one of the first "Strength-Through-Joy" units.

The technical organization of I.G. is an intriguing topic, but it describes only corporate superstructure. I.G. as another "big business" would have little novelty. But I.G. as a politico-economic entity, the embodiment of cameralist Germany, has the immediate importance of an additional army or a fleet. Again, no demon-theory is necessary in interpreting I.G.'s history from 1919 to 1939. I.G. is supervised by a "doctorate" whose ranks include today, as in its beginning, the scientific aristocracy of Germany. Nearly all of I.G.'s directors are doctors of chemistry, physics, engineering, or economics. For personnel, I.G. has been able to draw upon a populace which has been trained for generations in applied science. Herbert Hoover drew attention to the fact that there were two and one-half times the number of research workers in Germany that were engaged in comparable callings in the United States in 1925.

The sequence of events must be considered in recounting the part which I.G. played in German rearmament in the Inter-War period, beginning years before

Hitler appeared. The World War had shown up certain weak spots in the German armor. Continuing the lines of research begun before 1914 was not enough. The difficult task of rearming would be futile, unless any new war could be started with a wider margin of advantage than in 1914. This requisite superiority required that Germany become an absolute autarchy, able to supply *all* of its own domestic wants. Self-sufficiency, if complete, could withstand indefinite blockade.

On this score, I.G.'s intentions from 1919 onward are easily determined, and their fulfillment can be traced step by step. In addition to self-containment, however, Germany needed assurances that in her second gamble against the world, her former enemies would feel the grip of technological inferiority with even greater agony. I.G., whether it foresaw precisely the time and manner of the present war or not, used old and new methods to create this differential. Patents were applied for and obtained "en masse," in every country having a patent system, but largely in Germany, England, and the United States. But patents were the oldest and the least of I.G.'s tourniquets on the economic vigor of Germany's likely antagonists. The improved cartel device was used both to invade and to occupy strategic sectors in the economies of the then disunited nations. The cartel was I.G.'s formula for conquest.

Here, it is helpful to pass in brief review the specific utility of I.G. to the rebirth of German military prowess. I.G. had produced synthetic rubber during the World War, in relatively small amounts, but its quantity was insufficient and its quality unsatisfactory. I.G. therefore worked incessantly to make synthetic rubber on a large scale. The famous Buna rubbers were the reward of these experiments. The Bunas are made from petroleum.* Germany had little oil. I.G. hydrogenated coal into oil, and at a single stroke made possible the mechanization of the Reichswehr. The German Army at this very moment travels in tanks and trucks propelled by I.G.'s synthetic fuels, and shod with Buna rubber.

The production of new alloys and light metals by I.G. and its research colleagues, Krupp and Siemens-Halske, are the reason for the uncanny speed and dimensions of German rearmament. New aluminum and magnesium plants, and improved processes of production, largely I.G.'s own, were ready when the time came to fabricate planes. Beryllium, tungsten carbide, and new steels were forged to be used in armor plate, shell tips, and machine tools. Since all metals are precious in Germany, I.G. produced new plastics to take their place in consumer goods, and replenish many munitions supplies.

From the most universal raw material of the temperate zone—wood—I.G. produced substitutes for

* The essential ingredient of the Bunas is butadiene, a refinery by-product. This component can also be made from alcohol or coal.

metals, cotton, wool, explosives, fuel for vehicles, food-stuffs, medicines, and dyes. A whole new industry was developed from the chemistry of wood—a branch of science totally neglected in the United States.

Under the pressure of Allied blockade, the German disease rate had risen sharply toward the end of the World War. I.G. compounded vitamins and sulpha drugs to remove this danger in the future. If Germany was to regain her lost colonies, geopolitical analysis in-dicated that fighting would have to take place in the tropics. The quinine of Java was far away, and German troops would risk jungle fevers. I.G.'s answer to this prospect was atabrine—better than natural quinine for the quick cure of a sick soldier.

Lest it be thought that the relation between I.G.'s research and German aspirations is coincidental, the story of "Bayer 205" must be told. The number 205, like 606, stands at the pinnacle of a tireless series of experiments. Bayer 205 is a complex synthetic hydro-carbon. It was first announced by I.G. in 1920 that Bayer 205, rechristened "Germanin," was a cure for the dread sleeping sickness which the tsetse fly scattered over Africa. Sleeping sickness prevented the complete exploitation of Africa's wealth by the white race.

By indirect channels, I.G. made an offer to the Brit-ish Government—the secret of Germanin in exchange for the return of Germany's lost colonies. I.G.'s adroit-

ness is evident in the report published in the British
Medical Journal in 1922:

> A curious illustration of the German desire, not
> unnatural in itself, to regain the tropical colonies lost
> by the folly of the rulers of the German Empire, is
> afforded by a discussion which took place at a meet-
> ing of the German Association of Tropical Medicine
> at Hamburg. The *Times* correspondent in Hamburg
> reports that one of the speakers said that "Bayer 205
> is the key to tropical Africa, and consequently the key
> to all the colonies. The German Government must,
> therefore, be required to safeguard this discovery for
> Germany. Its value is such that any privilege of a
> share in it granted to other nations must be made
> conditional upon the restoration to Germany of her
> colonial empire." [14]

While no action by the British Government was ever
made public, and no official explanation ever given,
I.G.'s "bargain" was obviously not accepted. As it later
turned out, Germanin was not so effective in human
sleeping sickness as in mice or in test-tubes charged with
the causal parasite. But the motif of the episode ties
into and connects the pattern and purpose of I.G. research. Political control of Africa could not be bought,
but I.G. could still get economic colonies not only in
Africa, but elsewhere.

Whatever Germany needed, and modern science
could make, I.G. obtained for Germany, and tried to
keep from others. The combined effect of I.G. dis-

covery and I.G. cartel restriction on the development of other countries has only to be set forth to assume its true proportions. Every time some government official or industrial executive speaks of a scarcity of chemicals or metals, the chances are abundant that somewhere along the line there was an international cartel, and that the letters I.G. are inscribed on a supporting contract.

Although the internal organization of I.G. is an exciting subject, it is in the sphere of international industry that I.G.'s policies and practices assume their most sinister mask. The list of affiliations, associations, contractual agreements, and international cartels in which I.G. is either the promoter or at least a principal party reads like a bluebook of world industry. I.G. had cartel agreements with Standard Oil of New Jersey, with Aluminum Company of America, with Dow Chemical Company, with E. I. duPont de Nemours, with Monsanto Chemical Company, with Pennsylvania Salt Co., with Rohm & Haas, with Plaskon Corporation, with Hercules Powder Company, with Remington Arms, with the Unyte Company, and with numerous other American companies which will be referred to later. I.G.'s cartel agreements with Imperial Chemical Industries, with Norwegian, Dutch, French, Belgian, Italian, Spanish, and Polish concerns were, until the outbreak of the war, a true society of nations, industrially speaking.

In the Far East, I.G. was one of the principal sponsors of the Japanese chemical industry, forming an Axis which existed long before its political counterpart. It is interesting to note, however, that as early as the first World War, products were sold in the Australian market which bore the legend "Made in Germany," followed by a Japanese trademark.

Even greater weight must be attached to I.G.'s policies in this war than in the last. I.G.'s plans for postwar reconstruction are already provided for in its agreements with non-German concerns. Reports from France and the other occupied countries of Europe indicate that I.G.'s own staff has followed in the wake of Hitler's armies for the purpose of acquiring outright ownership of the entire European chemical industry. Inasmuch as superficially legal methods are used by I.G. in its acquisitions, as in the case of the Etablissement Kuhlmann, the French chemical company, I.G. apparently hopes to win its own war even though Hitler loses. In the case of American industry, I.G.'s foresight provided for a *modus vivendi* during the war and a settlement of claims afterward. American industry has been victimized twice. Will it be victimized in the future by the resumption of the same enticing "collaboration" in joint world-monopoly or by the "settlements" anticipated by I.G.?

4. THE FROZEN RAGE ACROSS THE RHINE

IT would be folly to indict an entire people. People in a nation, however, are part of an organic whole, whose way of life is ordained by the will of its ruling class. In Germany, this ruling class for centuries has consisted primarily of Prussian Junkers or those who would be like them. The Prussian feudal warriors have never been unsaddled by social change. Tacitus had recorded in the Roman era the ferocity of the Teuton. Heine, centuries later, warned the French of the "beast" that dwelled in the Prussian soul.

Since the days of Frederick William I, Prussian exaltation of military prowess has made German statecraft a succession of military plans. World domination is the pole, and blood and iron the compass, by which the German nation has been guided.

Is this to say that the people who have given birth to so many great musicians, poets, and scholars can be condemned? No. If the German people are to blame, as people, it is because they have failed for centuries to free themselves from the shackles of a small and ruthless group, whose traditions and ideas revolve about

49

absolute force. Mirabeau once exclaimed, "War is the national industry of Prussia!" Because Prussia won the sceptre of rule in the German nation, Prussianism became dominant in German Kultur, and tainted all it touched. The writings of Prussianized thinkers are saturated with the idolatry of power, and glorification of war as the way to German world dominion. From Friedrich List, to Heinrich von Treitschke, to Oswald Spengler, to Adolf Hitler, the belief has been proclaimed that Germany, by and with the virtue of the sword, should gain the world. In the pursuit of such ends, nations, like men, can sin against and lose the spirit of humanity.

The Prussian "Weltanschauung" of political and economic world hegemony is the well-spring from which both Hohenzollern Imperialism and National Socialism flow. This outlook envisages an administered economy, planned and ordered by the State as an adjunct to "Machtpolitik." Succinctly stated, ". . . there has been a certain logical sequence in Prussian-German history. It was and is the expression of cameralism, the peculiar German type of mercantilism." [1]

Werner Bruck, former Assistant to Walther Rathenau * in the German War Office, and later a department head in the Ministry of Economic Affairs in the Weimar Republic, says of Prussian militarism:

* Head of the German Economic War Ministry in the first World War.

This militarism has rightly been called the cement that bound the whole structure of society into an entity. It was, and still is, an outstanding expression of the national efficiency of the Supreme State. In the greatest degree produced by constant drill, everything had to be as on the parade-ground, where thousands of soldiers monotonously repeated the same movement. This spirit of prompt obedience extended from the army to industrial life: the local units responded to the least word from headquarters. The giant industrial plants, large savings banks, local branches of the social democratic party, and even the trade unions, functioned through men of the type of captains or non-commissioned officers.[2]

Of the commercial "arrivistes" who came into the picture with industry, Bruck says:

. . . these business men left no stone unturned, in business and society, to bring themselves into the machine. They joined noble cavalry regiments and acquired landed property. This union between the powerful old nobility and these upstarts, anxious for assimilation into its ranks, stood actually and morally in the way of every democratic and socialist movement.[3]

Bruck cites Friedrich Naumann, whose National Socialism, vintage of 1895, sanctified militarism as the foundation of order, without which the State could not exist. Bruck's opinion of the Weimar Reich deserves serious consideration. He points out that the war econ-

52   *GERMANY'S MASTER PLAN*

omy continued to operate after the Armistice. The thin
veneer of democracy imposed on this war economy by
the Versailles Treaty did not alter either the locus of
real rule or its concentration in the Junker military and
industrial oligarchy. As for the honest and sincere men,
some now dead, the rest scattered to the four corners
of the earth, living as refugees, who tried to make
democracy work in a military socialist state, the whole
group

> . . . was doomed to failure from the first by its lack
> of power.
> . . . No doubt, in many groups extending from
> the middle classes to the ranks of the Social Demo-
> cratic Party, a feeling for democracy existed. But
> among the population in general such feeling was
> very weak. The average German received this sud-
> denly-acquired individual liberty with indifference.[4]

Von Moellendorff, in the War Office until 1918, continued as permanent secretary for the Economics Ministry under the Weimar regime. Von Moellendorff, the
coiner of the term "Planwirtschaft" (economic planning), "succeeded in anchoring his ideas . . . in the
Constitution of the Weimar Reich." These ideas followed the ". . . administration of the economic system
of the War period." Von Moellendorff was a principal
promoter of the plan of self-sufficiency as an economic
weapon. Though Von Moellendorff departed from government, later to become a director of I.G., his ideas

remained. The cartels grew stronger in inflation. The
High Command bided its time, until the economic machine was again ready to do its bidding. As Bruck con-
cludes:

> The historian's interest is attracted by the fact that
> the Third Reich followed directly in its social and
> economic system the model given by the Weimar
> Reich. . . .[5]

I.G. and the Weimar Republic

The relationship between I.G. and the Weimar Republic is that of villain and victim, or co-conspirators,
depending upon whether we accept the sincerity of the
German Government from 1919 to 1933. I.G. executives commonly held cabinet posts, especially after Hin-
denburg's election. It is acknowledged without question
that both German industry and the German army re-
armed throughout the life of the ill-fated Republic.
Refugee scholars have maintained that the failure of
the Republic was directly attributable to these aims of
industry and the army. Franz Neumann, for example,
says of the Weimar Government that:

> . . . it did not see that the central problem was
> the imperialism of German monopoly capital becom-
> ing ever more urgent with the continued growth of
> the process of monopolization.[6]

The lines of evidence converge to the conclusion that
even if the constitutional German Government was

guiltless, it made no real effort to halt the training of troops in secret, the manufacture and export of arms, or the gobbling up of all key enterprises by I.G. or its followers. By 1924 Colonel William Taylor, duPont's Paris agent, could write to his company that "The European monopoly in military material [is] passing slowly into German hands." [7]

Article 170 of the Treaty of Versailles specifically prohibited German export or import of armaments or munitions. By 1925 it was known that:

> . . . in open violation of the Treaty of Versailles the Germans shipped munitions to the Argentines . . . Rottweil [I.G.'s wholly owned subsidiary] still makes and sells excellent military powders, and German factories for munitions have been built or openly offered to build in Spain, Argentina, Mexico, etc.[8]

Although these violations of the disarmament clauses of the peace treaty were known to the State departments of Great Britain and the United States, no action was taken. The Imperial Chemical Industries, formerly the British Nobel company, refrained from any protest because of its cartel agreements with I.G. As Sir Harry McGowan, the head of Imperial Chemical Industries, Ltd., stated, the British Chemical industry could not "achieve technical success without the help of the Germans." [9] What would Perkin have said to this?

1926—not 1933—was the year which really foreshadowed this generation's "rendezvous with destiny."

In 1926 the German army formed an Economic High Command. The truth of this assertion is independently documented from many sources, and Robert Strausz-Hupé has stated it pithily. In his words, the Economic High Command had as its express purpose:

> . . . studying the deficiencies of German economy and laying plans for transforming it into Wehrwirtschaft. . . . Rapid conquests alone could provide new resources before Germany's reserves, accumulated by barter, ruthless rationing, and synthetic chemistry, had been exhausted in the initial war effort. These new resources could then be poured into the war machine rolling on to ever larger territorial conquests, and as long as it kept on rolling, the economy of greater space need never fear a crisis.[10]

The liaison between I.G. and the High Command was maintained by direct and indirect means. I.G.'s policies and industrial relationships were charted thereafter as part of a "ruse de guerre." I.G. did rearm the German economy. The High Command took care of the training of troops in the Black Reichswehr, and in "private" volunteer groups. Pilots were trained in gliders— the phantom air force. Infantry was drilled in hiking clubs. The Reichswehr was limited to 100,000 men, but each name on its rolls stood for as many as 30 men, each of whom received training during the twelve-year period of enlistment. Colonel Taylor of duPont in 1932 reported:

. . . One of the motives back of the French proposal, that all countries should establish a conscription is to upset the present German system of handling their Reichswehr. The Reichswehr is limited to 100,000 men of 12 years enlistment, and it would appear reasonable to suppose that there should be at present a number of soldiers around the age of 33 or 34; the fact is that when one meets a soldier of the Reichswehr he is a young man in the early twenties, and it is pretty well accepted that there are several men available under the same name and hence training much larger number of men than permitted.[11]

The Weimar government could not suppress these activities. Instead, it conducted several hundred treason trials in secret against journalists and workmen who revealed the truth beneath the surface. As Dr. H. C. Engelbrecht and F. C. Hanighen state:

. . . It would seem then that, despite the Versailles treaty, Germany is again a manufacturer and exporter of arms.

This inference is confirmed by various incidents from the last ten years. There was the Bullerjahn case of 1925. On December 11, 1925, Walter Bullerjahn was sentenced to 15 years in prison for "treason." The trial was held in secret and the public was excluded. Both the crime with which the condemned was charged and the name of the accuser were kept deep and dark secrets. After years of agitation by Dr. Paul Levi and the League for Human Rights, the facts were finally disclosed. The accuser was Paul von Gontard, general director of the Berlin-Karlsruhe Industriewerke, the same man who had used the French press in 1907 in order to increase his machine gun business. Gontard had been establishing secret arsenals, contrary to treaty provisions, and this fact was discovered by the Allies. Gontard disliked Bullerjahn and had had serious disagreements with him. In order to get rid of him he charged him with revealing to the Allies the fact that Gontard was secretly arming Germany. This was termed "treason" by the court and Bullerjahn was condemned, although not a shred of evidence was ever produced to show his connection with the Allies. The exposure of the facts in the case finally brought the release of Bullerjahn.

*   *   *

A little later Carl von Ossietzky, the courageous editor of the *Weltbuehne*, was convicted by a German court of "treason," because he had revealed military secrets in his journal. The secrets he had published were closely related to the secret rearming of Germany contrary to treaty provisions.

There is also some evidence that Germany is importing arms and munitions from other countries. In a confidential report of the exports of Skoda for 1930 and 1931, classified by countries, Germany appears as importer of comparatively large amounts of rifles, portable firearms, aero engines, nitrocellulose, dynamite, and other explosives.

All of this occurred in pre-Hitler Germany.[12]

I.G., along with Krupp and Thyssen (who later regretted his complicity with the Nazis), financed Hit-

ler. In a memorandum dated March 22, 1932—a year
before Hitler took over—from the files of the Foreign
Relations Department of duPont, J. K. Jenney, now
the assistant head of this Department, wrote to W. R.
Swint, his chief:

> It is a matter of common gossip in Germany that
> I.G. is financing Hitler. Other German firms who are
> also supposed to be doing so are Krupp and Thiessen.
> How much truth there is in this gossip we are unable
> to state, but there seems to be no doubt whatever that
> Dr. Schmitz [director-general of I.G.] is at least per-
> sonally a large contributor to the Nazi Party.[18]

When the Nazis did take over, I.G. became in effect
the business partner of the Hitler Government. Ivy
Lee, the late American publicist, testified before the
Dickstein Committee in 1934 that he was hired as a
publicity agent in this country for the German Government by I.G. and paid by Dr. Schmitz in person. The
propaganda which Lee spread included both Nazi liter-
ature and I.G.'s self-glorifying handouts. Actually there
was little distinction between the two.

The War Economy of 1914 became the Cartel Economy of Weimar. Impregnated as it was by the smoul-
dering fetish of the Versailles Treaty, the militaristic
imagination of the people was kept at white heat by
the "invisible government" of the Junkers in Army
and Industry. When the necessary backlog of capacity

and invention had been accumulated, the torch was placed. Hitler was chosen to light it.

Thorstein Veblen stressed, in "Imperial Germany and the Industrial Revolution," the divergence between the *laissez-faire* of England and the United States and the authoritarian habits of thought traditionally associated with the Junker-mind. During the industrialization of Germany in the latter nineteenth century, economic liberalism was no more than an interregnum episode. Since the time of Bismarck, the German Government has sponsored industrial cartels because they made production lines goose-step in unison. Germany became "the classic land of the cartel."

Geopolitics has been called "the systematic struggle for space and power," with world-mastery its goal. Years prior to the World War, geopolitics was already a highly developed study in German universities and military circles. Geopolitics is a name for Prussian desires, whose military culmination must be a Global War.

In the folklore of future ages the Germans will be classed as the warlike race of modern times. No devil-theory of history is implied in this assertion, for the motives and acts of Germans are products of *Kultur*. It was, after all, a neglected American military genius who most mordantly defined the spirit of German militarism. Homer Lea, writing in 1912, prophesied the future in startling detail, and described the German nation as:

. . . a military power in which neither theories nor sophistry find a place, but where the intentness of its aims knows no discouragement, its progress no diversion of the terribleness of its energy nor fatigue. The movement of such a nation resembles that of fate in the certitude of its progression. The noise of its approach tallies the destiny of many states.[14]

5. PREVIEW

"THE remembrance of things past" is more than a Proustian image. Not as hindsight, but as hard-won knowledge does the narrative of history have meaning. For this reason it is necessary to pass in review the pattern of events in the United States in the years 1914-18, and in particular the circumstances attending the entry of the United States into war in 1917. A comparison between the experiences of the United States in the World War and in the Global War establishes parallels which cannot be considered accidental. They were and are the product of calculated military design. The German attack by cartels in 1914 had the same purposes, executed in much the same manner, as the attack on our economy today. The mistakes of public policy which were made at that time and in the years following the Armistice provide a significant commentary which has value for the future.

In many respects, the war effort of this country in 1917 was even more severely handicapped than at the present time, because our industrial structure did not have the resilience which technological advances during the past twenty years have given us, and because we were at war before any countermeasures could be set in motion. It is to provide a frame of reference for present and future strategy and to seek the causes of present conditions that the preview of cartel activities which was given to us in 1914 is outlined.

The most serious shortages in the United States at the time of the World War resulting from the action of German cartels were those of dyestuffs, nitrates and potash, medicines, military optical goods, surgical instruments, heavy ordnance, and radio and electrical equipment.

The first impact of war in 1914 was felt by the dyestuffs and textiles industries of the United States. Because "selective attack" by I.G. had aborted any effort to establish an American dyestuffs industry, we were entirely without the facilities or the know-how to meet the situation. Our total dyestuffs industry consisted of five very small firms employing collectively less than the entire number at work in a single I.G. laboratory. I.G. produced four-fifths of the world's total output of synthetic dyes, and provided more than 90% of the dyestuffs which this country consumed. The British blockade and the embargo placed by the German Government on exports of dyestuffs and medicines threatened the steady operation of American industrial life. In March 1916 the German Ambassador, Baron von Bernstorff, sent the following cablegram to Berlin:

It is reported to me by Hossenfelder [the German Consul-General in New York] that the stock of dyes in this country is so small that by a German embargo about 4,000,000 American workmen might be thrown out of employment.

On his part, Hossenfelder had written to Berlin:

Neither through money nor the granting of credit nor by any other means can that critical situation be relieved which has been called forth by the removal of certain articles which are obtainable only in Germany. These articles are chiefly potash, chemicals, and dyestuffs . . . to enumerate the industries which are suffering from the scarcity of German chemicals would lead too far. I may, however, mention that the cry for help which comes from the world of physicians is becoming louder and louder and more insistent.

The country, however, is being hit hardest by the lack of dyestuffs, which makes itself felt more and more every day. . . . In estimating the effect which will be produced by cutting off the importation of potash, chemicals, and dyestuffs, it should be taken into consideration that the circle of persons affected is very extraordinarily large. Through the lack of dyestuffs alone not only is a whole list of important industries . . . gradually made lame, but for the great public living becomes more expensive. . . . We are here unquestionably face to face with conditions which are without parallel in the past.[1]

The reasons for the strength of Germany and the weakness of America in the dyestuffs and organic chemical industries are not far to seek. By 1914 I.G. had achieved not only superiority but a world monopoly in the production of dyestuffs. The commercial practices and patent policies of I.G. were deliberately intended to prevent, so far as possible, the development of coal tar chemical industries in France, Great Britain, or the United States. While patents and patent privileges were the primary weapons which I.G. used in its assiduous effort to retain its supremacy, it did not allow non-German patents to block it at any point. The marketing tactics were equally effective: by dumping and by singling out particular products for cutthroat competition I.G. precluded any possibility that American or English firms could successfully enter the industry.

Where necessary, I.G. resorted to full-line forcing of its dyestuffs, by threatening to shut off the supply of any manufacturer who tried to circumvent its control. Bribery was a recognized practice of I.G., and a special fund existed for the purpose of corrupting opposition which could not otherwise be overcome. Organized propaganda was supported to discourage native initiative, and a doctrine of German invincibility in the organic chemical industry was pounded by every available means into the consciousness of both the United States and England. Belief in this notion of the incomparable ingenuity of Germany in the chemical field has been weakened by subsequent developments, and will not stand logical analysis, but it is still invoked to justify cartel agreements which cannot otherwise be defended. The secret of German industrial invincibility was not inherent genius, but singleness of purpose and an indomitable will to conquest.

Hossenfelder, in the cable quoted above, refers to the cry for help which came from American physicians. The shortages of medicine were perhaps even more critical than the lack of dyestuffs. All salvarsan used in the United States prior to the World War had been imported from Germany, and the stoppage of imports created so grave a situation that, even before we declared war, attempts were made to work the American patent owned by I.G. It was found that "the patent protects the product, but does not reveal the method." This use of "bogus" patents, containing nothing of the know-how, by German interests to further their grip on our economy was a settled policy throughout German industry. In this connection Sir William Pope stated in 1917:

> In fact, some German patents are drawn up for the purpose of discouraging investigation by more practical methods; thus, anyone who attempted to repeat the method for manufacturing a dyestuff protected by Salzmann and Kruger in the German patent No. 12096 *would be pretty certain to kill himself in the operation.*[2]

This device should be kept in mind when the claim is advanced that Germany "shared" her knowledge with other countries.

In the case of salvarsan, this country suffered throughout the war effects which intensive research could not mitigate. The drug prepared according to the specifications contained in I.G.'s patent was so toxic that many fatalities in the Army and Navy and among the public resulted from its use. Salvarsan, the "healing arsenic," Ehrlich's "magic bullet," became as effective as a sixteen-inch shell from a Krupp cannon, and produced as many casualties. When it is realized that an estimated ten million persons in the United States were afflicted with syphilis at that time, and that the larger dispensaries administered an average of 2,000 injections per month, the magnitude of the problem can be understood. The cost in time, health, and money exacted from us by German patent control in this instance was both incalculable and irreparable.

The shortage of salvarsan was not the only blow at our national health. The scarcity of novocaine resulted in a reversion in American surgery to "Bulgarian operations," executed without benefit of anaesthesia. This single lack, in the opinion of medical men, "threw us back fifty years in civilization" at a time when our need was more acute than ever before in our history.

In the case of luminal, a synthetic drug used to prevent epileptic seizures, the loss could not be made good, for its formula eluded us.

Even before we actively sided with the Allies, German economic warfare in this country was carried on through the agencies of the chemical, metal, and electrical cartels controlled by German interests. Planes which we were manufacturing for the Allies were held up fifteen months by the deceptive tactics of the Bosch magneto interests, and it was not until our own declaration of war that any measures could be taken against the Bosch company.

An even more insidious aspect of the patent agreements entered into between German and American concerns prior to the World War was the provision for an exchange of information on technological improvements and on the scope of their application. German companies, then as now, conducted the most comprehensive industrial intelligence service in the world. Although patent agreements were the principal means of obtaining such information, financial and commercial agreements were also channels by which vital knowledge of American industrial organization flowed to Germany.

Probably one of the most lurid affairs during the whole period of the war concerns Dr. Hugo Schweitzer, at that time president of the old Bayer Company in the United States. Dr. Schweitzer was an American citizen who became head of the German espionage service in America, known in the Secret Service in Berlin as "No. 963,192,637." Dr. Schweitzer was interned after America entered the war, but before that time was able to conduct a highly efficient system of industrial espionage and warfare. At one time he was able to corner the

American market in phenol, or carbolic acid, in order to prevent its transshipment to the Allies, and succeeded in achieving on the economic front a victory which was comparable to any gained by German arms in France. He was complimented by Dr. Albert, his superior, in the following language:

> The breadth of high-mindedness with which you at that time immediately entered into the plan has borne fruit as follows: One and a half million pounds of carbolic acid have been kept from the Allies. Out of this one and a half million pounds of carbolic acid four and one-half million pounds of picric acid can be produced. This tremendous quantity of explosive stuffs has been withheld from the Allies by your contract. In order to give one an idea of this enormous quantity the following figures are of interest:
>
> Four million five hundred thousand pounds equals 2,250 tons of explosives. A railroad freight car is loaded with 20 tons of explosives. The 2,250 tons would, therefore, fill 112 railway cars. A freight train with explosives consist chiefly of 40 freight cars, so that the 4,500,000 pounds of explosives would fill three railroad trains with 40 cars each.
>
> *Now one should picture to himself what a military coup would be accomplished by an army leader if he should succeed in destroying three railroad trains of forty cars, containing four and a half million pounds of explosives.*
>
> Of still greater and more beneficial effect is the support which you have afforded to the purchase of bromine. We have a well founded hope that, with

the exclusion of perhaps small quantities, we shall be in a position to buy up the total production of the country. Bromine, together with chloral, is used in making nitric gases, which are of such great importance in trench warfare. Without bromine these nitric gases are of slight effect; in connection with bromine, they are of terrible effect. Bromine is produced only in the United States and Germany. While, therefore, the material is on hand in satisfactory quantities for the Germans, the Allies are entirely dependent upon importation from America. [Italics added] [3]

Dr. Schweitzer's position and the weight of his authority made both profound and prophetic an article he wrote during the first World War. At the time of Dr. Schweitzer's death Government agents searched his apartment. Among his effects was found an unpublished article entitled "The Chemists' War." In this remarkable document Dr. Schweitzer records the plans for self-sufficiency which were to precede German conquest. He says "Germany deprived of all imports by the sea-power of England has been transformed into a self-supporting country by the chemists." Dr. Schweitzer relates that in 1910 large-scale experiments had been undertaken by the Institute for the Fermentation Industry in Berlin, looking toward the solution of the protein problem which was to plague Germany in the following war. He describes the way in which Germany had freed herself from nitrate imports, a discovery which, in his opinion, would some day produce a universal fertilizer.

"When English blockade threatened to starve the women and children of the Empire" fourteen substitutes were found for spinach, five for salads, and nine for foods rich in starch.

Dr. Schweitzer in this article raised the possibility that the cotton farmers of the South would some day be displaced by German production of textile fibre from wood. In ominous words he says:

All these endeavors to substitute cotton may appear ridiculous to us who have been brought up with the idea that "Cotton is King," and that we have been destined by fate to supply this fiber to the civilized world. The farmers who cultivated the madder root and the planters who raised indigo were also inclined to jest when they were appraised of the fact that German chemists had succeeded in reproducing in the laboratories the dyes which their crops furnished, but when the manufactured materials drove the natural products from the markets and left the farmers and planters without a job, hilarity ceased. History may repeat itself and willow bark and nettle, or some other substitute raised on German soil may, in the near future, depose King Cotton. The German chemist has a duty to perform, and with his perseverance and application he does not shrink from any problem however difficult it might appear to outsiders.[4]

Dr. Schweitzer discourses (*in 1916!*) on synthetic rubber, aluminum, and magnesium as a means of increasing Germany's self-sufficiency. He says:

Next to steel and iron, aluminum and magnesium play a prominent part as substitutes for copper. It has been found that an aluminum-magnesium alloy possesses great advantage over the latter as an electrical conductor. Magnesium is said to be useful for many purposes for which aluminum is being employed today. This is a very important discovery, because Germany has enormous supplies of magnesium chloride, a by-product of the potash industry, which has been considered worthless up to now. *Two large factories, started during the war, are now producing magnesium.* [Italics added] [5]

Because of these developments in Germany, Schweitzer saw that, win or lose, "there will be a big rush for the Teutonic bandwagon and all the ideas of a nation boycott of the Germans, or of an ostracism of Germany's traders and manufacturers, will quickly vanish in thin air." And he adds:

That this new scientific achievement will prove of momentous importance appears from the fact that the great chemical works which supply the world with dyestuffs, synthetic remedies, photographic developers, artificial perfume, etc., have entered the field and have become important factors in the artificial fertilizer industry of Germany. The peace negotiations will undoubtedly culminate in the conclusion of commercial treaties between the nations. What an enormous power will be exercized by that nation when possessing such a universal fertilizer and practically world-wide monopoly of potash salts will have something to sell that every farmer in the civilized world absolutely requires.

Schweitzer's role in attacking us, and his understanding of the importance of German technological plans, were forewarnings of what was to happen 25 years later in the Global War.

Dyestuffs, drugs, and potash were by no means the only industries in which the German-controlled cartels or German-held patents were able to cripple our aid to the Allies and our own war production. Only the most strenuous efforts by Government and industry could overcome the shortages of military optical goods controlled by the Zeiss works of Jena, whose American partner, Bausch & Lomb, had not theretofore produced military optical glass.

In this highly specialized field, as in the instances of radio apparatus, ignition systems for engines, and extremely technical metallurgical processes, the Germans exercised control both through patents and through cartel agreements which divided fields of endeavor. In other instances, they exercised outright monopoly, bolstered primarily by patents, and completely prevented the establishment of a domestic industry in this country. Thus, for example, even the surgical instruments so necessary in time of war were largely covered by German patents, and in 1914 over 80% of the surgical instruments in this country were imported from Germany.

Nor did the penetration of German interests into our domestic industrial structure stop with the accessories of war. The German Krupp company had "a long line of patents covering ordnance in this country, the most important of which was the split trail for field guns, 77 and 155 millimeter guns which we adopted and used during the war." The increased demand for these highly strategic tools of military science and industrial techniques made even more acute the pressure originating in the preemption of these fields by German cartels. So great were our deficiencies and so drastic our need that before 1917 our War Department took and tried to use patents covering vital processes and products, in an attempt to set up American industries to meet our requirements. In doing so they risked whatever future liability for royalties or damages might have been demanded after the war, as the "Trading with the Enemy Act" was not adopted until some time later.

Following our entry into the World War and the establishment of an Alien Property Custodian, a total of some 12,300 patents owned by German interests was taken over by the United States Government. Of this number, approximately 5,000 pertained to various branches of the chemical, dyestuffs, pharmaceutical, munitions, and explosives industries. The balance, which were placed at the disposal of the War and Navy Departments, also related to military and industrial supplies. After the war a number of these patents were placed in the custody of the Chemical Foundation, the rest remaining in the possession of the Army and the Navy.

Although the scarcity of dyestuffs and medicinals handicapped our conduct of war and enabled the Germans to produce and use poison gas almost a year before the Allies were in a position to retaliate, this situation was not the most crucial encountered by the United States. The problem of synthetic nitrogen in the years 1914-1918 corresponded precisely to the problem of synthetic rubber in 1942. Prior to 1914 the world's chief source of supply for nitrates was the Chilean fields. These compounds are the essential component of dynamite, T.N.T., and picric acid, the principal explosives of warfare.

About 1908, Professor Fritz Haber, with the full support and under the supervision of I.G. and the High Command, continued his initial experiments, begun in 1905, to make synthetic nitrogen for fertilizers and explosives. By 1913 a plant was erected at Oppau on the Rhine with 10,000 tons capacity. This was a signal event in the history of that era. Without it there would have been no war. Germany's diplomacy in the years immediately preceding the war was timed to correspond with the progress of research by which she intended to free herself from her dependence on imports of Chilean nitrates and to acquire her own source of fertilizers and explosives. Because her fleet could not command the sea lanes, Germany knew that war with England meant blockade. Blockade in turn spelled disaster if she lacked the nitrates necessary in the manufacture of munitions and the maintenance of agricultural production. The zeal with which the problem was attacked, and the scale on which the first manufacture of synthetic nitrogen was undertaken, leave but one conclusion—Germany was preparing for the "Chemists' War." Germany had determined to make synthetic nitrogen, *and she had succeeded.*

What was the reverse of the shield? When war did come, the United States had no plants for the synthetic fixation of nitrogen. Our absolute dependence on the Chilean nitrate industry was emphasized in the annual report of the Chief of Ordnance of the United States Army in 1915. As it turned out, not only were we restricted to very limited supplies of nitrate from Chile, but it later developed that many of the Chilean companies were controlled by German interests.

In 1916 Congress appropriated several million dollars and appointed a committee of scientists to study the problem of manufacture of synthetic nitrogen, and as soon as we entered the war, the Nitrate Division of the War Department undertook an extensive construction program. Four large plants were started for the production of synthetic nitrogen and nitric acid.

There were about 250 United States patents pertaining to nitrate fixation, all owned by German companies.

When these patents became subject to license under wartime legislation, an attempt was made to apply them. Nitrate Plant Number One was built at Sheffield, Alabama, at a cost of nearly thirteen million dollars. The anticipated capacity was 9,000 tons of ammonia and 14,000 tons of nitric acid per year. This expenditure of time, labor, and money was in vain. The German patents had failed to disclose the crux of the process, namely, the composition and preparation of the catalyst required to operate the method successfully. The United States remained dependent during the war for nitrates on the trickle of imports from Chile, which had to run the gauntlet of German submarines.

There were legal issues and intricate administrative problems met by the Government after the establishment of an Alien Property Custodian. The creation of the Chemical Foundation and the litigation which later occurred between the Foundation and the Government (terminating in three decisions upholding the creation of the Foundation and its custody of chemical patents) have only historical value. It should be noted, however, that, although the principal purpose in the establishment of the Foundation was the prevention of a recurrent subordination of the American chemical industry to the German trusts, the program of the Government consisted largely of improvisations. For this reason the measures adopted did not take into account the contingencies which were to arise after the cessation of hostilities, contingencies having their source in the militant nature of German industry. It was realized at the time, however, that the future might witness a renewal of the struggle with the German cartels or, what was worse, a reestablishment of their dominating interests in critical spheres of world economy.

One man, at least, saw through the German plans. Francis P. Garvan, head of the Chemical Foundation, understood the tactics and objectives of the cartels, and fought a lonely battle against them. Knowing that there could be no disarmament while the German cartels continued to function, Garvan sought to build America's chemical power. In his words:

> . . . we have learned to know that this was an industrial war, brought on by industrial Germany in her lust-made haste to capture the markets of the world. Industrial Germany, in its arrogance and pride, preferred the formidable hazard of battle to the progressive and sure infiltration which within ten or twenty years might well have given her the world domination she sought from complacent and unthinking peoples. Industrial Germany was in control of imperial Germany; industrial Germany sympathized and participated in the preparation for this war; industrial Germany waged this war; and industrial Germany was the first to see defeat and forced the military peace, in order that, with her industrial equipment intact, she might continue that same war by intensified and concentrated economic measures. It was Germany's chemical supremacy that gave her confidence

in her avaricious dream of world empire; it was Germany's chemical supremacy that enabled her to wage four years of pitiless warfare; and it is Germany's chemical supremacy upon which she relies to maintain the war, and for that supremacy she pays homage to her dye industry and counts upon that dye industry to maintain it.[6]

6. DU PONT

"YOU . . . are in a position to talk directly with a group . . . that controls a larger share of industry through common stock holdings than any other group in the United States. When I say this I mean that I believe there is no group, including the Rockefellers, the Morgans, the Mellons, or anyone else, that begins to control and be responsible for as much, industrially, as the duPont Company." [1] This estimate of the position of the duPont family in American economic life is set forth in a letter written in 1934 by John J. Raskob to a director of one of the duPont companies. Mr. Raskob's opinion is especially noteworthy, not only because of his own eminence in political and economic affairs, but because of his intimate acquaintance with duPont interests.

In any assessment of the military and industrial strength of the United States, the logical starting point is the firm of duPont de Nemours. Heaped with the scorn and abuse of pacifists, labelled as Merchants of Death, the duPont corporation is the largest chemical arsenal of this country. Since 1802 duPont powder mills

have been the major source of military explosives in all
the wars we have fought. During the World War, du-
Pont supplied not only the needs of the United States,
but 40% of all explosives used by the Allies.

The "men of good will," honest in their convictions,
who attacked duPont as a munitions maker, were more
than mistaken. Such attacks were based on an unreal
and visionary conception of the tragic evolution of history. Had they realized that Germany was planning to
plunge the world into another war, the sincerest believ-
ers in peace would have demanded that duPont continue its historic role. Not duPont's production of munitions, but the monopoly—pattern of the American
chemical industry—should have been the target. In retreat, duPont was pressed to withdraw more and more
from munitions to peaceful pursuits.

Like other American industrialists, duPont believed
far too much in normalcy as the principle of good business. Restriction of output, fixing of prices, and the
formation of cartel agreements which inhibited the full
maturing of technical change—these are the practices
which most weakened the American chemical industry.
The high-price low-output point of view, which, from
fear of competition, sacrificed industrial for financial
strength, has been the greatest curse of the democratic
economies. From a military standpoint, this type of
thinking not only helped Germany to outdistance the
United States, Great Britain, and France, but hobbled

last-minute preparation. Even during war, such aversion to change, expansion, or possible competition has gone on, reducing the momentum of our charge, and keeping us on the defensive.

What goes to make up this towering financial and economic structure beyond the bare facts of corporate size and cartel relations is the story of one of America's dynastic families, the sketch of which would be a fitting subject for the pen of a Sinclair Lewis or a Theodore Dreiser. Our attention, however, is not so much concerned with the "who" as with the "what" and the "how" of industrial empires. The principles which may be learned from the biographies of corporations affect far more than the immediate owners, and have bearing upon the social and economic destiny of the American Republic.

E. I. duPont de Nemours & Co. is the oldest and largest of the "Big Four" * of the American chemical industry, and one of the staunchest of the "old line" of industrial baronies in this country. Its activities are centered primarily in the heavy and light chemical fields, but financially, duPont connections spread into almost every major branch of commerce from banking, automobiles, and mining, to railroads, aviation, communications, and insurance. Within its own particular fields of production, duPont is a vertical and horizontal com-

---

* The other three are Allied Chemical, Union Carbide and Carbon, and American Cyanamid.

bination of specialized departments, wholly owned subsidiaries, and largely controlled corporations, each of
which operates as an autonomous unit with over-all
ownership and authority concentrated at the top of the
corporate structure in a single holding and operating
company. The latter is the familial organization which
coordinates the policies and functions of all duPont
interests.

While the number, extent, and size of duPont's pro-
ductive undertakings do not, on paper, equal those of
I. G. Farben or of Imperial Chemical Industries of
Great Britain, they are more varied than the compara-
ble operations of any similar enterprise in the Western
Hemisphere.

Internationally, duPont's status is of the same order
of importance as its domestic position, with the difference that in the world economy it is more narrowly confined to industrial affiliations without the direct financial and personal relationships which it possesses in
national economy. In certain basic types of chemical production, such as explosives, fertilizers, and dyestuffs,
duPont's international rank places it among the foremost group of modern chemical combines. No world
cartel in any important section of the industry could be
formed or operated without the participation or tacit
acceptance of duPont. Conversely, duPont's own control of its markets is largely dependent upon its membership in international cartels, especially that union

which it has established with the Imperial Chemical Industries.

As corporations go, duPont has had an interesting history, not only because of its place in American economy, but also as a case study in what might be called "industrial genetics." For it is as much the result of the personal traits and ability of the duPont family as it is of historical priority that the company early attained and maintained an unusual degree of prominence which carries over into political and social affairs.

High in any ranking of the industrial, social, and financial elite of America, the name of duPont has borne a distinction in the history of the United States seldom surpassed. The duPonts' connection with this country's development started illustriously, and has been developed by succeeding generations in a steady, at times romantic, but increasingly conservative pattern. As is often the case in the biography of noted clans, the "founder" of the family's importance in the New World was a personality characterized by "dash," élan, progressive and almost radical ideas. Pierre Samuel du-Pont de Nemours (1739-1817) possessed all the qualities of intelligence, glamour, and "drive" which are associated with the "Illuminati," the heterogeneous group whose brilliance of mind and spirit enlightened the late eighteenth century and blazoned the future of western civilization.

Pierre's son, Eleuthère duPont, started a powder mill

at Jefferson's request in 1802, near Wilmington. Eleuthère had been taught to make gunpowder by Lavoisier,
one of the giants of modern chemistry, and had further
experience in the government mills of France. His venture in the New World was to be the cornerstone of the
family's wealth.

The story of the duPonts now becomes a corporate
history. Later members of the family gained distinction
in many diverse fields, but it is primarily with the industry founded by Eleuthère that the name is identified
today. For ninety-seven years, from 1802 until 1899,
the company remained unincorporated, operating as a
partnership. During this span, which marked the building of America, the powder mills also grew, and went
through the stages by which most large American concerns pass from "enterprises" to "interests."

The period from 1802 to 1872 was one of even development for the duPont company. America was a
raw country; firearms were almost as universally used
as any other necessary tool, especially on the frontier.
Industry blasted paths and roads across the continent,
and three times the nation went to war. To the degree
that our national expansion was explosive, in a physical
as well as a figurative sense, the powder business was
ordained to prosper. As has been the case with so many
historic industries in the United States, the duPont concern, or rather its guiding minds, became increasingly
enamoured of size, and size in turn meant trustification.

The result was the formation of the so-called Powder Trust, which had the longest uninterrupted career of any American combine except the Standard Oil trust.

The formation of the trust is described melodramatically in an old article in the stately Harvard Quarterly Journal of Economics: "At ten o'clock on April 23, 1872, certain persons representing six gunpowder manufacturers held a meeting in New York City. . . ." The pool created at this meeting rationalized the powder industry of the United States.[2]

A revolution had occurred in the explosives industry. Nobel's invention of dynamite, intended to guarantee the peace of the world by making war too horrible to contemplate, had resulted in the emergence of a European dynamite cartel. In the United States dynamite was first manufactured in 1869, and had been included in the 1872 agreement. By 1897 the foreign cartel had decided to invade the American market, and began the construction of plants in Jamesburg, New Jersey. This threat to the American pool brought an instantaneous reaction. Emissaries of duPont, representing the American trust, journeyed to Europe for the purpose of making a satisfactory arrangement. Very little time transpired before a contract known as the International Agreement emerged from the series of conferences held between duPont representatives and the officials of the Nobel Company of London and the German dynamite trust. The terms of this document are interesting, not

only because of their connotation as a politico-economic
agreement, but because they show the way in which
German concerns used every device to insure their receipt of technological data on war material.

The "European factories," which included the Vereinigte Koln-Rottweiler Pulverfabriken and the English Nobel Dynamite Trust Company, agreed not to
erect any powder works in the United States. DuPont
agreed to refrain from undertaking any similar enterprise in England or on the Continent. The world
market for high explosives was divided into four dis-
tricts, with each of the members of the cartel having
a protected national market, and other areas, such as
South America, being designated as "syndicated territory," which might be exploited jointly. None of the
parties to the agreement was to undersell the others, or
to compete for orders from their respective governments. All technical information concerning processes
used in the manufacture of military explosives was exchanged, with the understanding that duPont would
keep the Nobel Trust and the German companies informed of all sales of powder to the United States Government, describing exactly the quality, quantity, and
requirements which the powder was to fulfill.

In 1910 the Department of Justice brought suit
against duPont, charging that both its foreign agreements and its domestic liquidation of competing firms
constituted violations of the anti-trust laws. The Gov-

ernment won the case, and a decree of dissolution was handed down by the Court, which resulted in the partitioning of the principal companies into three units. As the Court said at the time, "The dissolution of more than sixty corporations since the advent of the new management in 1902, and the consequent impossibility of restoring original conditions in the explosives trade, narrows the field of operation of any decree we may make." Nevertheless, the dissolution was carried into effect by creating the Atlas Powder Company and the Hercules Powder Company, both of which are in existence at the present time, and both of which are tied very closely to the parent company by patent agreements and by mutual membership in cartels in the powder industry.

Within a few years from the date of the decree the duPont company was reorganized in Delaware with a relatively modest capital of $120,000,000. The estimated assets of the duPont company at the present time are in the neighborhood of $700,000,000, but again this figure is based upon "visible" holdings, and is no indication of the real strength of the company.

The two most prosperous periods in the history of duPont were the years of the first World War and the period from 1929 through 1933. During 1914-1918 the gross income of the company was over a billion dollars, with a net profit close to $230,000,000. DuPont used part of this tidy profit to buy ten million shares of the General Motors Corporation, thereby obtaining the largest unified interest in the greatest of the Big Three of the American automobile industry.

The enormous expansion of duPont's facilities during the war, coupled with the many chemical shortages, such as dyestuffs and nitrates, which this country encountered, pointed the way toward the logical paths of development for the duPont endeavors. In rapid succession during the years after the Armistice duPont entered the fields of dyestuffs and other organic chemicals, paints and varnishes, electro-chemicals. It also inaugurated a progressive pattern of research. It combined with other chemical interests, and increased its general chemical manufacture so that between four and five thousand products bear the name "duPont."

The Armistice had hardly been signed before duPont representatives were on their way to visit I. G. Farben for the purpose of forming an alliance. In November, 1919, representatives of duPont and of the Badische Company, the principal corporate entity of I.G., met in Zurich, Switzerland, and worked out a tentative agreement for the organization of a "world company" to exploit the Haber-Bosch process for the synthetic manufacture of ammonia. Also, duPont sought know-how and technical instruction in the dyestuffs industry. Although I.G. was not averse to an agreement with duPont, the two could not reach complete accord on the relative division of control. DuPont sought to turn the "regulatory screw" of tariff legislation on I.G., but the latter, conscious of its real strength, could not be moved from its entrenched position. In fact, duPont's envoys were of the opinion that Dr. Carl Duisberg, who was in many respects the master mind of I.G. from its formation in 1904 until his death a few years ago, still believed that he could "bully the U. S."

I.G. was being courted at the same time by British chemical interests, and took full advantage of its strategic and technical situation in order to obtain the best possible conditions for the reestablishment of its world position. While the duPont-Badische negotiations did not result in the formation of a grand alliance, they were by no means without issue. DuPont's relationships with the Vereinigte Koln-Rottweiler Pulverfabriken (V.K.R.) became even closer. Both the V.K.R. and the Dynamit Aktiengesellschaft (D.A.G.), the successor of the German Nobel Company, became a part of I.G. Together with I.G., duPont and Imperial Chemical Industries, Ltd. [I.C.I.] both owned minority interests in the stock of D.A.G., and duPont at one time had about three million dollars invested directly in I.G.'s stock.

On January 1, 1926, an agreement was consummated between duPont, D.A.G., and V.K.R., corresponding to the Explosives Agreement of the same date between duPont and I.C.I., which effectually divided the world market for military powder. This agreement, discussed in the hearings of the Nye Committee in 1934, was found in the duPont files marked "Unsigned—in effect as a gentleman's agreement." Under this agreement, as under the arrangement with I.C.I., patent licenses and technical information were exchanged, and since, in deference to the provisions of the Versailles Treaty the German companies could not sell military explosives in other countries, duPont became, in effect, their sales agent. To quote the Nye report, "In other words, though German munitions companies cannot sell abroad, American companies can sell for them, and to our own Government at that."

Partly because of the failure of the conferences with I.G., duPont ultimately entered into as complete a union with I.C.I. as it is possible for two distinct groups to achieve and still retain even nominal individuality. I.C.I. was the combination of the British dyestuffs industry and the successor to the British Nobel company with which duPont had established relations in 1897. There are a series of agreements between duPont and I.C.I. pertaining not only to the general division of fields and markets between the two, but dealing also with special situations, such as that in South America and in Canada. In both of these latter areas, duPont and I.C.I. operate jointly-owned subsidiaries, known as Duperial in South America, and Canadian Industries Limited in Canada.

While the relationships between duPont and I.C.I. cover all branches of the chemical and explosives industries, both companies have, of course, entered into other commitments, principally with I. G. Farben, with the Mitsui interests of Japan, and with many other lesser concerns in the United States.

The hierarchy of agreements in the chemical and explosives industries approaches world-rationalization. Because of I.G.'s position, it has been able to use the apparently overlapping network of understandings to "divide and rule," in its campaign for world supremacy. Were it not for the consolidation existing between duPont and I.C.I., there would be no counterpoise to I.G. But because the duPont-I.C.I. alliance was based on commercial, not military, considerations, I.G.'s ulterior motives were not clearly understood. Both companies were therefore the more readily persuaded that I.G. meant no harm.

Because of duPont's position in our chemical industry in particular, and our economy in general, it is beguiling to many undemocratic minds to consider that duPont could be America's I.G. As the nearest facsimile of economic feudalism in this country, duPont men have flirted in the past with various reactionary organizations, such as the Crusaders and the Liberty League. While these tendencies are not visible at present, they are latent in duPont or any similar economic unit.

Monopoly in whatever guise means rigid control of economic life. A replica of I.G. in the United States, constantly spreading its spell over industry and government, would by the very reason of its being, tend to crush democracy. The political integrity of the individual, and the right to engage in enterprise, are the freedoms for which we fight. Democracy and an I.G. could not dwell together in Germany, nor could they do so here.

7. DYESTUFFS—THE KALEIDOSCOPE OF WAR

THE history of dyestuffs reveals the strategy and tactics of German Geopolitik from the time Germany became a nation to the present. An indication of the significance of the dye industry lies in the fact that, as we have seen, the center of the high command in Germany's economic war is I.G. Farbenindustrie, which, translated literally, means "Dye Industry." In the light of the importance of the dye industry in world affairs both past and present, it is logical that this should be so. The dye industry can be and has been mobilized for war almost since its establishment.

Explosives, poison and noxious gases, antitoxins and serums, so essential to warfare, belong to the same chemical category as do dyestuffs. The few basic coal tar and organic compounds are used to make several hundred types of so-called "intermediates," which may in turn be used with equal facility to make dyes, medicines, or explosives. Consequently, research in the dye industry has effects in all other branches of the organic chemical industry. Out of German dye laboratories have come

93

phosgene, among the deadliest of gases, as well as salvarsan and sulphanilamide, the magic bullets used to
destroy disease. The whole paradox of science is illustrated in these aspects of the dyestuffs industry. Compounds almost identical in chemical properties can be
used to kill or to cure, as weapons of man against man
or of man against the destructive forces of nature.

The story of the dye industry in the first World War
has already been told. It is with the sequel to the war
that we are now concerned. The Alien Property Custodian's office established by the American government
was an emergency measure. It is evident in the litigation
and confusion which attended the administration of this
office that, although the Alien Property Custodian was
intended to act as a trustee for the public, in effect it substituted itself for German patent holders. This statement is not intended to impugn either the motives of
the incumbents of that office or to cast aspersions on its
operations. No purpose would be served by discussing
the pros and cons of the disputes which arose during and
after the war concerning the disposition of German patents, or the claims made by various litigants.

One thing is clear. The spirit and purpose of the
Alien Property Custodian legislation, if not the letter,
were directed toward the establishment of American industries in lieu of those previously dominated by Germany. This was especially true of the pharmaceutical
and dye industries where, as we have seen, German con-

trol placed the United States in a precarious position when war began. Despite repeated warnings by those in Congress and those in industry that unless effective action was taken a return of German control would occur at the end of the war, the intent of the legislation was frustrated.

In retrospect the story looks quite simple. Those leading the fight to correct the evils revealed by the World War placed their reliance on a high tariff and, indeed, succeeded in achieving it. Once the security of the country was entrusted to the tariff law, there was no consideration of the possibility that this "Maginot line" could be pierced. Complacency, coupled with German ingenuity and the fact that Germany continued her economic war without alarming her opponents, were the chief conditions that ultimately lead to encirclement of the new American dyestuffs industry. If the analogy may be continued, the tariff wall about the dyestuffs and pharmaceutical industries was not pierced so much as it was flanked. It must be recorded to his everlasting credit that President Wilson not only recognized the need of a tariff, but realized that a tariff would be insufficient to assure the future independence of our organic chemical industry. In his annual message to Congress, delivered May 20, 1919, he said:

> Nevertheless, there are parts of our tariff system which need prompt attention. The experiences of the war have made it plain that in some cases too great

reliance on foreign supply is dangerous, and that in determining certain parts of our tariff policy domestic considerations must be borne in mind which are political as well as economic.

Among the industries to which special consideration should be given is that of the manufacture of dyestuffs and related chemicals. Our complete dependence upon German supplies before the war made the interruption of trade a cause of exceptional economic disturbance. The close relation between the manufacture of dyestuffs on the one hand and of explosives and poisonous gases on the other, moreover, has given the industry an exceptional significance and value.

Although the United States will gladly and unhesitatingly join in the program of international disarmament, it will, nevertheless, be a policy of obvious prudence to make certain of the successful maintenance of many strong and well equipped chemical plants. German chemical industry, with which we will be brought into competition, was and may well be again a thoroughly knit monopoly, capable of exercising a competition of a peculiarly insidious and dangerous kind.

In 1919 the Alien Property Custodian auctioned the Bayer dyestuffs and pharmaceutical interests, including seized patents, to the highest bidder, the Sterling Products Co. (Inc.) of West Virginia. This company, interested only in the pharmaceutical business, disposed of the dye business to the Grasselli Chemical Company.

Although there is no evidence to indicate that it was

the result of conscious planning, the divorcement of the dye and pharmaceutical enterprises is worthy of reflection. The German dye and pharmaceutical business is merged into one industry. This unification enormously increases the creative potentialities of the industry, because a great many medicinal and pharmaceutical discoveries of recent years are closely related to the chemistry of dyestuffs. For example, Ehrlich's cure for syphilis is actually a dye that kills the spirochete by impregnating it in much the same manner that indigo blue impregnates cloth. Sulphanilamide and the rest of the sulpha series of drugs belong to the sulphur and aniline derivatives which form the basis of our present dye industry. Wherever research laboratories experimenting in both dyes and pharmaceuticals are operated jointly, there is greater likelihood that discoveries having application in one field will be found to apply to the other. When such interests are divided, it is far less probable that the dual utility of such discoveries will be realized.

The need for the development of a dyestuffs industry in the United States under the control of bona-fide citizens, in view of the experience of this country during the World War, could not be ignored. It has already been remarked that before the war Germany supplied some 85% of the world's dyes and practically all of the intermediates.* The industry in the United States

* An intermediate is a semi-fabricated coal tar product which is necessary for the manufacture of any one of a large group of finished products.

was relatively infinitesimal, since there were only six dye plants in operation and these were dependent for their intermediates upon Germany. The American industry at the beginning of the World War employed only 528 people, and the value of its production was less than $3,500,000 per year. The famine of pharmaceuticals and dyestuffs caused this country to become acutely conscious not only of its lack of products but of its lack of productive facilities in this industry. So drastic was the shortage of dyestuffs and medicinal supplies during the war that when the German submarine *Deutschland* arrived in Baltimore with a cargo of these materials, it was an occasion for jubilation. The fact that a military vessel could make the trip in face of the British mastery of the seas, and the significance of such a voyage to our vaunted isolation, was overlooked.

The sale by the Alien Property Custodian of the German Bayer dyestuffs, pharmaceutical patents and operating units to Sterling Products, and the latter's sale of the dyestuff branch to the Grasselli Chemical Company appeared to be a step in the right direction. With the purchase by the Grasselli company of the dye business the seed of a large self-sufficient American-controlled industry was planted. There was one disturbing factor: the reemployment of many of the German personnel of the Bayer interests, but where else, it could be argued, were technicians in so highly specialized a field to be found? Rudolph Hutz, the manager of the former Bayer dyestuffs company in the United States, who had been interned during the war, became general manager of the Grasselli Chemical Company's dyestuffs division; there were many lesser figures thus transferred.

Shortly after the Armistice, and largely because of the many blunders of the Treaty of Versailles, as well as dissatisfaction with the British and French attitude concerning war debts, the post-war depression in the United States, and the sufferings of the vanquished Germans, American distrust of her former foe began to wane. Consequently, when in 1920 the German economic offensive began to roll, there was almost no alarm in this country. Frustrated to some extent by the tariff and by the loss of its valuable patents in the dyestuffs and pharmaceutical fields, two alternatives were open to the German interests: they could enter into agreements dividing world territory with the American group, or they could re-purchase as much of their former assets in the United States as could be bought. Since the alternatives were attractive, they adopted both. In 1920 the German Bayer Company executed an agreement based upon patents and trademarks with the Sterling Products Company.*

So far as dyestuffs were concerned, the German Bayer company made overtures to the Grasselli Chemical Company in 1923, and entered into a formal agreement

---

* This agreement will be discussed in the section on pharmaceutical cartels.

with them in 1924. Under this agreement, a jointly owned company was formed. Fifty-one per cent of the stock was vested in Grasselli, the remainder in German Bayer. The new firm, called the Grasselli Dyestuffs Company, was apparently controlled by the American participant, but this appearance was both fictional and ephemeral. For one thing, the German Bayer company carefully protected its dominance of the world market by providing that the new company could sell only in the United States and Canada. Hence, one of the most important elements in the infant dye industry was removed as a threat to Germany's new type of imperialism. Bayer also protected another part of its business by prohibiting the new dyestuffs company from engaging in the production of heavy chemicals. Finally, the monopoly movement in America was encouraged by the contract between Bayer and Grasselli, since it was agreed not to form any other dyestuffs company which might compete with their jointly owned enterprise.

Aided by the desire of the Grasselli Chemical Company to free itself from the fear of German competition in its domestic market, the Bayer company was able to sink the first shaft in the reconstruction of German control of the dyestuffs industry in the United States. Numerous ramifications of this early agreement were to ensue, causing much perplexity and grief to our government, as well as much embarrassment to certain industrial enterprises and highly placed individuals not sufficiently aware of German geopolitics to keep clear of "entangling alliances."

Thereafter agreements and reorganizations within the dyestuffs group went forward with unabated velocity, each time increasing German control. On June 17, 1924, a new agreement, basically the same as the earlier one, but including as a signatory Grasselli Dyestuffs, was executed. On March 23, 1925, another German dyestuffs manufacturer was brought into the scheme. The Hoechst Company joined in a new agreement and was given 30% of Grasselli Dyestuffs stock, with Grasselli Chemical and Bayer retaining 35% each. On the same day a supplemental agreement providing for a sales organization called General Dyestuffs Corporation, to market the dyes of Grasselli Dyestuffs, was executed. On July 31, 1925, all eight members of I.G. were included by virtue of still another series of agreements, which provided the same basic arrangements of the very first contract with the additional feature of profit-sharing by the various parties. This profit-sharing was not without benefits to Grasselli Chemical, but it parted with control of the former Bayer dyestuffs business in the United States. It was, therefore, left in 1925 with 35% ownership of Grasselli Dyestuffs, the remainder and controlling portion once again passing into the hands of the great I. G. Farbenindustrie. Wilson's prophetic apprehension was becoming a concrete reality.

By October 20, 1928, the Grasselli Chemical Company was eliminated entirely. The E. I. duPont de Nemours Co., desiring to purchase the Grasselli Chemical Company, would not do so until the latter was free of the dyestuffs business, lest duPont, now a dye producer itself, be liable under the antitrust laws for purchasing a competitor. On October 20, 1928, Grasselli Chemical Company sold out the dyestuffs business to representatives of I. G. Farben, and three days later duPont acquired the Grasselli interests itself. The Germans, through I. G. Farben, had in less than ten years after the Armistice regained the dye business which it had lost by confiscation. This left the Germans with control over a substantial part of United States dyestuffs production, although by no means as complete as during the period prior to the first World War.

The Germans, of course, were confronted with other problems incident to their loss of control of the dyestuffs markets during and after the first World War. Other concerns in the United States, such as duPont, Allied Chemical & Dye, American Cyanamid, and a host of independents, recognizing the fruitfulness of the dye business in this country, entered the field. Even before the war, the Swiss were beginning to develop a substantial business. The restrictive effect of the war upon German exports gave the Swiss an opportunity which they did not forego. In fact, the three Swiss producers, Ciba, Sandoz, and Geigy, formed a cartel group of their own under a "Community of Interests Agreement." Consequently, by 1920 the Swiss were ready for a fling in the major circles of international business.

Because of Germany's historical priority in the fusion of the dyestuffs industry within her frontiers, and because the other countries of the world had been held in subjection by the German cartel until the World War, the combination movement in the dye industries outside of Germany did not develop fully until the 1920's. But no sooner had England, the United States, and France succeeded in establishing their own domestic sources of supply than the shadow of the German trust again was cast over the markets. The new dye industries in these countries took no more than their first steps before the old urge to "get together" made itself felt. Combination became the object, and absorption or amalgamation the means, by which dyestuffs companies in the allied countries began their own cartellization. It may be argued that, despite tariff protection, the new entrants knew from past experience that the proficiency of the German trust's "selective attack" or "sharpshooting" exposed them to repeated subjugation. But it was also the desire of the "rookies" in England, France, and the United States to "play ball" with I.G. and thereby further their own monopolistic security. If the American, British, French and other non-German dyestuffs companies had heeded the warnings of history, they might have hesitated long before entering into any agreements with the German interests. Admonitions were voiced by many outside the industry, both here and abroad. For example, Henry Hauser, writing even before the end of the war, in his study "Germany's Commercial Grip on the World," counselled extreme caution. He said, "These attempts at international regulation of production and of sales appear singularly dangerous to anyone who knows the lion's share which Germany means to reserve to herself in the 'organization of the world.'"

Nevertheless, the avidity with which the managers of the dye industries looked toward the integration of the world's dyestuffs concerns was too strong to be stopped by fear. By 1922 negotiations were under way between the British Dyestuffs Company and the Germans, and between duPont and the British. Rapid co-ordination by agreements and mergers within each country, and higgling with each other occupied the years immediately following the Armistice.

In 1926, an executive of duPont, in a letter to du-Pont's European manager, outlining the formation of Imperial Chemical Industries, said:

> When Sir Harry [referring to Sir Harry McGowan] was in New York, he met Sir Alfred Mond there, and in the course of a couple of hours' conversation, these two had reached practical agreement to consolidate the British Chemical industries in a single company. The details of this agreement were arranged shortly after the return of Sir Harry to London, with the result which you now know. While in

New York, Professor Bosch [of the I.G.] was informed of the proposed amalgamation, and expressed himself as extremely well pleased, and it was arranged that he would stop off in London on his return to Germany.

Sir Harry explained . . . *that the formation of I.C.I. is only the first step in a comprehensive scheme which he has in mind to rationalize chemical manufacture of the world.* The details of such a scheme are not worked out, not even in Sir Harry's own mind, but the broad picture includes working arrangements between three groups—the I.G. in Germany, Imperial Chemical Industries in the British Empire, and duPonts and the Allied Chemical & Dye in America. The next step in the scheme is an arrangement of some sort between the Germans and the British. He appreciates fully, or at least he says he does, the supreme difficulty in the way of the final step, namely the personality of the management of the Allied Chemical & Dye. In spite of this, he is hopeful that a satisfactory arrangement can be come to. [Italics added] [1]

Although duPont and I. G. Farben never succeeded in establishing a general understanding such as that between duPont and Imperial Chemical Industries, they did work out a degree of "practical" cooperation. It was not lack of desire on the part of either to enter into restrictive agreements which frustrated the consummation of an entente. In the years 1927-1929 continuous nego-

tiations contemplating the establishment of a jointly
owned dyestuffs company to advance their mutual interests in the United States were carried on even to the
stage of working out the specific functions of the proposed American Dyes Company. The point of difference between duPont and I.G. which no amount of bargaining could overcome was the question of control of
the proposed company. I.G. demanded at least a 50-50
partnership. To duPont's offer of a 49% share, I.G.'s
response is summarized in a duPont memorandum:

> I.G. suggest a 50/50 stock ownership, so that they
> would have a veto power as to expansion, export and
> prices, and thus be able to protect their world mar-
> kets against American competition. We did not agree
> to this and stood firm that such an arrangement would
> be impossible. In connection with this proposition, the
> I.G. suggested the desirability of taking in the Allied
> Chemical & Dye Corporation. We gave it as our opin-
> ion that this was impossible on account of the Sher-
> man Law. They also suggested that it might be de-
> sirable to take in the Cyanamid Company.
> Dyes: The I.G. had no criticism of our suggestions,
> but stated that they must take the matter up with
> their American associates first before giving any an-
> swer. We understood that they had in mind Grasselli,
> and offered to approach Grasselli, with whom we are
> on friendly terms, but were requested to allow them
> to take the matter up first. In this connection, Dr.
> Bosch suggested the desirability of taking in the Swiss
> Company in America.[2]

When it was at last realized by duPont that further efforts to reach an understanding were futile, they contented themselves with an "amicable cooperation" embracing "on the one hand understandings about foreign markets and on the other . . . amicable settlements of all patent litigation in the United States of America."

In a report dated March 18, 1936, concerning duPont-I.G. relationships in patents and processes, it is stated:

> In the last few years duPont-I.G. relationships have notably improved, due partly to the personalities of individuals entrusted with negotiations and partly to an officially more friendly attitude from higher up in the I.G. organization. Also it is said that I.G. now wishes to put its patent office operations in this country on a profitable basis through a liberal policy in granting licenses.
>
> Various informal contacts and the cementing of more cordial relations have been achieved through the London Office but all actual patent licenses and agreements have been worked out with I.G. in New York.
>
> Orchem. [which refers to the Organic Chemical Division of duPont] has been notably successful in dealing with Mr. Duisberg and the I.G. patent firm of Hutz and Joslin in New York City. In the last three years some 42 licenses have been negotiated and interferences settled and these things are now more or less taken in their stride with the important and unimportant items all being run through the mill

together. Messrs. Holmes of Orchem. and Brownell of the Legal Department, have achieved excellent results in their handling of this situation.

*   *   *

The I.G. and duPont have an informal agreement that when we have German patents which seem to us might be profitably exploited in Germany, and when these patents cover subjects on which we have no prior commitments or moral obligations to discuss with anybody else, we will bring them first to the attention of the I.G. and they will do the same for the United States.[3]

It must be stated, in fairness to duPont, that in so far as its negotiations and transactions with I.G. are concerned, duPont exhibited far greater respect for the national interests of the United States than many of its monopolistic brethren in other industries. To the extent that they were aware of I.G.'s desire to obtain veto powers over various branches of American industry, duPont reacted in what could be called a patriotic manner. It was, of course, a favorite device of I.G.'s to obtain 50% ownership of joint companies formed as a result of its contracts with American industries and, where possible, to retain as a part of its prerogatives the ultimate power of decision over construction of operating facilities, development of output, general price levels, and export policies of such joint concerns. This device was successfully used by I.G. in the case of Grasselli Dyestuffs Company, which has already been discussed, and in the cases of the Magnesium Development Corporation, the Winthrop Chemical Company, Jasco, and others. A qualification must be entered concerning duPont's maintenance and regard for national interest. In the semi-annual report of its Foreign Relations Department dated February 9, 1940, duPont stated:

> I.G. have given evidence of the adoption of a policy of industrial development in South America through purchase of the Fluminense caustic-chlorine plant in Brazil and of shares of the Electroclor Company in Argentina. Arrangements have been made for the repayment to the I.G. of money advanced to Duperial for the purchase of shares in the latter company as it is impracticable for I.C.I. to be in partnership relationship with a German Company. *The duPont Company informed I.G. that they intended to use their good offices after the war to have the I.G. participation restored.* [Italics added] [4]

Turning now to other phases of the cartellization of the world dye industry, the most important interconnections are those between duPont and I.C.I., between I.C.I. and I.G., between I.G. and the European dyestuffs cartel, and the relationships between all of these and the Mitsui interests of Japan. Although each one of these associations could be the topic of a separate economic study, we can telescope the detailed arrangements in order to concentrate on their total effect. Very soon after the formation of I.C.I., duPont's representatives (in this case Lammot duPont was the chief emissary) conducted conversations in the years from 1927 to 1929 which resulted in an agreement which amounted to the complete alliance of duPont and I.C.I. in the world chemical industry.

This agreement, which is drawn up in phrases reminiscent of a major political treaty, provided for the exchange of information on all patented or secret inventions, for the exchange of exclusive licenses under each other's patents, and for the disposition of world markets. In a truly imperial manner the agreement provides that duPont shall have exclusive rights in the countries of North and Central America exclusive of Canada, Newfoundland, and British possessions, and that I.C.I. shall have exclusive rights within the British Empire. In the case of India, duPont was permitted to continue its activities subject to a future settlement.

In 1931, duPont and I.C.I. agreed to transfer all of duPont's assets in India to I.C.I. in exchange for the transfer to duPont of the entire ownership of I.C.I.'s American subsidiary, Dyestuffs Corporation of America. I.C.I. was careful to inform duPont of its 1931 agreement with I.G. and the European cartel, and to reassure duPont that their mutual understandings were in no way affected. In Canada, duPont and I.C.I. operated a jointly owned company, Canadian Industries Limited, whose supervision was somewhat informally entrusted to correspondence and meetings of the representatives of the principals. This method of administration proved satisfactory until 1936, at which time, because of legal considerations, duPont expressed its preference for a formal tri-party agreement to define C.I.L.'s status.

The original 1929 agreement between duPont and I.C.I. was automatically terminated on June 30, 1939, at which time a renewal contract was entered into, having substantially all the features of the earlier understanding.

One of the knottiest problems encountered by all direct and indirect participants in the world dyestuffs cartel was posed by the "gentlemen of Japan." Since 1931 the cartel, including National Aniline Corporation (a subsidiary of Allied Chemical & Dye), duPont, I.C.I., and the Europeans, had controlled the market in China on a formal basis in accordance with what was called "the China Six-Party Agreement." The Mitsui interests, having established themselves in the dyestuffs industry as the leader of the Japanese market, were successfully crowding out duPont, I.C.I., and the continental cartel. The members of the cartel felt that Mitsui could be brought in on the same basis as other national monopolies, but Mitsui's claims and aspirations, in line with its Asiatic plans, were somewhat larger than had been anticipated. Appeasement was the cartel's first plan, but with a readiness for "war" if that should be necessary. In 1934 A. C. Lumley, far-eastern repre-

sentative of the National Aniline Corporation, wrote
that:

> We therefore believe it will be wise to attempt to
> ascertain the limit of the Mitsui ambitions by meet-
> ing them in conference with the avowed object of at-
> tempting an amicable arrangement. Mitsui may re-
> fuse to enter such a conference; if so, nothing is lost
> and the fight can begin exactly as it would have begun
> without any conference proposal. Even if we get
> Mitsui into a conference, their ideas may be too big
> and they may demand a share of the world market
> larger than other indigo manufacturers are willing to
> give them. If so, again, the fight can begin as if the
> conference had not been held. On the other hand,
> there is just the chance that a satisfactory arrange-
> ment can be reached and a price war averted, and it is
> my firm conviction that such a possibility should be
> investigated.[5]

Mitsui became a member of the International Committee on Dyestuffs and Sulphur Black, which allocated
the bulk of dyestuffs consumed in Asia. In 1934, at
which time Mitsui was included on the committee, it is
evident that the Japanese intended if possible to use
their membership simply as an operating base. In 1938
the Foreign Sales Manager of National submitted a
report on the China market, setting forth the average
sales by the Japanese and indicating that there were
grounds for disturbance so far as the activities of the
Japanese were concerned. He stated:

The above figures are emphasized because Japan as yet is not totally independent of imports of Miscellaneous Colors into Japan proper, and Japan's existing manufacturing capacity . . . is still very inadequate to support Japanese ambition within the occupied Chinese area, regardless of what is undoubtedly a fundamental policy now with the Japanese Government; namely, to consolidate her commercial position in the occupied Chinese area to the exclusion, if at all possible, of foreign manufacturers, with the possible exception of what may be a co-operative plan with the German I.G.[6]

In reviewing the operation of the dye cartel up to the outbreak of war, there are certain features which may be emphasized by recapitulation. Without considering for the moment the relative positions of the individual concerns involved, it is apparent that the entire world, with the exception of Russia, was organized in a more or less complete fashion. All of Europe, all of North America, all of the major countries of South America, and all of Asia were divided up among the principal dyestuffs producers. Allocation of territory, interchange of patents and technical information, fixing of production quotas and prices, and all other behavior characteristics of international cartels are to be found in the web of agreements and understandings that has been sketched. In the center of the web, spinning out a filament in every direction, was I.G.

Like all able military commanders, the Germans carefully reviewed their earlier campaigns so that for future battles past mistakes could be avoided, weakness in the enemy more readily exploited, and instruments and devices which proved themselves worthy more fully utilized. Rarely has this been so true as in the development, scope, and operation of the American I.G. Company. Disguise, surprise, and the economic counterpart of a fifth column were all to be found in its arsenal. Where devices and instruments of the World War proved inadequate, new ones were substituted; where they had succeeded, they were sharpened and employed again.

In 1929, for the ostensible purpose of merging all of I. G. Farben's interests in the United States, the American I.G. was formed. Included in this network was the General Aniline Works, described earlier as Grasselli Dyestuffs; the Agfa-Ansco Corporation, a large photographic manufacturing and supply group; a 50% interest in Winthrop Chemical Company, which served as I. G. Farben's link to the pharmaceutical business of the United States, and a little later a 50% interest in the Magnesium Development Company, which was the vehicle combining I.G.'s light metal interests with the Aluminum Company of America. Through the ownership of a large block of Standard Oil of New Jersey stock, American I.G. was close to this company. Walter Teagle, the President of the Standard Oil Company of New Jersey, was a member of the Board of American I.G., as was Edsel Ford.

The German dyestuff interests had learned their lesson well. In addition to securing membership on the board of directors of these two prominent American industrialists, the German ownership of the organization was also concealed. In 1928, I. G. Farben organized in Switzerland a company known as the Internationale Gesellschaft für Chemische Unternehmungen A. G. (I. G. Chemie), and transferred to it I.G.'s holdings in American I.G. *It was then often and loudly proclaimed that American I.G. was Swiss-owned,* and had no German connection, notwithstanding the fact that until 1940 the head of I. G. Farbenindustrie, Hermann Schmitz, was also president of Swiss I. G. Chemie, and that the directorate of American I.G. was *in the control* of former officials of I. G. Farbenindustrie, including its president, Dietrich Schmitz, the brother of Hermann Schmitz.

The desire of I. G. Farben to retain an American façade and the magnitude of its power were responsible for its ability to refuse successfully permission to Walter Teagle to resign from the board of American I.G. He tried to do so continuously after 1933, when he was advised of the implications of his presence on that board. "The cartel control was . . . strong enough . . . to keep Mr. Teagle . . . upon the board of this I. G. Farben company against his will." [7]

In 1939, the eruption of war between Britain and Germany was also the signal for the German affiliates in the United States to take their designated posts. This will become clearer as the rest of the cartel story unfolds. By December 1939 the American I.G. was somewhat reorganized and its name changed to General Aniline & Film Company. Every charge that General Aniline & Film was German-owned was answered by statements of its officers that it was Swiss-owned. The Board of Directors took on a more American complexion with the addition of some new directors. "American I.G." may have become General Aniline & Film, but it remained I.G. in America. A soldier without uniform is still a combatant, except that he may be known by a more unsavory term.

Audacity is a quality not lacking among the Germans. Willingness to do the bizarre and unexpected has been an exceptionally effective weapon in their successes. Nevertheless it is still somewhat breathtaking to note that I.G. made arrangements for its agencies in the British Empire to continue business despite the war. On September 19, 1939, just sixteen days after Britain and Germany were at war, I.G. cabled General Aniline & Film:

> . . . IN ADDITION TO CANADA WE RELEASE YOU FROM EXPORT RESTRICTION IN REGARD TO FOLLOWING COUNTRIES GREAT BRITAIN, BRITISH INDIA, AUS-TRALIA, NEWZEALAND BUT ONLY FOR DURATION OF

PRESENT STATE OF WAR AND AS FAR AS SUPPLIES TO
FOLLOWING FIRMS ARE CONCERNED
IG DYESTUFFS LIMITED 14 BRIDGE STREET MANCHES-
TER 3 CHEM DYES LTD WITTET ROAD BALLARD ESTATE
BOMBAY DYCHEM TRADING CO PTY LTD 573 LONSDALE
STREET MELBOURNE CONE DYES AND CHEMICALS LTD
15 COURTENAY PLACE WELLINGTON C THREE PLEASE
CONFIRM [8]

Thus an arrangement was made whereby the I. G.
Farben agencies in the British Empire were to continue
throughout war with General Aniline & Film providing
the necessary dyestuffs. Note should be taken that General Aniline & Film could not sell generally in the British Empire but only through I. G. Farben's agents.

Acting a little more cautiously than its government,
which thought the fall of France would end the war,
I.G. recognized that even the possible fall of Britain
might not end "the present state of war." I.G. thereupon amended its cable by sending another on September 21, 1939.

. . . REPLACE IN FIRST TELEGRAM "FOR DURATION
OF PRESENT STATE OF WAR" BY "UNTIL FURTHER
NOTICE" AND ACT ACCORDINGLY [9]

On October 16, 1939, the pinch of the blockade was
felt by I.G.'s agency in Colombia, South America, and
General Aniline & Film received a cable from I.G.
granting permission to sell there, but only to the I.G.
agency. By January 8, 1940, General Aniline & Film

was permitted to sell to all of Latin America, and a list of I.G. agencies was supplied. Sales could be made only through these agencies. This simple device of protecting the I.G. distributive outlets in Latin America may have serious military consequences some day. Of immediate importance was the fact that the British blockade was disrupted.

8. PLASTICS—THE TEST-TUBE METAL

GERMANY'S metal reserves have never been enough to fill the maw of Mars. In her search for "ersatz," Germany years ago saw in plastics the ideal material with which to round out the stock-pile.

But plastics are more than ersatz—they are a new frontier of science. By exploring every source and every application of plastic materials, Germany has created an almost inexhaustible well of novel and useful products. The role which plastics take in war is larger every day. The 10,000-mile bomber of the future may be pressed out of plastics lighter than the light metals and equally as strong.

The emergence of plastics on the industrial scene is relatively new. The industry in this country at present produces annually about 300,000,000 pounds of plastics, valued at approximately $500,000,000. Their uses have not only been of a substitute variety, but because of their many new characteristics, they have probably supplanted many uses of glass, metals and wood permanently. Plastics are the genies in the test tube, which are called up to remedy shortages.

119

The functions of plastics in war are manifold, including service as windshields on all airplanes, parachute flares, navy mosquito boats, crash helmets, bayonet sheaths, gunstocks, bayonet handles, and a variety of other military goods. This merely scratches the surface of their diverse applications. Suggestion has been made that modern soldiers should wear coats of plastic armor. The Ford Motor Company has already experimented with an all-plastic automobile body. Plastics' domestic uses have already invaded the fields of jewelry and ornamentation, kitchenware, furniture, clothing such as belts and suspenders, optical lenses, and medical instruments. Plastics have practically eliminated rubber as a material for dental plates. Some plastics can "bend" light, and this peculiar property has made it possible that in the future windowless offices, factories, and homes can enjoy "piped sunshine." Still in its infant stages, the future of the industry is already assured.

The fields of organic chemistry, as already noted, are so complex, and have so many ramified interrelations, that developments in one have applications and effects in others. Pharmaceuticals and dyestuffs have already served as examples. Plastics are endowed with similar physical and chemical properties, and their history is complicated by similar commercial and geopolitical difficulties. Their development, therefore, is replete with international cartel agreements, involving division of territory, patents, and all those characteristics which identify German Economic War.

There are many kinds of plastics. Germany has channelized its indefatigable science in the development of one of the most important, namely, methyl methacrylate, which is probably better known here under the trade names of Plexiglass and Lucite. This plastic is made from coal, oil, and air.

Research on the problem of eliminating excess weight in aircraft is among the major projects of aeronautical laboratories. The less weight, the more gasoline, hence greater range; the less weight, the more weapons, hence maximum destructiveness. The needs of the Luftwaffe have therefore governed the experiments with plastics in German industry.

This special type of plastic is more transparent than glass. It increases a pilot's range of vision, while giving him greater protection, for it is shatterproof. Cockpit enclosures, the noses of Flying Fortresses, and all parts of a plane that must give the crew greater visibility with a minimum of risk are made of Plexiglass.

As its name implies, this plastic is readily shaped into any form desired. It can be machined, sawed, or moulded better than any metal. In fact, it can be best defined as a kind of wooden glass. The value of plastics to Germany is transparent.

Back in 1903 a Dr. Otto Rohm and a Mr. Otto Haas formed a partnership in Darmstadt, Germany, to manufacture and market a substance known as Oropon, which is used in the tanning of hides. Shortly thereafter, Otto Haas came to the United States, and another partnership, called Rohm & Haas, was formed in Philadelphia. The Oropon business was highly successful. Dr. Rohm remained in Germany to run the German end of the business, while Mr. Haas in due time became an American citizen and conducted the business in the United States.

Shortly after the United States declared war on Germany in 1917, it was decided to incorporate the partnerships. The German firm was incorporated in Darmstadt, Mr. Haas receiving a minority interest. The American firm was incorporated on April 23, 1917, in Delaware, with both partners receiving 50% of the common stock.

In due course, the Alien Property Custodian seized the stock owned by Dr. Rohm in Rohm & Haas (Philadelphia). This was sold by the Alien Property Custodian to the Tanners' Products Company of Chicago for $300,000. In 1924 the original German owners of the confiscated stock regained control. Otto Haas paid approximately $500,000 for it, and turned the stock over in the form of a trust to Otto Rohm. Thus this important part of the tanning industry, scheduled to be a support of America's war-born chemical facilities, had been recaptured.

Rohm & Haas (Philadelphia) was technically independent of Rohm & Haas (Darmstadt)—they were merely owned by the same stockholders. The spirit of cooperation prevailed, and their relationships were very close. On October 14, 1927, this propinquity was consolidated by an agreement between the parties. The familiar pattern of division of territory was in evidence. Rohm & Haas (Darmstadt) received exclusive rights to Europe, Africa, and Asia, while the American company received North and South America, Australia, New Zealand, and Japan. Although the leather tanning business was the main object of the agreement, provision was made for negotiating along similar lines the development of future discoveries which might be of interest to the parties.

It must be remembered that the major business during the period 1920-1930 of both Rohm & Haas companies was in the field of Oropon and general chemicals. The seed for the plastic, methyl methacrylate, however, was sown a long time ago. Dr. Rohm, in achieving his Ph.D. made it the subject of his thesis. It was not until the first World War that he obtained patents covering this product. These were, of course, licensed to the Rohm & Haas Company of Philadelphia.

When the development of Plexiglass blossomed into commercial practicability in 1934, a new agreement was entered into between Rohm & Haas (Darmstadt) and Rohm & Haas (Philadelphia) covering the field. The division of territory this time was not so generous to the American company. Rohm & Haas (Philadelphia) was limited to the United States and Canada, and received the exclusive rights to patents in this territory. The right to export elsewhere was prohibited. The German company, on the other hand, retained rights to the rest of the world. The American company even agreed to do whatever they could to prevent their customers from reselling into the territory of the German company.

It will be recalled that invention has the unbusiness-like habit of spilling over into fields where it was not intended to go, and plastics are no exception. They had application outside the scope of glass, metal, and wood substitutes, and adhesives. The processes involved could also be employed in the fields of photography, dyestuffs, artificial rubber, pharmaceuticals, abrasives, and cellu-loid-like masses. From these broad pastures Rohm & Haas (Philadelphia) was specifically excluded.

A crystal ball is not necessary to see the omnipresent shadow of I. G. Farbenindustrie. These six fields were squarely within I.G.'s preserve, and any permission to engage in them was theirs to grant or deny. Thereupon, in the same year, 1934, I. G. Farben entered into agreements with both Rohm & Haas (Darmstadt) and Rohm & Haas (Philadelphia).

In the agreement between the German companies a straight division of fields was negotiated, reserving for the Darmstadt company the solid plastic field which, roughly speaking, concerns itself with structural material like Lucite and Plexiglass. I.G. retained the generic chemical field from which plastics are derived.

The I.G.-Rohm & Haas (Philadelphia) contract was a masterpiece of diplomacy. Because of I.G.'s many agreements and interests in the United States, the contract had to be drawn without disturbing the web already spun. The division of territory was simple: Rohm & Haas (Philadelphia) was limited to the United States and Canada, I.G. ruling the rest of the world.

The division of the fields of operation was somewhat more involved because of these other contracts. Accordingly, Rohm & Haas (Philadelphia) was prohibited from engaging in the six areas of photography, dyestuffs, artificial rubber, pharmaceuticals, abrasives, and celluloid-like masses. Since the products Rohm & Haas was permitted to manufacture had uses in zones allocated to so-called "friendly firms" * of I.G., however, it was agreed that Rohm & Haas (Philadelphia) would be the sole supplier of the raw materials on the basis of cost plus 10%. "Friendly firms" * included General Aniline Works and Standard-I.G. Corporation.† Neither party could grant sublicenses without the consent of the other, except that I.G. did reserve the right to grant these licenses to "friendly firms." The contract is described by a Rohm & Haas (Philadelphia) official as follows:

---

* Those American firms either owned by or having agreements with I.G.

† A company owned jointly by Standard Oil of N. J. and I. G. Farben.

We already have an agreement with I.G. in which we divide the acrylic and methacrylic field between ourselves and I.G. Under the agreement with I.G. certain uses of the products are reserved to I.G. and certain ones to us. We, ourselves, no longer have the right to use the products in the field for certain purposes, . . .[1]

And by another Rohm & Haas official:

. . . But one thing was clearly provided, namely, that *third parties should be prevented from entering into the fields* and therefore the exceptions were stated in the contract. Only the "friendly firms" and acquirers of licenses as to synthetic rubber should be included in the contract. . . . [Italics added] [2]

The freedom of activity and degree of domination of the chemical industry by German interests, which characterized the years prior to the World War, was no longer so great. Others were becoming active. On July 1, 1929, duPont and Imperial Chemical Industries entered into a gigantic cross-licensing agreement * covering a multitude of chemical fields, including "Acids, both organic and inorganic, for both the heavy chemical industry and special industries." This latter clause included acrylics.

At first the "division of territory" clause resembled the usual German cartel agreement. Imperial Chemical Industries received the British Empire and Egypt, while

---

* The same duPont-I.C.I. agreement mentioned in Chap. 6.

duPont operated in North and Central America. Canada and Newfoundland were to be free territories. In 1934 this agreement was somewhat modified to prevent the exchange of secret military information and to change the "division of territory" clauses so that the owner of a basic patent, the licensor, had the right to sell the product concerned all over the world. Actually, however, this was merely a change in form, apparently to correspond with the Antitrust laws of the United States, but in fact competition did not revive. In the opinion of the Antitrust Division, "the right of the licensor to sell in the licensees' exclusive territory was not exercised, but merely inserted to mask illegality."

These concerns had extensive research facilities, and it was not unlikely that acrylics would come within their camp. This is just what happened, and the usual patents ensued. Some of the more basic patents conflicted with those of the German-dominated cartel, and patent interferences arose. By this time the acrylic field was already complicated by a maze of agreements. Although the usual practice among large combinations finding themselves in patent conflicts is to settle them without resort to a full-dress legal battle, this case was complicated by the diverse interests of the various parties.

The negotiations between Rohm & Haas (Philadelphia) and duPont continued through 1935 and part of 1936, when an agreement was finally made. The points raised indicate clearly the problems involved. On one

side were the patent applications of Hollander and
Neher, inventors for Rohm & Haas (Philadelphia),
while on the other side was the Hill patent, covering an
invention by Rowland Hill, a scientist for Imperial
Chemical industries. Under Hill's patent an exclusive
license had been granted to duPont for the United
States. Neither side felt too secure as to the validity or
priority of their inventions. DuPont in particular was
worried. The General Manager of their Organic Chemicals Department wrote:

> If the Hill Patent were strong and would give us
> a dominating position in the field of methyl metha-
> crylates, we might hesitate to give up that position
> . . . if, however, there is a considerable doubt as to
> its validity, a settlement may be the best method of
> safeguarding our position. . . .[3]

Vigorous competition in the market place was contrary to the traditions of both corporations. Both were
interested in achieving a stabilized and controlled situation. Patents formed excellent instruments with which
to achieve this end. The greatest difficulty was met in
achieving an agreed-upon cartel which would control
the fields of endeavor, the prices, and divisions of territory. For almost the whole of 1935 these negotiations
continued.

Among the difficulties that presented themselves was
the fact that both had relations with foreign companies.
Rohm & Haas, for instance, stated:

. . . we could think of a price agreement on the finished product, or a division of our interests. *I told him we have not only our own interests at stake, but also the ones of our German house and the I.G.* [Italics added] [4]

DuPont had its own agreement with Imperial Chemical Industries. Rohm & Haas was concerned lest Imperial Chemical Industries upset the arrangement by selling in the United States. DuPont reassured Rohm & Haas:

> . . . I.C.I. reserves to itself the right to sell in the United States in emergency cases, but Mr. Wardenburg assured me that although this has been in force for many years, such an emergency has never arisen. . . . [5]

Rohm & Haas, however, was not convinced and could not accept the various proposals of duPont or assurances about Imperial Chemical Industries, because they had *"responsibilities to other parties to whom I have to explain the situation and I do not see how I could do this without embarrassment."* [6] Finally the duPont company wrote to Rohm & Haas (Philadelphia):

> As pointed out to you in our letter of March 5, I.C.I. retains the right to sell the patented products in this country. However, it happens that one of our principal men was able to visit the I.C.I. plant on a trip to Europe, which he was making in connection

with another matter. It was learned that their work in developing the marketing of the materials covered in our license agreement is along quite different lines than those which seem to us to be attractive in this country. We would assume from our observations, therefore, that there is little likelihood of their exercising the right which they retain to sell the products in question in this country.[7]

With this Rohm & Haas was convinced.

The purpose of settling the interference ran along with cartel tradition. Writing to the Philadelphia firm on February 22, 1936, Darmstadt said as follows:

Who has the advantage of this exchange? The party which at present or in the future has the technically most valuable inventions appears to be at a disadvantage because they will have to share their rights with the other party without compensation. Therefore, the incentive to push the development forward would be influenced, and only the party who could sell the cheapest would have any advantage. We believe that an arrangement of this type would only be justified if at the same time there were made an understanding concerning the market and price. It does not appear that there has been any discussion on these points with duPont.[8]

Darmstadt's belief "that an arrangement of this type would only be justified if at the same time there were made an understanding concerning the market and price" was answered by Rohm & Haas (Philadelphia):

Before going into the interference situation at all I had told the duPont executive who had made the overtures to us (Mr. F. A. Wardenburg) that it is necessary to consider what to do after we have exchanged licenses. I told them that they would have to stay out of the laminated glass field and the acrylic acid field, i.e., that they cannot expect any licenses from us in these two fields and that it is advisable to have an informal understanding how to act in the fields where both firms have the right to proceed. We arranged that in the case of products where we compete, we shall consult with each on prices, etc., in order to avoid destructive price cutting. *A matter like this cannot be put into the contract, because it would be against the law. We have to rely on our verbal assurances and our experience with duPont during the last fifteen years has proven that they can be relied upon to live up to an arrangement of this kind.*

Please treat this confidentially. [Italics added] [9]

Once the crucial point of creating a stabilized noncompetitive cartel situation was agreed upon, it was arranged to concede priority on the patents. Rohm & Haas received the laminated glass patents, while duPont received the methyl methacrylate patent.

The American producers were now tied to the cartel. It was necessary to bring one more group within its orbit, namely, Imperial Chemical Industries, of London. This was done by an agreement between Rohm & Haas (Darmstadt) and Imperial Chemical Industries.

During the negotiations Rohm & Haas (Philadelphia) cautioned Darmstadt that, before any "satisfactory arrangement" was entered into, it would be necessary to check with duPont and Rohm & Haas (Philadelphia). Rohm & Haas (Philadelphia) was given complete information on negotiations, and on August 31, 1936, an agreement between Imperial Chemical Industries and Darmstadt was signed.

The agreement, in effect, provided for division of territories in which I.C.I. received the United Kingdom and the British Empire, while Darmstadt received Europe, including the U.S.S.R., except Holland, Denmark, Norway, and Sweden, which were to be common territory. When third parties entered non-exclusive territory, I.C.I. and Darmstadt agreed either to meet the competition or bring it within the cartel. Prices were to be fixed in the "free" territory.

In 1939 duPont discovered that Rohm & Haas (Philadelphia) had an excellent process for making cast sheets of methyl methacrylate, which had been kept secret from duPont. A supplemental license agreement was negotiated whereby Rohm & Haas (Philadelphia) and duPont cross-licensed each other on the new process. Since Rohm & Haas (Philadelphia) insisted upon the maintenance of its domination of the cast sheet field, and also was the owner of the most important patents, it pledged duPont to manufacture no more than one-half the quantity Rohm & Haas might make in any given year.

By 1940 the United Nations, under the pressure of war with Germany, were beginning to order enormous quantities of Lucite and Plexiglass. DuPont, because of the restriction under the contract, was unable to expand. Thus, during one of the most critical periods in our history, when our very security depended on straining every muscle to increase production of a vital material, our greatest chemical company was forced by contract to restrict its output. Thereupon, the general manager of duPont wrote the following interoffice memorandum dated January 15, 1941, indicating the drastic lengths to which duPont was willing to go to free itself of the "dead hand" of this agreement:

> *I explained to Mr. Haas that we were booked up solid until October of the present year under this restriction and asked him whether he wanted us to tell the Government that we were limited by the license or whether he preferred to lift the restriction. He agreed to lift the restriction during the present emergency.* [Italics added] [10]

DuPont apparently was not averse to calling in the law when its interests were served thereby. Although duPont did not resort to complaining to the Government, the Government nevertheless stepped in with a Grand Jury proceeding, and both Rohm & Haas (Philadelphia) and duPont were indicted on August 10, 1942.

The Rohm & Haas Company of Philadelphia oc-

cupies a very uncomfortable position at present. Its early
history indicating its German origin, and the seizure of
some of its stock by the Alien Property Custodian during the World War have already been recounted.

Sensitive to all charges impugning its patriotism, the
officers of Rohm & Haas (Philadelphia) let no stories
in the press or charges before Congressional committees
go unanswered. This defense is accomplished with gusto
and vigor. The charges arise, however, not because of a
lack of patriotism, but from the unfortunate position in
which cartel members find themselves when entangled
with nationals of a country where the cartel system is a
weapon of war itself.

In addition to the agreements with I. G. Farben and
Rohm & Haas (Darmstadt), Rohm & Haas (Philadelphia) also has agreements with Theo. Goldschmidt, another German company. With the latter company Rohm
& Haas (Philadelphia) entered into an agreement in
1934 covering Tego gluefilm, an adhesive extensively
used in the production of plywood, especially for aircraft and marine vessels. Rohm & Haas (Philadelphia)
had other agreements with I.G. and Rohm & Haas
(Darmstadt) concerning tanning agents. All these agreements had one common characteristic: *The world outside the United States was German territory*. As a result,
the German companies had achieved, as in dyestuffs, a
very large system of distributive outlets throughout the
world—especially in Latin America.

The declaration of hostilities in September 1939 found the German plans ready for execution. Rohm & Haas (Philadelphia) was notified by its German cartel associates that it now had permission to ship to Mexico, Central and South America. In some cases it was given permission to sell to Japan, China, and Siam.

Rohm & Haas (Darmstadt) received royalties which amounted to a substantial share of the profits on these sales of Plexiglass, I. G. Farben protected its network of distributive outlets, and Theo. Goldschmidt protected its customers. *In all cases the business of supplying these markets was to revert to the Germans at the conclusion of the war.* Every item sold under the arrangement helped frustrate the British blockade of Germany. The correspondence of I. G. Farben with Rohm & Haas in particular is worth quoting:

> I. G. Farbenindustrie Aktiengesellschaft
> Frankfurt (Main) 20, den 22nd Dec. 1939

Abt. G. Kp/Br.
Mr. Otto Haas,

> c/o Messrs. Rohm & Haas, Philadelphia.

Dear Mr. Haas: The arrangements which we have with your firm about synthetic tannings limits the markets where you are free to sell your synthetic tannings to the United States of America and Canada, whereas we supply the rest of the world. In previous years we have in some exceptional cases allowed you to make certain shipments to the South American markets. Most of these markets can at present not be supplied by us regularly and in order to allow our friends in those markets to maintain their position, we should very much appreciate if you could supply them which certainly would also be in the general interest of the business in synthetic tannings.

We have therefore informed our friends in the South—and Middle American States to approach you through the Advance, Solvents Chemical Corp., New York, in case they are in need of synthetic tannings and Tamol and hope you will be in a position to supply them; only in the case of Mexico, where our business friends report you already for Koreon, you will receive enquiries directly.

I take the opportunity to send you my best wishes for a merry Christmas and a happy New Year.

With best regards, I am yours very sincerely,

W. E. KEMP.[11]

Replying to this letter, Otto Haas stated:

I am in receipt of your letter of December 22nd. Of course, we shall be glad to follow your wishes in every detail.

I attach herewith a list of the shipments which we have already made to Bogota, Lima, and Rio. These orders have come to us entirely unsolicited, and we thought that it was to your best interest to fill them.

I wish to assure you that no matter who is doing the shipping we shall revert to the status quo antem as soon as normal conditions have been restored.

The thought uppermost in my mind is to serve you in the most faithful and most efficient way possible in this emergency.

Yours very truly,

Otto Haas.

9. DRUGS AND GEOPOLITICS

THE pharmaceutical business occupies a unique position in the realm of German cartel activity and economic warfare. Its significance is derived from the absolute dependence of tropical countries on the constant use of medicines to stave off disease, and tropical countries are the most fertile territory for the ravages of plague. The experience of Bayer 205 bears witness to the relationship of pharmaceuticals and the tropics in Germany's plan. As already noted, Germany's earlier experiment in warfare during the first World War placed great reliance on the control of pharmaceutical preparations. The activities of Bayer Company during that war had extreme value to Germany's schemes of aggression.

The Sterling Products Company, which purchased the Bayer interests confiscated by the Alien Property Custodian, chose to dispose of the dyestuffs branch and retain for its own operations the pharmaceutical assets. Most important of these was the Bayer Cross, the long-established trademark of Bayer of Germany. Throughout the world this trademark had received acceptance as a representation of the traditionally high quality of

138

German chemical commodities, and as a result, the German company built up a very profitable business.

The acquisition of the Bayer properties by the Sterling Company had hardly been accomplished when the international scope of operations of the Bayer Company became apparent. Although Sterling had the right to use the Bayer Cross in the United States because of its purchase from the Alien Property Custodian, its title could hardly be called clear in other countries of the world. This was particularly true in South America, where the German Bayer interests were poised to strike at Sterling's legal title to the Cross. Rather than risk endless litigation in a continent where the Germans had already made deep inroads, Sterling decided to avoid this difficulty at all costs.

On October 28, 1920, therefore, Sterling made its first agreement with Farbenfabriken Vorm. Friedr. Bayer & Company of Leverkusen, Germany. This company was, of course, a member of the I. G. Farbenindustrie. The preamble to this agreement reads as follows:

> In order to develop a large business in South and Central America and Mexico (hereinafter called the Territory) the two parties have concluded the following heads of Agreement for the purpose of particularly exploiting Acetylsalicylic Acid (Aspirin) or its compounds in connection with the trademark Aspirin, the trade name Bayer and the trademark referred to

as the Bayer Cross Mark or under any other trademark or name in the Territory and also for dealing
with other goods as hereinafter mentioned.[1]

While it related basically only to aspirin, the agreement
broke the ground for future dealings. In effect, the
agreement provided that competition between Bayer
and Sterling in South America was to be eliminated, and
that the company with the cheapest costs would supply
the market. Profits on this business were to be divided,
with 75% going to the Germans and 25% going to
Sterling. For almost a generation this proved to be a
highly profitable agreement for both parties. It is interesting to note that at no time during this period did
Sterling sell in South America, Bayer supplying the
market until the outbreak of Global War.

With the initial resolution of the difficulties between
the two parties, the road was paved for future agreements, and in 1923 a second agreement was entered into
between the Sterling interests and the I. G. Farben interests, covering practically the entire field of pharmaceuticals. This included:

Substances used in medicine or pharmacy, perfum-
ery and toilet articles of all kinds including cosmetics.
Products used or intended to be used for agricultural, horticultural or veterinary or sanitary or disin-
fecting or preservative purposes or insecticides or
germicides.
Substances or articles used or intended to be used

for photographic (except photographic papers) or scientific purposes.

Chemicals or substances of any kind to be used in the production of any of the foregoing products.[2]

In addition, territory was divided so that Sterling received the United States, which included Puerto Rico, the Philippine Islands, the Hawaiian Islands, and the Panama Canal Zone, as exclusive territory free from I. G. Farben's competition. The agreement was to last for fifty years. Coincident with this arrangement, I.G. received a 50% interest in Winthrop Chemical Company, a subsidiary of Sterling which marketed most of the pharmaceutical products other than aspirin. I.G. protected its other cartel agreements in the United States by specifically exempting a number of products.

> . . . all photographic articles, including photographic and moving picture papers, heligraphic papers, artificial silk and artificial silk products, dyes and colors, carbide and carbide derivatives and products made from carbide derivatives, as, for example, acetic acid, acetic acid anhydride, acetone, acetaldehyde, butanol, organic products used in the varnish, lacquers, paints and solvents industry, as, for example, artificial resin, camphor and camphor substitutes, softeners, etc., also products in which wood pulp or cotton are component parts, as for example actyl- and nitro-cellulose, viscose, etc., heavy chemicals, prussic acid, cyanide of sodium and all other cyanide compounds, *and also excepting all products regarding*

*which the I.G. is prohibited from selling by now ex-
isting contracts with others in the United States.*[3]

In 1926 this agreement was amended to include all
of I. G. Farbenindustrie, which was reorganized at that
time. From time to time other agreements were entered
into whenever particular exigencies arose.

Once again the Alien Property Act of 1917 was nulli-
fied. In the plans of the Germans for economic as well
as military domination of the world, South America has
always loomed high in their calculations. It is not without significance that the first agreement between Sterling and I.G. related specifically to South America.

Sterling, of course, not unlike many American corporations, was fully aware of the commercial advantages of an agreement with the German I.G. interests.
Like almost all American corporations, it knew little
and cared less about German plans for international
hegemony. The main question rested on the pivot of
profitableness and freedom from German competition.
This arrangement was specifically desirous from Sterling's point of view since it was new to this business, and
the Germans were "old hands." A deal was certainly
preferable to competition.

While some of the American corporations which became entangled with German interests may have been
mere dupes, German cartels did not always rely on native firms to carry out their ends. In certain instances,

the Germans set up their own subsidiaries, which were then camouflaged to look like independent concerns.

Although it is difficult for one to think of sex hormones as an important industrial product entering into international intrigue and economic warfare, it nevertheless occupies a special position in just that field. Its history demonstrates almost perfectly the utilization of a device based upon patent controls, specialized skill, and legal subterfuge as a method of turning the cartel into an instrument of warfare directed against the United States by Germany.

The Schering Corporation of Bloomfield, New Jersey, has, for the past few years, been recognized by doctors as the manufacturer of the finest quality sex hormones in the United States. Its scientists contribute to various technical periodicals, and its laboratory is considered to be the best of its kind in this hemisphere. In effect, as far as high quality sex hormones are concerned, it has built up a monopoly.

The German control station, which directed the affairs of the Schering Corporation of Bloomfield, was Schering A. G. of Berlin, a key factor in the economic war, and one of Germany's most important pharmaceutical and chemical manufacturers. Under the aegis of Dr. Julius Weltzein, former president of Schering A. G., Schering built up an export system throughout the world which had as its purpose not only the enlargement of Germany's foreign trade but also the develop-

ment of what might be called "colonial settlements" in
the form of distributing agencies. These were used as
outlets for Schering A. G.'s products, and at the same
time were the foci of German political intrigue in various regions of the world, in particular, the British Empire and Latin America. With the advent of Hitler in
1934, the Schering outlets were cleansed of any non-
Aryan influence, and were staffed with either loyal or
Nazi Germans. By 1938 this cleansing had included Dr.
Weltzein.

It is reputed that before this war Schering's largest
business outside of Europe itself was in Latin America.
It is the largest German exporter of pharmaceuticals,
medicinal specialties, which include sex hormones, vac-
cines, anti-venereal toxins, laxatives, anti-shock serum,
fine laboratory, and plant protection chemicals. Its export business is large enough to accord it a principal
place in Germany's system for securing foreign cur-
rency, which has been called *devisenbringer*.

Schering A. G. was not without fear of competition
throughout its empire by American producers. It therefore was a prolific applicant for patents in the United
States Patent Office, and in 1929 it established a subsidiary in the United States known as the Schering Corporation, not only as a means of protecting its empire
but as a device for exploiting the market in the United
States. The Schering Corporation, finally domiciled in
Bloomfield, New Jersey, was one of the few Schering

satellites which did its own manufacturing, and so developed that it was a miniature replica of Schering A. G. of Berlin.

The Schering Corporation, protected by patents and supplied with the ex-president of Schering A. G., who became a refugee in 1938, as its own president, prospered so that in 1940 its profits were estimated to be $2,350,000. Considering its capitalization of $499,000, this was an excellent business venture.

Toward the close of 1937, Schering A. G. of Berlin, recognizing the delicate state of the international situation, did what was characteristic of many other German enterprises during this period—it transferred the Schering Corporation of Bloomfield's ownership to Swiss interests, which are in effect controlled by the Swiss Bank. At the same time a contract was executed between Schering A. G. and its daughter company Schering Corporation, by which the latter agreed to buy all basic raw and intermediate materials from the parent concern, and not to export its own products except with the consent of the latter. These stipulations applied not only to materials produced in Germany but also to products from other parts of the world, such as Holland and British India, with the result that the Schering Corporation was forced to pay an added toll simply to maintain the position of Schering A. G. As usual, in accordance with this agreement, Schering of Bloomfield was not permitted to export outside the United States.

The effect of this served Germany's interests well. In the first place, it disguised the true ownership of Schering of Bloomfield with a Swiss cloak. Thus, should the United States and Germany be at war with each other, there was at least a chance of frustrating the operations of the Alien Property Custodian. In the second place, it circumscribed the American Schering's operations to preclude any interference with the German Schering's international markets.

There have been many who have maintained that the sale of American Schering to the Swiss was a bona-fide transaction. Whether or not this was true can be judged by the conduct of American Schering Corporation since the outbreak of war between Germany and Great Britain.

At about the time that Great Britain and Germany began hostilities the Schering A. G. of Germany advised the Schering Corporation of Bloomfield that the latter could now export to the markets belonging to the German corporation's sphere. There were, however, certain restrictions:

(1) Schering of Bloomfield would export to those portions of the world denied to Schering A. G. by the British blockade, with the understanding that this was either for the duration of the war or until further notice from Schering A. G.;

(2) the material sold outside the United States was

to be labelled with the Schering A. G. trade-mark;

(3) there was to be a division of profits on this business, with Schering A. G. receiving the larger share;

(4) Schering of Bloomfield was to deal only with the Schering A. G. agencies in South America or other parts of the world. Under no circumstances was Schering of Bloomfield to set up its own agencies.

The effect of this arrangement is apparent:

(1) It provided a means for Germany to circumvent the British blockade;

(2) it provided exchange for the German agencies in South America which were well staffed with Nazis, enabling them to continue political and other subversive activities;

(3) it maintained the German monopoly of manufacture and distribution of these medicinal commodities in South America;

(4) it prevented the establishment of an American distributive setup for these materials in South America.[4]

The Germans prepared for retaliatory measures long in advance. When the Black List was issued including all of the known German Schering agencies in South

America, dummy firms were already in position to function in the place of the blacklisted parties. The Schering Corporation of Bloomfield continued to put German labels on the goods shipped to South America.

Because of the effect of monopoly created by the Schering Corporation in the United States, highly critical materials such as anti-shock serums and others could only be purchased from one source—the Schering Corporation.

The Department of Justice intervened and smashed the American Schering's operations in the South American market. Shortly after December 7, 1941, the Alien Property Custodian seized all assets of the company. This seizure could not mitigate, however, the adverse effects deriving from the careful preparations of Schering A. G., a province in the dominion of I. G. Farben.

10. PRIVATE GOVERNMENT AND
INDUSTRIAL MUNICHS

"AS a principle in which the rights and interests of the United States are involved . . . the American continents . . . are henceforth not to be considered as subject for future colonization by any European power. . . . We should consider any attempt on their part to extend their system to any portion of this hemisphere as dangerous to our peace and safety." These clarion phrases of the Monroe Doctrine strike the one consistent note of American foreign relations.

Promulgated over a century ago, this doctrine excluded for all time any effort by foreign imperialism in Europe or the Orient to gain a political foothold in the Western Hemisphere. It has been a cornerstone of our national policy toward South America. The slightest suggestion that it was in danger has been sufficient to arouse both government and public. What we do not realize is that, for the past twenty years, this principle has been systematically subverted by the establishment of economic colonies subject to German political control in Central and South America. In accordance with

149

the German Plan, the penetration of South America was carried out by "diplomacy and trade."

South America has always been a plum in German eyes. Under the Kaiser's regime, German representatives and commercial attachés were trained to study every nuance of thought and custom of the Latin countries. Germans who went to South America spoke impeccable Portuguese and Spanish. They married into the best families, and became a part of the native culture. But at all times the military aspirations of the Fatherland were kept in mind. Profits from the sale of goods, and detailed surveys of the wealth and resources of our Southern neighbor were sent back to enrich and to inform both German industry and government. When the Nazis started their "Auslands" organization, the basic personnel and data were at hand. To the training of German agents and diplomats who were to be sent to South American countries, the political and racial theories of Nazism were added. Dr. Rosenberg himself, the official philosopher of Nazism, supervised this training. "Diplomacy and trade" now meant Nazi penetration. In Nazi schemes, this means prelude to invasion.

The danger is real. Although the Monroe Doctrine has always been the measuring-stick of our armies and navies, its main reliance has been the width of the oceans. Airpower has narrowed the ocean barrier. Generals Arnold and Eaker subscribe to a statement made by an American air expert, who said:

If Germany flew 1,000 bombers to Brazil, and landed them on airdromes prepared by the millions of Germans now resident there, supplying through the air the necessary bombs and fuel, it would be necessary for the nation which would enforce Western Hemisphere defense to drive those bombers out. But no land or water-borne army can approach Brazil under the sphere of influence of those 1,000 bombers until the bombers have first been destroyed or driven out. That means, then, that the nation which would dislodge those German bombers must have an air force with sufficient range to destroy those bombers on their Brazilian bases.

If such an air force were available and were directed energetically at those Brazilian based Europeans, they might be flown again home to Germany, or be reinforced. The ensuing air engagement would largely determine the issue. Certainly it would settle the first or the air phase. This is how easily an aggressive foreign power could test our doctrine of hemisphere defense.[1]

When war broke out, the United States faced two grim prospects: the British fleet might be destroyed, and South America invaded.

Isolationists demanded that we stay out of Europe's squabbles. Interventionists viewed with alarm. The country was in an uproar of disunity.

Underneath all this chaos an orderly development of Germany's economic war was unfolding. It will be recalled that, throughout the maneuvering of I. G. Farbenindustrie in the United States to regain their position in the chemical industry, they were always careful to restrict their American affiliate from entering the world markets. When World War II broke out, England's main weapon was the naval blockade. This normally would have meant that Germany's world markets would be lost, at least for the duration. Germany, however, was prepared for this attack.

During the twenty preceding years, a network of distributing outlets for German goods was established throughout the world. Denied colonies by the Versailles Treaty, Germany was able to circumvent this obstacle through clever manipulation of patents, agreements with competitors to divide territory, which generally left Germany with the lion's share of the world to exploit. Not without effect in these arrangements when the Nazis came to power was the barter system of trade. As a result Germany was given a relatively free hand to set up a vast and cleverly manipulated system of distribution. Especially effective and important was this network in South America. The size of the Blacklist, on which 7,500 names now appear, shows the dimensions of the bridgehead.

Germany did not have to fight for the South American market. The entire continent was handed over to German cartels by American businessmen. The consequences of this investment of South America by German interests are both military and economic. We are

suddenly awakened to the realization that economically
we have been flanked, and that this fact is a threat to our
military security. How strong the grip of German economic interests is in South American countries has been
demonstrated both in Chile and in Argentina.

What must be understood is that German preemption
of South American markets was possible only because
American concerns agreed not to compete in that area.
What our government would never have agreed to,
cartels could do: give consent and support to the insti-
tution of economic and financial salients which became
outposts of Germany. In almost every instance in which
South America was reserved by cartel agreements to
German monopolies, their subsidiaries and agents were
the entering wedge by which it was hoped to accomplish two ends: first and foremost, in the war which was
to come, economic control in South America could be
used to defeat the blockade of Nazi exports. The export
of German goods, important to German commercial
prestige, could be maintained in plain view of the Latin-
American countries. English and American influence
would correspondingly be injured. Thereby, extension
of German power over the market structure of South
America became more easily the nucleus for German
propaganda and espionage. Because Germany and I. G.
Farben were ready with plans based on Total War and
charted long in advance, American companies are faced

with the appalling task of overcoming the power of the German commercial barrage.

Democratic government has no adequate defense against this type of subterfuge. Dollar Diplomacy long ago was supplanted by the Good Neighbor Policy. But neighborly friendship unsupported by economic ties is a fragile bond. Our government could not form such links because the cartels had made other dispositions.

The fact that cartel policies could frustrate the desires of the American government is the clue to their real nature. Cartels are private governments. To American concerns, cartels could grant stability and profits. To the Germans, cartels were protégés of the Reich—precursors of conquest.

Perhaps the most striking correspondence between the character of cartels as private governments and the powers of sovereign states is in the conduct of foreign affairs. A sovereign political entity is, in the last analysis, one which can subscribe to treaties and wage war. Cartels do both. The difference lies in purpose and responsibility.

All commitments of government are made in national interest and for the purpose of promoting general welfare. When war is necessary to their survival, governments embark on military ventures for the purpose of maintaining the integrity of the nation which they serve. In the case of cartels, treaties are made for private, not public, ends. The consequences of their acts may be vital to society, but their aims are framed with reference only to their own welfare. In the purview of cartels, the whole world economy is an area of exploitation. From this perspective they determine spheres of influence and divide hemispheres by treaties which require no consent either from the public or from legal governments.

When, for instance, the United States enters into a treaty with a foreign nation, its acceptance must be ratified with the advice and consent of two-thirds of the Senate, in the light of national policy. When a monopoly enters a cartel agreement, which equally affects the foundations of our national economy, no voice can be raised to question or approve. In fact, it is characteristic of cartel agreements, which, because of their economic importance, may be of greater moment than political understandings, that they are arrived at secretly and maintained in silence. There are no "open covenants, openly arrived at." There could not be, for otherwise it would be too evident that cartel agreements transcend any standard of national interest. Indeed, in one respect, the contracts executed by cartels are stronger and more durable than any treaty between governments, for cartels by prearrangement discount the contingencies of war. No democratic government could afford to do this. The only eventuality which cartels need or do recognize is that of *force majeure*, pressure exerted by law which cannot be evaded or foreseen.

Force majeure was the legal protection which German concerns invoked whenever their obligations under cartel contracts interfered with their role in German expansion. Nothing could stand in the way of German national interest. This contrasts in sharp relief with the industrial defeats suffered by the democracies because of "loyal adherence" to cartel agreements.

By their nature, cartels are paternalistic and totalitarian organizations, and their policies consequently cannot be thought of as truly capitalistic. Capitalism is based on freedom of enterprise; cartels are based on rigidity, stabilization, and private economic planning. They are the forerunners of the managerial revolution. Because they must play safe and avoid risk, they cannot be progressive. They fear two things, competition and technological change, for their existence depends upon concentration of ownership and control over patents, raw materials, and resources.

The greatest technological revolution of modern times inhered in Germany's plans for conquest. Every manifesto of discovery made by German industry was a step toward power, but each new development ran counter to the security of democratic businessmen. Not desiring to compete with such ruthless opponents, they were easy targets in the industrial offensive. Every time German industry presented a new development which threatened the financial stability of democratic monopolists, an industrial Munich ensued. Germany was appeased with territorial grants, royalties, and ever larger segments of world industry over which it might rule. Each conquest was a springboard for the next.

11. SAMURAI—ORIENTAL JUNKERS

GERMANY'S blueprint for conquest was truly global. It included the vast reaches of Asia and the riches of the Indies. To deprive its enemies of this wealth and to encircle Russia were the ends of Germany's eastern strategy.

In the ancient rivalry of peoples, no quarrel has burned more steadily or bitterly than the antagonism between the Teuton and the Slav. From Adolf of Holstein, the leader of the Teutonic Knights in the twelfth century, to Adolf Hitler, the concept recurring over and over again in German dreams is the Drang Nach Osten —the Drive to the East.

The land ocean of Russia has surged across the path to German world dominion. To the West lay Britain— the gateway to the seas. To the North were the silent wastes of ice. The Russian land bridge to the East was, therefore, the path across which German armies were to trod. The fertile valley of the Ukraine would supply the food for the German nation on the march. What was more important, beyond the bridge of Russia was the fabulous wealth of Asia. All the ersatz materials which Germany so painfully contrived in its laboratories existed in natural abundance beyond the Caucasus. There were whole forests of rubber and quinine, mountains of tungsten and tin. From the Caucasus to the Indies were endless deposits of oil. The virgin resources of Asia beckoned. Only the Russian Bear stood guard.

Along this road to Asia the invincible hosts of the Wehrmacht could storm their way. The ramparts which guarded Asia could thus be scaled and British sea power frustrated.

In the World War Germany's campaign in the East could not batter down the door to Asia. The schedule of Berlin to Bagdad did not run on time. In making global plans, the scope of Germany's ambitions in the East increased. Iran, Iraq, and Afghanistan were stations on the time table of German conquest. The terminus was India—the battleground of East and West.

German militarists had studied Japanese ambitions in the same minute detail with which they analyzed Allied strategy. Japan was the perfect foil for German aims, and could be used to stab the democracies from the rear, and give Russia a two-front war.

Japan nursed its own vainglorious schemes. The Tanaka Memorial propounded the limitless hopes of Japanese imperialism. Germany fostered these views for their immediate value. The strength of Japan could be utilized now, and its weaknesses noted for future reference. The westward flow of *Kultur* would in time engulf Japan.

In Japan, as in Germany, the development of modern industry occurred primarily during the latter half of the nineteenth century. In each country there was a military caste—the Samurai in Japan, corresponding to the German Junkers—who saw in the machine technique an instrument of national aggrandizement. There are, both industrially and in military affairs, almost identical characteristics in the last century of Japanese and German history, differentiated more by geographic conditions than by any other consideration. This parallelism illustrates the importance of the form of social institutions in the modern world, because in both of these aggressor nations the existence and promotion of military ambitions and the assumption of superiority to other peoples have produced corresponding modes of conduct.

It is enough to turn attention to the outstanding industrial group in the Japanese Empire, the Mitsui Gomei Kaisha (Mitsui Partnership Company), which ranks first among the four largest monopolist combines in Japan. The Mitsubishi, the Sumitomo, and the Yasuda, in approximately the order named, are all smaller than the Mitsui combine. It has been estimated that these four groups control over 70% of Japanese industry, and are the principal beneficiaries of Japanese aggression throughout the East. Indeed, these powerful companies have been the vanguard of Japanese armies, for in every area in which they have succeeded in establishing a commercial foothold, an excuse has later arisen for military action.

The Mitsui group has perhaps the longest history of any large modern corporation, tracing its family tree to the seventh century.

The Mitsui were among the first Japanese business-men to carry on trade with foreign merchants. Even be-fore the treaties of 1854, by which Japan established uneasy relations with western civilization, the Mitsui had carried on some trade with Dutch commercial agen-cies. Following the removal of the barriers to trade, Mitsui became the most important trading concern in Japan, accounting for nearly one-half of the total im-ports and exports. This branch of its business alone makes Mitsui the greatest single trading company in the world.

After the restoration and the fall of the Shogunate, the Mitsui banking house became for a time the unoffi-cial treasury for the Emperor Meiji Tenno, and is still the most important "private" bank anywhere in the East. Since that time the number and scale of Mitsui enterprises have grown until they are, collectively, among the world's largest business groups. The central holding company and general headquarters administer-ing all the Mitsui interests is the Mitsui Partnership

Company, membership in which is restricted to the heads of the eleven Mitsui families.

Feudal succession determines the selection of the president of the concern, and the lesser offices are allotted to representatives of each family group. The entire assemblage of Mitsui enterprises is operated according to a family constitution originally drawn up by the son of Hachirobei, the founder of Mitsui's dynasty. This constitution, in the main, consists of Oriental maxims intended to assure prosperity and the retention of control within the membership of the eleven families. The constitution was redrafted in 1900, and now requires every member of the family at the time of majority to swear an oath of allegiance to the House of Mitsui. It is interesting to note that among its clauses is the command to serve the Emperor before all else, and, as the Mitsui have stated themselves, this precept "has never been forgotten."

The branches of the House of Mitsui are divided into domestic and foreign enterprises. The Mitsui Partnership Company itself does not often deal directly with the representatives of industry outside Japan. This function is performed by the Mitsui Bussan Kaisha (Mitsui & Company, Limited), which has branches in all of the principal countries of the world.

The major fields of operation in which Mitsui is engaged are banking, mining, insurance, engineering, steel, coal, silk and cotton textiles, electrical machinery, aviation, chemicals, cement, transportation (rail, marine, automobile, and airplane transport and manufacture), and armament production. For many years it has been virtually impossible for any foreign concern to operate in the Japanese market without the consent of Mitsui. As a consequence, commercial and contractual relationships existed up to the time of the war between Mitsui companies and nearly all of the major industrial enterprises carrying on business in Japan or China.

In some instances British, American, and German companies conduct joint enterprises with Mitsui. For example, the Shibauri Engineering Works is a joint enterprise of Mitsui and International General Electric; the Japan Steel Works is a joint enterprise of the Mitsui and the British companies of Armstrong and Vickers. Many of the Mitsui firms operate under license from American, British, and German companies. Mitsui has relationships with duPont, General Electric, I. G. Farben, Imperial Chemical Industries, Sperry, Pratt & Whitney, the Mond Nickel Company, Aluminium Limited, to mention only a few.

Mitsui is itself a cartel, and is a member of the principal dyestuffs and chemical cartels of the world. It may be noted, however, that in none of its connections with foreign industry, even in the case of German industry, has Mitsui exhibited the slightest compunction at any time in forcing acceptance of its own terms, and in establishing a bargaining position intended eventually to eliminate all foreign control or participation in Japanese industry. As stated by an American cartel member expert on the ways of Mitsui, the Japanese plan was to accomplish "the exclusion . . . of foreign manufacturers with the possible exception of what may be a cooperative plan with the German I.G."

This in itself is only nationalistic; Mitsui's aims, however, are international. In the chemical industry Japanese ambitions, executed primarily by Mitsui, approximate those of Germany. Their object is the control of world markets in chemicals, and the support of the military regime to obtain those markets by conquest.

Asia constitutes today the greatest market on the earth. No subtle insight is required to deduce the economic incentives which have motivated Japanese foreign policy since the first World War. It should be pointed out that, contrary to a commonly held opinion, there is no conflict between Japanese industry and Japanese militarism. The "co-prosperity sphere" of greater Asia, which is the aim of the warlords, is also the goal of Mitsui and its lesser companions in monopoly in the Japanese economy.

The relationship of Mitsui to American, English, and German financial and industrial groups has significance, not only because of the technical knowledge and capital introduced into Japan by these channels, but also because of their cartel character. The cartel form in

Japan, as in Germany, is admirably suited to industrial organization under a totalitarian regime.

In its intercourse with the western powers, Japanese industry has found cartel agreements most useful in gaining freedom from competition, and at the same time acquiring through patent agreements, licenses, and jointly owned concerns, the scientific knowledge necessary to the erection of a military state. Because of cheap labor and the imitative ability of their race, Japanese industry even before the war had become a serious threat to America's international trade position; indeed, to the very same firms with whom agreements had been established either by Mitsui or by the other members of Japanese industrial oligarchy, Japanese competition was a nuisance.

In 1937 the Japanese were included in the Axis. The elements of German strategy were complete.

When war began, Japan hung back, awaiting the test of German ability to execute the plan successfully. One by one, such doubts were dispelled. Every German victory was an argument with cogent force. Japan determined to come in and take its share.

The last weeks before Pearl Harbor disclose the pattern. German armies battered their way to Moscow's gates. Despite the approach of winter, the Wehrmacht did not retire when tactical principles indicated strategic retreat. Political reasons held them there. Retreat might have discouraged Japan. The moment had come when

Japan must act to divert the energies of the United States, and lock the "Open door."

On the very day that Japan had lashed out at British, Dutch, and American possessions, the German army withdrew to its winter lines. The United States was no longer the isolater, but the isolated.

Pearl Harbor, Singapore, and Java smashed the complacency with which the Japanese peril had been regarded. Those who had believed in the myths that Japanese could not fly, that their navy was inferior, and that they would not dare to cross our path had deceived themselves.

What was even more appalling, the strategy of blockade had been turned against its makers.

12. MOSQUITOES, MALARIA, AND MONOPOLY

THE Global War is measured around the girdle of the Equator. Africa has its effect on the Russian front, and Singapore was the key to the whole Pacific. In all the wars of history, disease has been the invisible foe of armies. But the Equator is the fever line of the earth. When soldiers from temperate zones are sent to jungles and deserts, their bodies must be conditioned, and ample supplies of medicine must travel with the men.

Among the scourges of mankind throughout recorded history, none has been more widespread in its incidence, and only the "black death" has been more devastating in its immediate effects, than the disease known as malaria. In any German plan of war, this problem had to be resolved. As early as the World War, I.G. produced a substance called Optochin, which had some properties of the quinine which Germany could not get. Optochin was not successful in its action, and I.G. continued its search.

Spurred by Germany's desire for colonies, I.G. at last succeeded. Atabrine, a synthetic specific which produced amazing cures in malarial patients, resulted, for I.G. knows no fatigue. Thereby hangs a tale of equatorial war.

As Dr. William Osler said, "No infection except perhaps tuberculosis compares with it in the extent of its distribution or its importance as a killing and disabling disease." The frequency and persistence of malaria have probably exacted a greater cumulative toll of human health in the span of history than all the wars ever fought. There is a close connection between malaria and war. Like other diseases to which man is subject, malaria increases its inroads whenever the sanitary barriers of peace are overthrown by war. It is recorded that Egypt was saved from the Assyrian armies of Sennacherib in 712 B.C. by an outbreak of malaria which debilitated that tyrant's hosts. During the Civil War in our own country, malaria was the leading cause of death on the Southern side.

In the present war, with our troops spread around the world, especially in tropical regions, the threat of malaria to soldier and civilian alike is enormously increased. Dr. John E. Baker, former director-general of the Burma Road, stated recently that if some means were not found to check the spread of malaria in China, the Japanese would soon be able to let the mosquitoes do their fighting.

Even in peacetime, however, large areas of the world are constantly subject to the disease. It is estimated that there are some 800,000,000 sufferers from malaria in the world today, more than 100,000,000 of whom are in India alone, accounting for 1,000,000 of the 3,000,-000 deaths annually. In the United States, it was estimated in 1937 that there were more than 4,000,000 cases, the majority of which were in the southern states.

More than a thousand years ago it was suggested that mosquitoes carried the disease, but it was not until the discoveries made by Sir Ronald Ross, C. L. A. Laveran, and others, definitely proved the guilt of the anopheles and similar mosquitoes, that it was possible to institute the preventive measures developed in sanitary engineering. When the French first attempted to construct the Panama Canal under the direction of Ferdinand de Lesseps, they were forced to abandon the project because of the malaria and yellow fever which struck down the laborers. Sir Richard Gregory, in his book "Discovery," says—"It has been stated that before the work was finally abandoned by the French, a human life had been sacrificed for every cubic yard of earth excavated." Not until Colonel Gorgas was able to destroy the principal breeding places of the carrier mosquitoes could the canal be completed.

No real relief from malaria was found until the early part of the 17th century. Nevertheless, long years were to pass before the knowledge of the specific cause and care of the disease were to be known or used widely in Europe. When Torti gave name to malaria, in belief that it was caused by "bad air," there was as yet no real understanding of the mode of transmission or the physiological effects of the quinine used as a remedy. Spanish Jesuits in Peru had used the bark of the quina tree in treating fevers. It is believed that they obtained their knowledge of this bark from the native Incas. Even at that early date, the sale of quinine was a monopoly of the Jesuit order. Dr. Victor Heiser, in "An American Doctor's Odyssey," says, "The priests received its weight in gold from those who could afford to pay; to the poor it was free. The supply was never equal to the demand, and in the effort to adjust the balance, the trees of South America were stripped of their bark and largely destroyed." The later monopoly in quinine was to prove not so philanthropic in dispensation of the drug.

The haphazard and reckless methods which depleted the supply of cinchona bark in South America led to attempts to cultivate the tree in other countries. As was the case with rubber, the seeds of the cinchona tree were taken to the East Indies, where by careful botanical study it was found that the tree could be improved and would grow readily in the rich earth of Java. Just as the English attempted to protect the rubber plants, so the Dutch sought to guard their knowledge of the methods of cultivation and extraction. It may be remarked, however, that whereas the English failed to keep their secret, the Dutch were entirely successful, so much so that even up to the present time no one has succeeded in determining exactly what methods they used in caring for the tree or what are the actual costs of production of quinine. Since 1865 the Dutch have maintained one of the tightest of all monopolies by the usual methods of market control, but with consequences more immediately and dramatically tangible in the casualty lists of those stricken by malaria.

Dr. Heiser graphically describes the care used by the Dutch Quinine Syndicate to keep its knowledge hidden, stating, "Not many miles from the Botanical Gardens lies a mysterious plantation, encircled by a high stone wall. Within this enclosure, which no visitor ever enters, grow the cinchona trees of Java. The secret of cultivation and extraction thus jealously guarded have made the Dutch supreme in the production of quinine." [1] The 37,500 acres of trees supplied over 95% of the world's quinine. As with the Jesuits, the supply has never been equal to the demand, not because more could not be made available, but because the government-sponsored syndicate of planters and manufacturers, the Kina Bureau of Amsterdam, maintained a high-price, low-output policy. Regardless of actual need or effective demand, only a limited amount of quinine was sold to each country. The annual harvests of cinchona bark, no longer necessitating the killing of the tree, were often larger than the quotas. In such cases, the excess bark was stored, or more often, burned. It has been estimated that about 50% of the bark produced was burned in some years.

The little quinine produced outside the Netherlands Indies was, through international agreements, subject to the same price-fixing arrangements. Since the unconscionable high price precluded its purchase by the people of the areas where malaria occurs most frequently, the cartel's monopoly was criticized by social and medical workers in the East. The Health Section of the League of Nations, at Dr. Heiser's suggestion, periodically published the production and price record of quinine and its derivatives, which so clearly bespoke the unrelenting control, which had, with more efficient methods, made greater output possible, but increased prices and withheld "surplus." It is not too much to say that these practices were directly to blame for the continuance of a much higher death rate than that which would have obtained if maximum production and competitive price levels existed.

The international cartel in natural quinine was indicted by the United States Government in March, 1928. Twenty-five manufacturers, Dutch, German, French, English, Japanese, and American, of quinine and other derivatives of cinchona, and a number of individuals were charged with violation of the antitrust laws. The indictment summarizes the activities by which the cartel was accused of enforcing its artificial control over the world market.

First, the indictment charged that imports of cinchona bark and quinine derivatives into the United States were restricted as to quantity, and shared by various American manufacturers, such as the Merck Company and Mallinckrodt Chemical Company, on an allotment basis. Prices of all cinchona products were fixed at both wholesale and retail levels. Any firms failing to observe the prices fixed by the cartel were threatened with boycott, and shutting off of further supplies of the drugs, and this "policing" of the market was rigidly enforced. *All* the manufacturers of quinine derivatives in the world were compelled to pool their profits under an arrangement known as the "Aussgleich," or equalizing agreement, which apportioned quotas of bark and quotas of profit, among the members of the cartel. Manufacturers who sold less than their quota, and who did not reach their fixed profit level, received contributions, presumably on a pro-rata basis, from those selling in excess of quota.

The indictment was filed in March, 1928, and in September of the same year a consent decree was entered which enjoined further operation of the cartel within the United States. But the jurisdiction of one government was limited, and the cartel continued to function in the world market. Obviously, the isolated "competitive area" of this country could not escape the effects of an entirely monopolistic market outside its borders. And to make the decree effective, it would have been necessary to break the grip of the cartel on the source of supply. This could not be done, and no measures short of an international decree could make this "natural" monopoly, as it was euphemistically termed by its beneficiaries, a competitive industry.

That the cartel's continued functioning in the international market remained unimpaired is borne out by considering the long-term price record of quinine, and by the situation which existed when war began in 1939, and again when Japan attacked and conquered Java. In 1914, quinine sulphate, the principal form in which cinchona is given to malarial sufferers, cost about twenty-five cents per ounce. In the middle twenties the price had risen to nearly fifty cents an ounce, reached sixty-seven cents in 1939, and is now over eighty-five cents per ounce. Only control by the Federal Government of the available stocks of natural quinine has held down the lid on prices.

The Dutch monopoly on cinchona, and the manufacturers' cartel which held so long to a competition-proof market were not free from the ever-present threat to all cartels: market rivalry based on technological change. It will be recalled that it was during an effort to produce quinine synthetically that Perkin discovered aniline dyes. I.G.'s continued search developed atabrine, a coal-tar derivative. It is taken in tablet form, and occasionally causes the skin to become yellowish, because it is made from a yellow coal-tar dye, known as acridine.

Atabrine is in some respects more efficient than natural quinine. A ton of atabrine can be used in treating about 600,000 cases of malaria, while a ton of quinine is sufficient for only 30,000 cases. Since 1932, because of its higher price, and especially because of the restrictive production policy of I.G. and its licensees, atabrine did not displace any substantial part of the quinine market during peace time. In the United States the Winthrop Chemical Company, a subsidiary of Sterling Products, with whom I.G. had other dealings, obtained an exclusive license under I.G.'s atabrine patents. By limiting access to technical knowledge of a vital product, I.G. had added a link in the German counterblockade.

As the Assistant Attorney General Thurman Arnold stated in the Oct. 1942 *Atlantic Monthly:*

A single patent, controlled by I. G. Farben, dictated the terms by which this essential drug could be manufactured in the United States. Sterling Products had an interest in this patent, but even during our lend-lease program officers of Sterling Products gave assurance to Germany that their interests would be protected during and after the war. Sterling Products is now rid of German domination. Today the situation is further safeguarded by the seizure of the German rights by the Alien Property Custodian. But the spectacle of the production of this essential drug, left so long to the secret manipulation of a German-American combination during a period when Germany was preparing for war against us, is too shocking to need elaboration.

The Dutch, with short-sighted stubbornness, clung to their cinchona plantations in Java and their rigid commercial practices in marketing. These policies have boomeranged not only on themselves but on all the United Nations. When the Japanese overran Java, they came into possession of more than nine-tenths of the world's supply, since the only other source of natural quinine is the scattered and relatively undeveloped industry in South America.

Present evidence indicates that this hurdle is being surmounted. Bataan was lost in part because of a shortage of quinine and atabrine. With the forces of this country and its allies engaging the enemy or guarding salients in tropical regions, which have been among the most active theaters of this war, every precaution should be taken to insure an adequate supply of these synthetics at prices sufficiently low to be within the reach not only of the fighting services but of the civilian populations. Malaria has not yet been defeated. It has only been checked in a relatively narrow segment of the world's populace, and that by strenuous efforts with little help from either the quinine syndicate or the I.G. controlled cartel.

Germany cracked the Dutch cartel, and permitted the United Nations to be "hoist on their own petard."

13. COAL, OIL, AND FIREPOWER

OIL is the blood of mechanized armies—the richest prize of battle. No sacrifice in lives or money has been judged too great to pay for its possession. Denied oil by the Allies for four years, the Imperial German Army had finally gasped and halted.

Like a phoenix rising from the ashes of its defeat, Germany emerged from the postwar years clutching the secret by which its basic need could be fulfilled. In 1926 I.G. belligerently announced to an unperceiving world that in due course "it would make all the oil the world required" from coal.[1] From that day forward there was no chance for peace.

The core of Germany's greatest military problem had been pierced. The oil which her ancient foes withheld could now be synthesized.

What did this mean in specific terms of global strategy? The oilbearing lands of the world were almost without exception located in countries which had been Germany's enemies. Consider where the oil deposits of the world are found. The United States has the largest fields; South America, China, the Dutch East Indies,

the Middle East, all of these were far away—their oil
was owned by enemy interests. Every well was protected by a hostile navy. The deposits of Roumania were
British-owned, and Roumania itself was a member of
the ring of buffer states which France would use as
shock absorbers when war should come again. Any effort
to reach Russian oil would mean the expenditure of
countless German lives with no guarantee of success.

What did Germany have? It had I.G. and coal. But
coal was of no use in planes. If I.G.'s magic could con-
jure oil from coal, then Germany could begin to calculate, free from the torment of knowing that the noose
of Allied strategy could garrote her war machine.

Coal became the denominator of Germany's future.
The sandbox of German earth would yield the vital
elixir to fuel her mechanized might.

There is a profound message for all nations in Germany's escape from her prison. Surrounded, and lacking the most essential material of motorized war,
Germany once more placed all her hopes on her technological skill. She was not disappointed.

This technological cataclysm was not recorded on the
seismograph of politics, yet its tremors were to rend
the fate of nations.

Not in the ledgers of government, but in the balance
sheets of finance were tallied the first accounts of this
discovery. In 1927 the largest industrial corporation in

the world, Standard Oil (N. J.) felt the shock to its foundations. It was as though all their wells had exploded at the same time. Every coal mine became a potential gusher.

Like the legendary giant which it resembles, Standard's strength is drawn from the earth, each renewed contact adding to its vitality. Standard's geologists ripped up a continent in their search for the precious fluid. In time they traversed the earth, seeking in remote corners of Asia, Africa, and South America, any trace of oil. Control of oil resources, oil refineries, and markets spread around the globe, has been Standard's sustenance. As late as 1941 Standard owned some 14% of the tanker shipping tonnage of the world.

Because modern civilization flows on a river of oil, Standard's every act is reflected in some manner in the ebb and flow of economic affairs. An outstanding authority on international industry has said of Standard:

> [It] has extended its influence over the whole world. In China it has made large advances to the government in return for valuable concessions. In Mexico . . . it has been engaged in a struggle with British capitalists for the control of oilbearing lands [and] it has been at times one of the principal instigators of civil disturbances there.[2]

This agitation is attributed to Standard in other countries, and was undoubtedly one cause for the expropriation of British and American oil properties by the

Mexican Government a few years ago. This same authority states:

> In Germany it attempted to defeat by force the plan of an oil monopoly aimed against it. Wherever oil is discovered, it tries to create a sphere of influence; it has branches in more than fifty countries. . . .

The convergence between the interests of I.G. and Standard Oil was a meeting of elemental forces in world industry. It loomed as a titanic conflict, it turned out to be a study in appeasement. Standard made the overtures and I.G. responded readily. The resulting deal set in motion a wave of events which ten years later would harass Standard's management. In Standard's own words, the essence of their basic understanding was that:

> The I.G. are going to stay out of the oil business proposition and we [Standard] are going to stay out of the chemical business in so far as that has no bearing on the oil business.[3]

I.G.'s position was clear. As long as it retained control of the production of oil in Germany, Standard could have the rest of the world—for a while. The orbit of I.G.'s interest was fixed by German aims. Standard thought only in terms of the geopolitics of its financial investment.

The division of fields of technology was settled in a series of agreements beginning in 1927 and concluding in 1929. I.G. retained for itself all rights to the basic chemical techniques, products, and markets by which it controlled its world domain. Standard was a great oil company, and was interested in chemistry only as it affected petroleum. I.G. was a great chemical company, and therefore was concerned in the commercial sense with the chemicals that might be derived from petroleum.

In 1929 what has been described by both Standard and I.G. as a "full marriage" was consummated. This marriage was witnessed by four documents dated November 9, 1929: (1) the Division of Fields Agreement, (2) the Four-Party Agreement, (3) the Coordination Agreement, and (4) the German Sales Agreement.* The parties to these nuptials dowered each other with exclusive monopolies in their respective holdings, vowing "loyal adherence" to each other's welfare for such time as the marriage should endure. In more concrete terms, the effects of this marriage may be summarized as follows: First, under the Division of Fields Agreement, Standard and I.G. agreed to eliminate all competition between themselves. This was done by recognizing the position of Standard in the oil industry and the position of I.G. in the chemical industry. Standard received carte blanche in the oil industry of the world *with the exception of the domestic German*

---

* Thus designated by the Government.

market. I.G., in turn, was assured a free hand in the entire chemical industry of the world, *including the United States,* a differential which was to embarrass Standard at a later date.

To grasp the magnitude not only of the Standard-I.G. cartel but, in particular, the potency and proportions of I.G.'s grip on technology, we must understand the nature of hydrocarbons. Hydrocarbons, compounds containing hydrogen and carbon, are the basis not only of petroleum products and of hydrogenated coal products, but are the fundamental constituents of a whole range of organic substances. A variety of techniques, such as hydrogenation, hydro-forming, hydrocarbon synthesis, polymerization, alkylation, and catalytic cracking, may be applied to carbonaceous matter. From the solid, the liquid, or the gaseous states of primitive materials, coal and oil, it is possible to produce a myriad of petroleum and chemical products.

Thus, whatever is made in either industry, chemical or petroleum, can in large part be created from the raw materials of the other. Moreover, the vast array of synthetics which can be formed by these processes includes those specialized commodities which spell the difference between a vigorous industrial system and an unbalanced second-rate economy. Judged by military potential or by modern peacetime production, no nation which does not have some source of hydrocarbons and the facilities and knowledge necessary to their transformation can be strong.

Coal, oil and air are the triangular arch of the modern chemists' war. The advances in chemical science have given hydrocarbons the quality and status of the magic philosopher's stone which can make a poor nation rich. The list of war matériel which can be brought forth from coal, oil, air and wood reads like the order-book of an army's ordnance command: toluol, tetracene, T.N.T., high octane aviation gas, plastics, synthetic rubber, dyestuffs, explosives, medicines, artificial silk, optical lenses, poison gas, food (the high-vitamin content oleomargarine fed to the German troops comes from this source), paraffin, clothing—what cannot be drawn from this cornucopia of slime and soot?

The patents of I.G. and Standard were pooled so that Standard received not only the benefits of its own research in oil technology, but also received the benefit of any discoveries made by I.G. Moreover, it was intended that this patent consolidation would so fortify Standard that all other oil refiners would be reduced to a subordinate position, thus rendering them susceptible and indeed suppliant to the formation of a gigantic patent pool covering the entire oil industry.

The second agreement in this contractual marriage is the Four-Party Agreement, formed for the purpose of executing the Division of Fields Agreement. It was agreed that I.G. would transfer to a joint corporation,

Standard-I.G. Corporation (S-I.G.), any rights upon patents affecting the oil industry. Standard in turn would transfer to this offspring its present and future rights under the hydrogenation process.

With regard to the exchange of experience between Standard and I.G., it was stated that:

> . . . the parties agree to work together on the technical development of the hydrocarbon field, to communicate to each other during the life and within the scope of this agreement all technical knowledge and experience, past, present and future, patented and unpatented, of which the parties are now possessed or which hereafter be possessed in the sense of having the power to dispose of them, and also to help each other in their efforts to obtain adequate patent protection.[4]

The merger of petroleum and chemical technology thus brought about could be held in check, "regulated" in business terms, only by a condominium of such size as the Standard-I.G. combine. Within the hydrocarbon and allied fields, the Standard-I.G. agreements must be considered as the radial hub from which other ancillary accords sweep out to all sectors of the oil and chemical industries.

The architecture of Standard's relationships with I.G. is constructed on foundations which, when uncovered, advertise the true purposes of the edifice and explain its use. Once past the façade of "cooperation," the

structure is seen to be a fortress to withstand any assault
by the forces of competition on the territory of Standard
or I.G., and a salient base from which both might conduct sorties into adjacent industries.

This stronghold was built, to adapt a phrase used by
Standard, by "piling patent upon patent," and the analogy is therefore not too remote. In the judgment of
the Senate Committee investigating the National Defense Program, "to obtain such a patent structure Standard paid a heavy price which, as in the case of other
companies creating such patent structures, had to be
borne by the entire nation."

The Standard-I.G. cartel was in its scope and implications larger, more powerful, and in some respects, at
least, of greater significance, than any other economic
"junto" with which we have dealt or shall deal. But
the characteristics of I.G.'s marriage with Standard are
so similar to its agreements with other American and
European industrial interests that no doubts can be
entertained of I.G.'s purposes.

The primacy of oil in international affairs and the
influences which oil's development has exerted on the
history of the twentieth century are traceable in British
imperial strategy since 1911. In that year Winston
Churchill, at the request of Lord Asquith, entered the
British Admiralty. Germany was increasing the size of
her fleet and the firepower of her naval rifles. Churchill
grappled with the enormous task of modernizing Brit-

ain's seapower in order to meet the new German naval threat. Churchill's problem was clear. He must build new ships with firepower beyond anything contemplated by Germany. Churchill knew that a second-best navy was like a second-best poker hand, and that the security of Britain's empire rested on the fleet. Every change in the structure of battleships was a gamble with the future.

Churchill himself relates a parable which shows his grasp of the basic nature of technological change. He says:

> In one of those nightmare novels that used to appear from time to time before the war, I read in 1913 of a great battle in which, to the amazement of the defeated British Fleet, the German new vessels opened fire with a terrible, unheard-of 15-inch gun.[5]

Churchill knew that war was the "art of calculated risk" and that there are other ways for a soldier to die for his country than on the battlefield.

In determining to equip the British fleet with 15-inch guns, he would encounter not only the opposition of Parliament but the natural conservatism of the British Government. Nevertheless, he made up his mind to proceed.

To put 15-inch guns on a battlefleet meant the redesign of all the ships on the ways, but in redrafting them, other problems arose. "The gun dominated the ship," and in order to reduce weight elsewhere without sacrificing armor, it was necessary to change the fuel energy from coal to oil. By eliminating coal bunkers and introducing oil, the fleet would gain at every point. Oil meant greater speed; oil gave ships a greater range of action; oil permitted the refueling of fleets at sea; but most of all, oil eliminated the dead weight of coal.

In moving forward Churchill encountered another obstacle, this time an oil cartel. He says:

> To change the foundation of the Navy from British coal to foreign oil was a formidable decision in itself. . . . First there must be accumulated in Great Britain an enormous oil reserve large enough to enable us to fight for many months if necessary without bringing in a single cargo of oil. . . . Fleets of tankers had to be built to convey the oil from the distant oilfields across the oceans to the British Isles, and others of a different pattern to take it from our naval harbours to the fleets at sea.
>
> . . . And beyond these difficulties loomed up the more intangible problems of markets and monopolies. *The oil supplies of the world were in the hands of vast oil trusts under foreign control.* To commit the Navy irrevocably to oil was indeed "to take arms against a sea of troubles." . . . If we overcame the difficulties and surmounted the risks, we should be able to raise the whole power and efficiency of the Navy to a definitely higher level; better ships, better crews, higher economies, more intense forms of war power—in a word, mastery itself was the prize

of the venture. A year gained over a rival might make the difference. Forward, then!

Churchill's understanding of the relationship between military strength and technology gave the British Navy its saving edge. The new 15-inch guns were a success. When the Battle of Jutland was fought years later, Churchill's actions were more than justified. If the German High Seas Fleet had met ships less powerful than the new British Fleet, the whole war might have been lost in the space of hours.

Churchill's decision precipitated a struggle for oil in which the British Empire became a major contestant. England entered into the oil market itself and ultimately formed the Anglo-Iranian Oil Company which, in turn, entered the world cartel.

If Churchill had held high office in the post-war years, who can say, when Germany declared its intentions, that Churchill would not have awakened Britain. After all, it was during the years between the wars that he wrote "While England Slept."

14. RUBBER—A LESSON IN LOGISTICS

PANZERS and armored cars are the cavalry of modern war. Their wheels and treads are rubber-shod—without rubber they must halt.

With every increase in the use of oil in engines of destruction, the need for rubber grew. For Germany the problem of rubber was, therefore, another hurdle to be leaped.

Rubber grew in far-off Malaya, and Britain rationed it to the world in war and peace.

Germany endeavored to achieve in the synthetic rubber industry the same success she attained in the manufacture of synthetic nitrates. The Bayer Dyeworks at Elberfeld, an arm of I.G., took up the problem of synthetic rubber, intending to make Germany independent of Britain's monopoly in the coming World War. At a dramatic meeting of the International Congress of Applied Chemistry in New York in the year 1912, Dr. Carl Duisberg of I. G. Farben delivered an address in German on the subject of synthetic rubber, which he illustrated graphically by displaying tires produced in I.G. laboratories. Although Germany was not completely able to master the problem at that time, by the end of the World War her annual production of synthetic rubber was between three and five hundred tons. When the war stopped, this production ceased, but I.G.'s research did not.

In both England and the United States large supplies of natural rubber as well as the interests of the rubber planters and fabricators precluded any large scale efforts to develop synthetic rubber beyond the stage of the laboratory.

After the World War I.G. resumed the study of synthetic rubber. During the years 1925 to 1933 I.G. obtained a number of patents on various processes necessary for the manufacture of synthetic rubber, and was able to produce several types of so-called Bunas. In this same period, in the United States, the DuPont Company, the Dow Chemical Company, and the rubber manufacturers also undertook some study of synthetic rubber. DuPont produced a substance known as Duprene, later called Neoprene, made from coal, limestone, salt, and water, which entered into some commercial use, since its resistance to oil, grease, and sunlight was superior to that of natural rubber. Other brands of synthetic rubber produced during this earlier period were, in the main, restricted to specialty uses.

As a product falling within the general scope of the Division of Fields Agreement between Standard Oil and I.G., synthetic rubber fell within the latter's exclu-

sive province. Research was carried on by both Standard and I.G., contemplating the development of
synthetic rubber, although I.G. excluded Standard's
commercial efforts in this respect.

Under the agreements, however, it was understood
that all know-how and experience obtained either by
I.G. or by Standard in the synthetic rubber field eventually would be pooled for their mutual benefit. The
remilitarization of Germany, however, as well as the
motives of I.G., did not permit the latter to turn over
its information to Standard. In fact, no more than the
barest patent specifications of the technique necessary
for the polymerization of the Buna-S and Buna-N rubbers were ever conveyed to Standard by I.G.

On its own behalf, Standard had developed in the
period 1930-1938 a form of synthetic rubber known as
Butyl, having a petroleum base, concerning which it
transferred to I.G. full and complete information.

In the agreements which Standard and I.G. made,
Standard held the position of junior partner in the
chemical field. I.G. had the last word on all questions
of general policy. When, therefore, four rubber manufacturers and one chemical company in the years 1932-
34 applied to Standard for licenses under the Standard-
I.G. synthetic rubber patents, I.G.'s decision determined
the result. Realizing that their own position would be
jeopardized by the new developments, the fabricators
of rubber wanted to enter the field. An agreement was

proposed between the Goodrich Rubber Company and
Standard which I.G. refused to ratify. Standard's own
attitude was intended to discourage the fabricators from
entering into production of any synthetic goods. As the
Goodrich Company stated:

> Certain it is that little enthusiasm will be aroused
> in a development where the question of terms on
> which it can be placed in commercial production is
> left to future negotiations, where there is a possibil-
> ity that these terms may be of onerous character as to
> preclude its employment or where there is even a re-
> mote chance that the result of our development will
> be passed on to another to the exclusion of ourselves.[1]

For the entire decade after 1932 Standard endeavored to keep its control untouched. There were two
chief difficulties. First, the rubber manufacturers might
seek to develop their own synthetics, which would make
void Standard's control. That Standard was aware of
this possibility is shown in a statement made in 1936:

> . . . following our refusal to deal with Goodyear
> on synthetic rubber several years ago, Goodyear went
> to work rather vigorously on its own behalf in this
> field and recently has succeeded in making some very
> interesting looking products.[2]

The second burden under which Standard pursued its
policy of averting independent research in synthetic
rubber came from I.G. I.G. prevented Standard from
committing itself to a positive program of synthetic rub-

ber development, and withheld the necessary know-how. As early as 1935 Standard knew that I.G. was not living up to its agreement to exchange full and complete information on Buna rubber because, in Standard's own words:

> . . . The Hitler Government does not look with favor upon turning the invention over to foreign countries.[3]

I.G.'s attitude was motivated by military expediency; war was coming and the German Government would not arm its enemies.

Despite I.G.'s refusal to adhere to its own side of the bargain, Standard, as a "loyal partner in marriage," decided to give its own knowledge of butyl rubber, a Standard Oil development, to Germany. Evidence indicates that Standard's butyl rubber can be made more easily, using less critical materials, than Buna. Butyl rubber, in the opinion of some experts, is substantially cheaper than Buna or natural rubber. The quality of butyl as it has been improved is almost the equal of Buna. Standard conveyed this information because of commercial considerations: it had too much at stake.

> . . . Certain difficulties still exist which prevent our I. G. friends from giving us full technical information and proceeding in the normal manner with the commercial development in the United States. . . .

In view of the very genuine spirit of cooperation which [I. G.] displayed, I am convinced that it is not only the right thing to do, but the very best thing from every standpoint to pass on to them full information on the copolymer [butyl] at this time. I do not believe we have anything to lose by this which is comparable with the possible benefit to all of our interests.[4]

In Standard's own words, it was felt that:

Until we have this permission [from Germany], however, there is absolutely nothing we can do, and we must be especially careful not to make any move whatever, even on a purely informal, personal or friendly basis, without the consent of our friends. We know some of the difficulties they have, both from business complications and inter-relation with the rubber and chemical trades in the United States, and from a national standpoint in Germany, but we do not know the whole situation, and since under the agreement they have full control over the exploitation of this process, the only thing we can do is to continue to press for authority to act, *but in the meantime loyally preserve the restrictions they have put on us.* [Italics added] [5]

Axis plans were reaching a culmination; Pearl Harbor was drawing closer. No synthetic rubber was being produced in this country on any commercial scale. The reason again was I.G.'s persistence in denying to Standard either permission or information necessary to begin large-scale development in the United States. As Standard stated at the time:

> The thing that is really holding us up, however, is not the lack of a plan either from Goodyear or ourselves, but the inability of our partners to obtain permission of their government to proceed with the development in the United States.[6]

Came September 1939 and war. In the following month, October, a vice-president of Standard Oil went to Europe and wrote back to Standard's president what is now the classic statement of "business as usual":

> Pursuant to these arrangements I was able to keep my appointments in Holland, where I had three days of discussion with the representatives of the I.G. They delivered to me assignments of some 2,000 foreign patents and *we did our best to work out complete plans for a modus vivendi which would operate through the term of the war, whether or not the U. S. came in.* All of the arrangements could not be completed, but it is hoped that enough has been done to permit closing the most important uncompleted points by cable. It is difficult to visualize as yet just how successful we shall be in maintaining our relations through this period without personal contacts. [Italics added] [7]

As a consequence of these arrangements, the strictures which I.G. had placed on Standard were slightly relaxed. Standard was now free if it chose to license the

rubber companies under the I.G. patents to make Buna.
On its own behalf, Standard retarded the pace of these
negotiations because of its instinctive desire to protect
and perpetuate its monopoly in the United States. That
these were its purposes is substantiated by two documents. The first is a memorandum by a Standard official
describing the type of license to be offered to the rubber
companies:

> The most important terms of the licensing agree-
> ment are:
> 1. The rubber company takes a license to produce
> for consumption in its own products but not for sale
> otherwise. It gives us an option to buy one-fourth of
> its plant capacity for distribution to the trade gen-
> erally.
> 2. A high royalty rate (7.5¢ lb.) is fixed so as to
> make the operation practical for the rubber company
> only so long as the product is used as a relatively high
> cost specialty.
> 3. The rubber company agrees to license back to us
> its improvements.
> The effect of these terms is to limit rather drasti-
> cally what the rubber companies may do under their
> license and to leave Jersey free to itself manufacture
> and sell, or participate along with rubber companies
> in a manufacturing organization, or confine its activ-
> ities to licensing and supplying raw materials. There-
> fore, the licenses offered may be considered as a stop-
> gap arrangement to permit the rubber companies to
> get into quick production of Perbunan for specialty

use if they so desire. Beyond this, there has been no decision as to how the development will be advanced.[8]

In analyzing the effect of these proposals, Standard's patent attorney stated:

> The agreement as it is now drafted will lead to the centering of all patent rights of licensees in the hands of licensor, with no outflow of these rights except to customers of licensor (and on two minor phases of patents to licensors' licensees).
>
> All manufacturing patent license of licensees will help to build up licensors' dominating position, but no licensee will get the benefit of any other licensees' manufacturing patent rights. In other words, this is not a cross-licensing agreement, but one in which patents are piled on patents in the hands of one centralizing company.[9]

How perfectly Standard's desire to look out for its own commercial future coincided with Axis plans!

The Pacific relations of the United States were becoming tense. Standard remained firm in its determination that no rubber company should make synthetic rubber tires until such time as Standard felt that its own control was secure. Two companies had the temerity to try. Goodrich started to fabricate Buna. Three months prior to Pearl Harbor Standard started suit against Goodrich for infringement of the I.G. patents. At the same time, a notice of similar action to follow was sent to the Goodyear Rubber Company.

The ensuing months after Pearl Harbor were to teach the American public the real meaning of "too little and too late."

A Lesson in Blockade

Synthetic rubber has become a military and economic keystone of American strategy. There would be no synthetic rubber problem if we could grow enough rubber or if the natural rubber industry, over the last twenty years, had not used a geographical monopoly as an opportunity to create one of the most important of raw material cartels. We have seen that patents can be instruments of power politics and warfare. Natural monopolies based upon the concentration of raw materials in favored areas of the world have played an equal part in international relations. In the case of natural rubber, the consequences of monopoly and cartellization have affected the course of the greatest war in history.

The colorful story of the natural rubber industry has been told and retold. Originally, natural rubber was found only in Brazil. As the uses of rubber in industry increased, this source became unable to supply the world's demands. Seeds and plants of the Hevea Braziliensis were smuggled to England, and eventually cultivation of rubber was begun in British Malaya, Ceylon, and the Dutch East Indies.

In a few years the monopoly which Brazil had enjoyed passed into the hands of the rubber plantations of the Far East. In time more than 90% of the cultivated rubber output was produced in British and Dutch colonies and plantations.

This situation was always a problem to the United States, because this country consumed more than three-fourths of all the rubber grown in the world. The large American rubber manufacturing companies in some instances were able to invest in Far Eastern rubber plantations, and eventually their share of ownership became substantial. During the first World War, before our own entry, we were cut off from our supply, but we failed to grasp the moral at the time.

At the end of the World War, the Dutch and British planters had accumulated large stocks of crude rubber. As output continued to increase in 1919 and 1920, the rubber market broke sharply. During 1920 and 1921 the British Rubber Growers' Association made strenuous efforts to obtain the intervention of their government on behalf of the industry. A special Parliamentary committee was appointed, and in 1922 a program of compulsory restriction, known as the Stevenson Plan, was put into operation.

The Stevenson Plan, acting in light of what it deemed to be imperial policy, undertook to rule out competition within the industry, to regulate the export policies of all the planters, and to set up a quota system of production. Negotiations were undertaken with the Dutch

Government, but the latter stubbornly held out and would not consent to the terms of the plan.

Despite this refusal of Dutch cooperation, the British Government enacted the plan into law late in 1922. The outcry in the consuming countries, principally the United States, was loud and long, and to mollify this agitation some concessions were made, without abandoning the principal provisions of the plan. As Great Britain's share in the world rubber market began to decline and that of the Dutch to rise, the first Stevenson Plan ultimately defeated its own ends. In 1928 it was supposedly shelved.

The cessation of the measures intended to maintain artificially the price structure of the rubber market coincided with the onset of the Great Depression. Efforts were made to declare a "tapping holiday" in 1930, but these were futile. Crude rubber stocks rose. Prices and exports fell. The entire industry suffered severely.

In 1933 conferences were begun to re-institute the cartel. In 1934 an intergovernmental agreement was drawn up between Great Britain, India, Holland, France, and Siam, governing world rubber production. An administrative body, the International Rubber Regulation Committee (I.R.R.C.), was set up to allocate production and export quotas. Accumulation of excess stocks of rubber was prohibited, as were new plantings of rubber trees. Nothing was overlooked. The export of "leaves, flowers, seeds, buds, twigs, branches, roots, or any living portion of the rubber plant that may be used to propagate it" was forbidden. Here indeed was the ultimate in cartel regulation of nature's processes.

The intergovernmental agreement was renewed in 1938 for a period of five years. Ostensibly its aims were the establishment of "equilibrium" and "fair and equitable" relationships between the planters and consumers. Such apparently lofty principles, however, could not conceal the fact that, like all such artificial restriction schemes, the agreement was based on the canons of monopoly. Thus, for example, when Germany sharply reduced its imports of natural rubber in the years immediately preceding 1939, the I.R.R.C. cut production and export quotas correspondingly, lest there should be any "surplus" on the world market.

It was, of course, typical of the purblind statecraft of those years that the governments supporting the cartel could not read the handwriting on the wall which, when translated, meant that Germany had overcome one of her worst problems in the World War, and was now prepared to try again. Furiously stirring its cauldrons on the Rhine, I.G. had learned to brew synthetic rubber, and, as with so many other materials, Germany could now discount in advance the blockade which war would bring.

Even after the blitzkrieg started, the I.R.R.C. continued the smooth tenor of its way. The Rising Sun of Japan glared ever more fiercely on the plantations of the East, but the cartel saw nothing beyond its own immediate shadow. The pettifogging behavior of the cartel aroused no alarm in any of the governments dependent on Malaya and the Indies for rubber.

From the military point of view, as well as from the economic, it is almost incredible that great states should permit themselves to be placed at such obviously geographical disadvantage. Pearl Harbor, Singapore, and the Dutch East Indies were a large fee to pay for a lesson in elementary logistics. The cardinal principles of military and economic warfare, the provision of ample supplies, had been violated.

15. *THE BATTLE OF ALUMINUM*

THE battle of aluminum is one of the major campaigns affecting the outcome of this war. Aluminum is the basic source of airpower. Because of its importance, Germany's aluminum industry was expanded to unprecedented size in the years of nervous "peace" before the war.

The industrial war is a series of campaigns. Measured by the yardstick of aluminum production, the United States and the United Nations are fighting desperately to match the output of the Axis. We lost the first round in this struggle, for the disparity remained in Germany's favor in 1942.

Since the outbreak of war, our pitiful capacity, stunted by high price, low-output policies, brought cries of anger from a public taken by surprise. The realization that aluminum production was now a fighting front precipitated a crisis. Men were toppled from high positions in our government because they had underestimated the need for this strategic metal. Charges of waste, inefficiency, and monopoly were freely hurled because of the shortage. Senate Committees held harrowing sessions, delving for the truth. Recrimination was the order of the day.

Once more monopoly was our undoing. The Aluminum Company of America, sole producer of aluminum in the United States, was harshly criticized.

Other ages have used iron, bronze, copper, steel and tin, but aluminum metal is entirely a product of modern times. It is the forerunner of the "Age of Light Metals." There is some slight evidence that "alumen" was known in the Roman Era, but it was not until 1825 that Hans Oersted, the Danish chemist, successfully isolated small quantities of aluminum in the laboratory. His feat was later duplicated by Woehler, the German chemist, who was able to determine more accurately the properties of the "silver found in clay."

Interest in the new metal, and realization of its possible applications, was immediate. Napoleon III, sensing that aluminum might be used for military equipment, subsidized Henri Deville, the brilliant French chemist, to discover economical methods by which aluminum could be produced on a commercial scale. Deville had exhibited a bar of aluminum at the Fair in Paris in 1855, and is credited with the major pioneering which ultimately led to the establishment of the industry. At the time Deville started his productive experiments in 1856, aluminum cost about $500 per pound, and ranked as a precious metal. Napoleon did not live to see his own augury vindicated, but the correctness of his premonition has long since been proved.

Aluminum is one of the most plentiful substances in nature, exceeded in its frequency of occurrence only by oxygen and silicon. It forms the metallic base of a variety of compounds, such as bauxite, alunite, leucite, feldspars, and common clays. In commercial production, the ore used is bauxite, which is richer than the others in its aluminum content. Characteristically, bauxite occurs in "pockets," or localized deposits, and this fact has been of extreme importance in the monopolistic development of the industry. Bauxite beds are found on every continent, and most of the higher-grade deposits are now worked.

The properties of aluminum which account for its uses are its light weight, its resistance to corrosion, its electrical conductivity, and its malleability. Aluminum can be forged, cast, and machined with precision, and when properly alloyed has a tensile strength equal to light steel. Because of these properties, aluminum has come to the fore as an ideal material for the manufacture of aircraft, ships, and other military and civilian vehicles. Aluminum cooking utensils and food receptacles are standard supplies of the home. The World War enormously enhanced the consumption of aluminum for military and transport uses and the interim between 1919 and 1939 saw its increasing application throughout industry.

The initial discovery which transformed the industry

was made by Charles S. Bradley, who filed an application for a United States patent in 1883. Bradley's application set forth a process for manufacturing aluminum by conducting an electric current through an aluminous ore, such as cryolite.* His patent was not granted until 1892, a circumstance which changed the later course of the industry.[1]

In 1886, Charles M. Hall, an American, and Paul Heroult, of France, filed claims almost at the same time, in their respective countries, describing the method of making aluminum by the electrolysis of alumina (aluminum oxide) in cryolite. Hall's patent was issued in 1889, and in the same year the Pittsburgh Reduction Company, which had been formed to exploit his process, began production of aluminum.

In 1907 the name of the Pittsburgh Reduction Company was changed to the Aluminum Company of America, and as a corporate entity Alcoa has been altered only once since then, when it merged with a Canadian power company in 1925. The duration of the corporate name is the only static feature of the company. In all other respects it has enlarged upon its original holdings. The ownership of Alcoa, however, has always been closely held by its directors, their families, and descendants, including the Davis group, the Mellon group, and the Hunt group.

---

* Cryolite is sodium-aluminum fluoride, occurring in large deposits only in Greenland.

The Hall patent expired in 1906, and the Bradley patent in 1909, and theoretically the aluminum industry was thrown open to all who would enter. Why others did not, and in fact could not do so, is explained by the policies which had governed the company's development from the outset. The patents were the first and the crucial factor which inflected the curve of the industry toward monopoly. But between the date of its establishment and the expiration of the patents, Alcoa took steps to nullify the loss of its patent protection. As a rule, patents and control of raw materials are the two strongest pillars of monopoly. Therefore, Alcoa, anticipating the removal of the first, sought to acquire the next best prop by engrossing the bauxite supplies in the United States, and later, in South America.

Having preempted the field, Alcoa grew to become one of the industrial giants of our economy. Its organic integration was carried forward by buying up the most favorably located water power sites that could be found. Alcoa was a member of every world aluminum cartel until 1915. Thereafter, while Alcoa did not directly participate in cartel agreements with foreign producers, no aluminum cartel could have existed had Alcoa chosen to compete.

Whether or not there were any tacit or "gentlemen's" agreements, the price, output, and sales records suggest that the Europeans have not sought to invade Alcoa's American stronghold, and Alcoa has abstained from any extensive effort to enter the European's sphere of influence. There is, however, indication that Alcoa's acquisition of European water power sites, bauxite holdings, and reduction facilities has had the purpose, and the beneficial effect (for Alcoa), of keeping the European producers "in line."

Alcoa was, until the war program of the government resulted in bringing the Reynolds Company and the government-built plants into the field, the single source of virgin aluminum in this country. Moreover, in the fabrication of aluminum products, such as aluminum sheet, automotive parts such as pistons, cooking utensils, and aluminum cable, to mention some of the larger items, Alcoa and its subsidiaries have maintained an unbroken "leadership."

By 1928 Alcoa had a corporate structure which could be used in any study of integrated "big business." Following the 1925 merger with the Duke interests in Canada, Alcoa had an authorized capital stock of 1,500,-000 shares, par $100 per share, and the same number of shares with no par or nominal value. Its wholly owned subsidiaries included thirty-two companies, ranging from railroads, bauxite mining companies, fabricating companies, sales companies, and power companies in the United States, Canada, South America, and Europe. In addition, it controlled a score or more of affiliated companies in partnership with others. These affiliated concerns included several European fabricating companies, Norwegian, Jugoslavian, Italian, French, and other firms producing bauxite, power, aluminum, and finished goods. What the total value of Alcoa's assets was by 1928 must to some extent be conjecture, but they were conservatively between one billion and one and one-half billions of dollars. At one time the market value of its stock alone was over one billion dollars. During its early period, Alcoa's profits permitted stock dividends on several occasions, and estimates have been made that for every dollar invested in Alcoa the annual profit to its stockholders has been in the neighborhood of 100%. Since much of this has been put back into the business, a fifty-year average return on the total equity would be about 13.5%, far higher than in comparable industries not completely monopolized.

In 1928, Alcoa executed what can be regarded as one of the shrewdest strokes any similarly situated company ever attempted, or one of the most unbusiness-like, depending upon the perspective from which it is viewed. Quite deliberately, Alcoa created the Aluminum Company, Ltd., in Canada, and "sold" to its own offspring all foreign properties which it possessed, with the exception of its Dutch Guiana bauxite mines and a few minor holdings. The consideration for this sale consisted of 490,875 shares of Alted's stock, which were distributed proportionately to the principal stockholders of Alcoa. Formally, and as Alcoa insisted, actually, Alted and

Alcoa were completely independent entities. As late as 1940 the owners of 81.53% of Alcoa's stock also held 83.93% of Alted's stock. We are faced, therefore, with a unique example of corporate development which economically reproduces the biological phenomenon of fission, by which bacteria reach a given size, and automatically divide into two. But analogy ceases with the act.

What was Alcoa's motive in forming Alted? Its own reasoning, at least as stated publicly, was to conduct business more efficiently in the British Empire and other foreign countries. Is this acceptable or plausible from an economic standpoint? It is not, because there is no economic or technical advantage in business operations which could not have been served by simply creating a subsidiary. As long as Alcoa retained Alted's stock in its own treasury, the latter was a subsidiary. By issuing the stock to Alcoa's own shareholders, did Alcoa free Alted completely? The questions which arise immediately are first, could it be contended that Alcoa deliberately created a competitor? Secondly, despite the technical independence of Alted, was there any change in *interests* which it served? To the first, it may be replied that not even the most altruistic corporation would set about consciously to destroy its own foundation and market. To the second query, the record answers that the controlling interests in Alcoa and Alted remained identical, with the exception of minor changes in proportionate holdings of stock by individuals. E. K. Davis, the brother of Arthur V. Davis, became President of Alted. The principal officers of Alted were all former Alcoa employees. The controlling shares, as has been stated, were held by the same groups in both companies.

Why, then, was Alted formed? It will be recalled that under the 1912 decree Alcoa was enjoined from entering into further cartel agreements with European producers by means of a Canadian subsidiary. While it may be legally moot, it is clear that Alted as an "independent" company could do what a subsidiary could not. Within three years after its formation, Alted entered into a world cartel agreement, to which only Alcoa, among all the major producers, was not a signatory.

Since Alted's formation, Alcoa has been able to enjoy to the full its monopolistic position in the United States market. Acting as a monopoly must, it has done four things: Restricted production, administered its price schedules, parried all threats of competition, and, as will be demonstrated hereafter, successfully checked a technological rival. The results of these policies became starkly and fearfully apparent when our national defense program began. The United States was no longer the world's largest producer of aluminum; this title had passed to Germany.

Through the cartel device Germany achieved a victory which a thousand bombers could not have won.

Force Majeure

The formation of Aluminum Company, Ltd., by Alcoa, as an "independent" corporation, even if it were credited completely, does not alter the aftermath of Alted's association with the aluminum cartel. After the World War, the European producers had joined in a series of cartel agreements, with the German producers, who had been completely united in a war-cartel, again coming to terms with the other aluminum manufacturers. Both the Vereinigte Aluminium Werke (V.A.W.), the government-sponsored cartel, and the Aluminum Werke, a subsidiary of I.G. (and of Metallgesellschaft, which I.G. controls), acted as one in their foreign relations after the war. There are close connections between the I.G. and V.A.W., through the Metallgesellschaft.

In 1928, the year in which Alted came into being, the European producers were joined in an Association. Alted did not enter immediately the Association, but did not in any way transgress its rules.

In July, 1930, Alted was a party to the "Zurich Agreement," by which the Japanese market was divided. Alted received 52% of this territory, the other 48% being divided between the British, French, German and Swiss producers. Alted was made exclusive sales agent in the Japanese market for the other signatories, therewith receiving the right to fix the price of all sales. This agreement prevailed until Pearl Harbor, although the growth of native Japanese production lessened Alted's grasp. During the years 1928-1931, there were also separate agreements concerning sales to Russia and India, in which Alted received proportionate quotas.

The year 1931 marked the end of the "Association," and the formation of a full-fledged cartel between Alted and the European producers. In October, 1930, Mr. A. V. Davis, of Alcoa, took a trip to Europe. The Europeans knew of it, and "anxiously" awaited his arrival. The chairman of the European cartel, M. Marlio, conferred with Davis, spoke of "harmony," and pointed out that "it was difficult to have harmony in the industry if the European producers were in a cartel and Aluminum were not." And the European producers, as E. K. Davis stated, regarded participation in a cartel "the acid test of good will." Whether M. Marlio succeeded or not in enlisting A. V. Davis' influence to persuade Alted to join in a formal cartel, shortly thereafter E. K. Davis, President of Alted, began work on a plan for a cartel, the principal features of which were known, at least in a general way, by his brother. At the latter's suggestion, Alcoa's own attorneys acted on behalf of Alted in the conferences in Montreal which were held in April, 1931, between Alted and the representatives of the Europeans.

These conversations were continued later in London, and on July 3, 1931, the so-called "Foundation Agreement" was signed in Paris. In performance of this agreement, the Alliance Aluminum Compagnie was incorporated in Basle, Switzerland. The Alliance issued 1,400 shares of "A" stock, subscribed by the members in the ratio of one share of stock for each 100 metric tons of their respective annual capacities. These proportions also governed the relative votes of each member company in defining Alliance's policies, and determined the quota of total production which each member would receive. The total annual production was to be fixed by Alliance. The entire executive staff of Alliance consisted of Ludwig Braasch and George Hodson, who had been for many years in Alcoa's employ. As E. K. Davis stated, Alted obtained the right which it asked for, i.e., ". . . to exercise a predominant influence over the administrative set-up of the Alliance . . ." It was at the request of Alted that the cartel placed Swiss bankers who were "friendly to Alcoa" on the directors' board of Alliance. (Swiss law required that some nationals be on boards of Swiss corporations.)

The ratios of ownership, and therefore of whatever maximum output might be fixed by the Alliance, were as follows:

Aluminum Ltd.	28.58%
French	21.36%
Germans	19.64%
Swiss	15.42%
British	15.00%

The Alliance also had the duty of fixing prices periodically, by setting minimums on aluminum ingot and
fabricated products, below which the cartel members
were not to sell. To enforce these decrees, Alliance was
empowered to deal in aluminum metal, so that it could
buy and sell excess stocks or surplus production of the
cartel members. The "buying price," set by Alliance,
allowed the members of the cartel to dispose of any
unsold aluminum at a price which was high enough to
deter them from any "dumping" at lower levels.

One feature of this cartel departed from the standard
pattern, and from the provisions of the former agreements in the industry. Instead of reserving particular
markets to each member, the quota system applied universally. By restricting total production and fixing prices
in all markets, there was no need to distinguish between
domestic and foreign outlets. The resultant supervision
covered the world market, with the conspicuous exception of the United States.

The Aluminum Company, since it was not a direct
member of the cartel, was not legally bound by its provisions. The cartel, on the other hand, could never have
functioned unless by design or accident Alcoa did not
disturb their markets.

One pertinent question stands out concerning the
Foundation Agreement and the Alliance. How could
any such contract or cartel hope to operate effectively
if Alcoa, not being a member, could at any time it chose

rip assunder the whole carefully planned program of the Alliance? The answer is that Alcoa did not do so, and that the members of the cartel acted as if it would not. As E. K. Davis stated (or understated?), "I am not conscious of ever having felt any apprehension about the selling of Alcoa metal on market conditions as they have been the past several years."

The Alliance, like all international cartels, thought and acted as a sovereign body. This presumption is explicit in a letter from E. K. Davis to M. Marlio, in December, 1935, concerning Russia, whose possible exports perturbed the cartel. Mr. Davis said, "The other thought that occurred to me was that the Alliance might be well advised to seize this opportunity presented by the Russians . . . particularly their desire for alumina concerning which you have already written me—to enter into a treaty with them whereby, for supplying them with the desired quantity of alumina and a considerable tonnage of aluminum, they will join the Alliance under some special understanding or agreement relative to their exports, thus safeguarding the Alliance from possible future annoyance from that source."

One year after the formation of the Alliance, that is, in 1932, the Board of Directors of the cartel decreed that the unit of production per share was to be reduced from 100 metric tons to 53 metric tons. The production records for the years 1930-1932 present an interesting

commentary on the coincidence of output policy between
Alcoa and the cartel:

	1930	1931	1932 [2]
Canada	34,900 *	31,000	18,000
France	24,640	18,152	14,360
Germany	30,700	27,100	19,200
Switzerland	20,500	12,200	8,500
England	14,000	14,200	10,300
United States ...	103,891	80,534	47,577

* Figures in metric tons.

Alcoa "happened to be" the only producer in the United
States, and its figures of reduced production followed
the cartel line. These years were, to be sure, a depressed
period, but the reductions in output by the Alliance were
only incidentally made with such adjustment in mind.
The Alliance was interested in "maximizing" revenue,
by maintaining price and lowering output, and in "stabilizing" the world market.

That Alcoa was a factor was recognized by I. G.
Farben in a memorandum concerning I.G. contracts
which "extend to the United States." I.G. stated:

> The firms jointly agree to avail themselves of the
> cancellation possibility of the Alliance Aluminium Co.,
> within five years, calculated from Jan. 1, 1932, only
> in the event that Aluminum Co. of America, which
> hitherto has not exported any aluminum from
> U.S.A., should commence to export aluminum or dis-
> turb in any other way the stipulations of the agree-
> ment with Alliance Aluminium Co.

To be sure, the cartel never was disturbed by Alcoa's expansion, and therefore no members withdrew.

In 1934 the German government harnessed the industry to its armament Juggernaut, and correctly saw the outstanding value of aluminum in the war they meant to loose on Europe. The policy of the Alliance as it was then formulated ran directly counter to the war program, so far as Germany was concerned. Germany would need aluminum and still more aluminum to fit its plans of conquest. Vereinigte Aluminium Werke and I.G.'s Aluminum Werke at once sought to be released from the quota restrictions placed on them by the cartel. Continued restrictions on the production of the democracies would not be hard to induce. Therefore, the German members could afford to show their hand.

The non-German members, including Alted, at first balked at the proposals made by the Germans. But the spirit of appeasement soon led the cartel to capitulate. At first, the members tried to satisfy the demand of the Germans by supplying them with extra metal, without lifting the bars the cartel had set up. These half-way measures did not find approval in Germany. V.A.W. was adamant in its attitude: not only must they be allowed to produce to capacity, but to expand their capacity without stint. As in political and military affairs, so in industrial agreements the Germans were ready to regard treaties as "scraps of paper" binding on others, but not on themselves. As E. K. Davis expressed it:

The German producers stated that they were going to produce in excess of their production rights whether the Alliance authorized them or not. The Germans stated in effect that they considered themselves to be subjected to *force majeure* in the matter, and asked to have their situation recognized.

This was done.

The Germans agreed not to export, and this sop proved sufficient to keep the cartel in operation as it applied to other countries, for a time. This stipulation also removed Alted's objection, since the Germans promised to buy a ton of aluminum from the cartel for every ton exported, so as not to affect the world market. As a further mollifying move, the Germans agreed to advance the price of aluminum sold for non-government purposes in Germany. This was no more than a gratuitous gesture. Germany restricted civilian consumption, which should have served warning on the other members of the cartel, had they not been so obtusely bent on preserving the market arrangements which their commercial instincts inclined them to place foremost.

E. K. Davis, in opposing the original demands of the Germans, portrayed accurately the nature of the scheme and the "business-like" basis of the objection. In a letter to M. Louis Marlio, chairman of the Alliance, Davis stated:

> *We and the others who are about to be sacrificed to this cold-blooded scheme have carried in silence*

*our respective burdens under the Alliance, awaiting
the time when we can enjoy some of the benefits of a
strict application of the association's rules.* [Italics
supplied]

Morituri te salutamus!

The action of V.A.W. and Aluminum Werke so disturbed the program of the Alliance that the Foundation
Agreement was abandoned. On January 1, 1936, the
Foundation Agreement was superseded by a new cartel
agreement. Alliance and its Board continued to regulate
output, but instead of fixing a "buying-price" at which
surplus products would be bought by the Alliance, a
royalty was placed on production above quota.

The demand for aluminum expanded generally after
1936 to such a degree that output-restrictions (but, on
the whole, not price levels) could no longer be enforced.
Hence, the Alliance has been dormant since about 1938.
But it is still in legal existence, ready to resume its
"burdens" as the future permits.

The "cold-blooded scheme" engineered by the Germans worked, and effectively hampered the armament
of the democracies. Germany became the world's principal producer of aluminum, and created an "aluminum
economy." The statistical record of output tells the story
in the barest terms:

	1933	1934	1935	1936	1937	1938 [3]
Canada	16,200 *	15,500	20,556	26,900	42,550	50,000
France	14,300	15,100	22,000	28,300	34,500	40,000

	1933	1934	1935	1936	1937	1938
Germany ...	18,900	37,200	70,800	97,500	127,500	175,000
Switzerland .	7,500	8,200	11,700	13,700	25,000	28,000
England	11,000	13,000	15,100	16,400	19,400	24,000
U. S.	38,614	33,647	54,112	102,027	132,759	130,129

* Metric tons.

Since 1938 the ascendancy of Germany in aluminum has been unimpaired and the disparity made greater by German conquest. It is reliably estimated that in 1941 Germany produced more aluminum than the *combined* United Nations. The collection of kitchen utensils in this country, occasioned by the shortage of aluminum for bombers, excited public question of such a scarcely-credible lack. The slow-down of aircraft production lines because of insufficient aluminum continued, in 1942, to hinder our "all-out" effort. The reasons for the scarcity of aluminum in this country are partly attributable to domestic monopoly, partly to the cartellization of the world market, and the concurrence, conscious or not, of the production policies of both monopoly and cartel.

Again, Germany took advantage of the "natural propensities" of cartel-makers, so as to weaken other countries, while leaving German industry free from external restraint, but completely "geared" to a war economy. In the case of France, the world's leading producer of bauxite for many years, the adherence of her aluminum producers to the cartel until the last hour before war is one direct cause of her downfall. When the Luftwaffe debouched from its hangars across the Rhine, to triumph swiftly over the comparatively miniscule French Air Force, the outcome was foregone. France could not remedy her aluminum shortage in the time allowed sufficiently to muster more than a token assemblage of planes. The moral needs no pointing.

16. MAGNESIUM—METAL OF MARS

TO Germany, magnesium was a discovery of great military importance. Its sources are virtually unlimited. It is found in seawater and in widely distributed ores. No blockade can cut off its supply, and only production facilities limit its output.

To a monopolistic aluminum industry, magnesium meant a technological rival of formidable properties. Its mere existence was a nuisance.

In these two sets of conditions magnesium developed to take its place among the lightest of light metals. Germany, since 1915, has constantly pushed onward in magnesium production. The democracies not only lagged behind, but sought to throttle magnesium, because it threatened to make obsolete the interests vested in aluminum. Once more monopoly must guard against both competition and technological change.

With Mephistophelean guile, Germany's minister of industrial war, I. G. Farben, lulled Alcoa into dreams of security, while Germany made magnesium in ever-increasing amounts.

Both I.G. and Alcoa "knew what they wanted." I.G.

desired magnesium. Alcoa wanted to erect a *"cordon sanitaire"* around the industry. I.G. lent willing aid.

Aluminum, as has been noted, is considered almost indispensable for some purposes which copper, steel, and other metals cannot economically fulfill, and is competitive with these metals in common use. Within its own special niche, aluminum is not, however, free from the threat of substitution by a competitive, and in many respects, a superior product, the metallic element magnesium. Although it has been known scientifically for some time, magnesium was first produced commercially in Germany in the early part of the World War. The General Electric Company, in 1915, produced magnesium in the United States, and during the period 1915-1919 some eight American companies entered the field. The initial impetus to the industry was both economic and military, since magnesium was used in making flares, tracer bullets, and incendiary bombs, and sold at a price of about $5 per pound.

Technologically, magnesium is in all important respects the greatest rival to aluminum. Magnesium can, when properly alloyed, fulfill any of the functions of aluminum with greater efficiency, since it is one-third lighter in weight, it is more easily shaped in the machining process, and has greater tensile strength. Chemically pure magnesium is extremely inflammable because of its affinity for oxygen. This characteristic impeded somewhat its introduction into commercial use, but accounted for its inauguration as a military essential, since magnesium generates extreme heat when it burns. Magnesium alloys, consisting of varying proportions of magnesium and aluminum or magnesium and other suitable alloy metals, possess great advantages as material for the construction of aircraft, the manufacturers of which are engaged in a never-ceasing search for lighter weight. The Minerals Year Book for 1940 reported:

> The highly destructive German-made aerial bomb used in Spanish Civil War raids on Barcelona consisted of ammonium nitrate, powdered charcoal, and aluminum, enclosed in a magnesium-alloy shell.

The use of magnesium reduced the weight of the bombload, permitting either more bombs or greater range.

At the end of the World War, the demand for magnesium declined, as did the output, and as a result, the price fell to one-third of its former level. Of the eight concerns which had been engaged in magnesium production, only two continued in the industry. These were the Dow Chemical Company and the American Magnesium Company, a wholly owned subsidiary of the Aluminum Company of America.

In the years 1920-1927, A.M.C. and Dow competed for the existing magnesium market. Dow produced magnesium by the electrolysis of magnesium chloride, and considered the metal a by-product of its chemical operations. A.M.C. used magnesite as its raw material, obtaining magnesium by the thermal reduction of the ore. Since Dow's process was more efficient, and its costs less than A.M.C.'s, it had the better of the struggle. Both companies, until 1927, probably sustained a small net loss on the total output. During this entire period, the weight advantage of magnesium over aluminum was offset by a much higher price. In 1926 Dow reduced the price from 90¢ per pound to 55¢ per pound. Immediately Alcoa recognized that if, as output increased, price reductions occurred in proportion, its own aluminum business would be threatened. Alcoa was also aware, about the same time, of the possibility that imports of magnesium from abroad would further augment the threat to its own position in the light metal market.

Constitutionally opposed to competition, and at the same time desiring to obtain a grip on the magnesium industry, Alcoa in 1927 permitted its subsidiary to cease production, and in July of that year contracted to purchase its entire requirements of magnesium from Dow. A.M.C. became Dow's largest customer, and under subsequent sales agreements was granted preference as against all other customers of Dow. At the same time the purchase agreement was signed, a cross-licensing agreement covering certain fabrication patents was executed between A.M.C. and Dow. Both A.M.C. and

Dow still retained the privilege of dealing with others, and A.M.C. could, of course, reenter production at any time.

During the years 1927-1928 the ubiquitous I.G. again became a member of the *dramatis personae* of the magnesium industry in the United States. I.G. approached Dow and several other companies in an effort to enter the American market with the aid of an American concern. Dow reacted negatively to I.G.'s advances. It was therefore almost inevitable that I.G., in making its rounds, should establish contact with Alcoa.

The first negotiations occurred in 1928; after a period of study of the process used in production and fabrication, and of discussion of the terms of agreement, Alcoa and I.G. signed what is known as the Alig Agreement, in October 1931. This agreement became the charter of the magnesium industry in this country until war supervened. Here again I.G. pursued one of its favorite practices in dealing with American industries: a joint corporation, the Magnesium Development Company, was formed, in which Alcoa and I.G. each held 50% of the stock. Magnesium Development Company was a patent-holding organization to which I.G. transferred a number of fabrication patents and to which Alcoa contributed some process patents, although not as many as I.G.

In addition to its participation in M.D.C., I.G. eventually received a 50% interest in American Magnesium,

Alcoa's own subsidiary, via General Aniline & Film.* The Alig Agreement provided that any licenses issued by M.D.C. for the production or fabrication of magnesium were to be restricted to the United States. The Alig Agreement stipulated that

> As long as magnesium is produced by any . . . producing company under a license or licenses granted . . . the holders of the I.G. shares in Alig . . . shall have the right to limit the increases in production capacity of every such producing company after the initial contemplated production capacity shall have been reached. The initial contemplated production capacity *shall in no case be more than 4,000 tons per annum.*[1] [Italics supplied]

It is significant to note that the sole producer of magnesium in the United States, while not a party to the Alig Agreement, never produced above 2,200 tons before the war emergency. This section of the Alig Agreement revealed in the light of later developments that I.G. was carrying out not only its own purposes in the magnesium industry of this country, but had actually invested, in a military sense, a strategic branch of production. I.G. had been insistent from the outset that Dow be included in the general plan formulated by itself and Alcoa. Dow was recalcitrant, not only because it felt that its own patent position was as strong as that of M.D.C., but because it did not relish dealing with

* See Chapter 7 (Dyestuffs).

I.G. To overcome this reluctance on the part of Dow, Alcoa inaugurated a familiar type of "squeeze play" intended to bring Dow into a more conciliatory frame of mind. In 1932, Alcoa's patent attorney, in a letter to Walter Duisberg (I.G.'s principal representative in M.D.C.), stated unequivocally:

> Dow is either going to play with us or is not going to play with us. If they do not play with us, we have two courses before us. One is to enter into an oral argument over the entire industry with Dow. The result of this argument would simply be that a great deal of time, paper and energy would be wasted to no particular effect. The other course is to sue Dow with two objects in view, the first object being to bring Dow to terms, the second object being to actually prosecute the suit to its logical end. As a patent company, MDC has nothing to offer at the present time except patents and technical information. Since they cannot make money on their technical information without their patents, they cannot deliberately refuse to recognize an outright challenge of the validity of their most important patent structure.[2]

This maneuver succeeded, and in 1933 Dow and A.M.C. entered into a five-year purchase contract reaffirming A.M.C.'s position as a preferred customer. On January 1, 1934, Dow entered into a patent-pooling agreement with M.D.C., cross-licensing each other on certain fabrication patents. The strength of Dow's patent position had been recognized much earlier. In 1930

H. E. Bakken of Alcoa, in a report concerning possible
arrangements covering the industry, stated:

> For the immediate present, with Dow as sole pro-
> ducer and ourselves and I.G. Farbenindustrie A.G.
> following up fabrication processes and fundamental
> research to increase the use of magnesium, it is ex-
> tremely doubtful whether anyone else would attempt
> to break into the magnesium business. As has been
> pointed out before, the two companies together would
> have a very strong patent situation. It is felt that
> this situation alone would make the entry of other
> interests unattractive. Even Dow Chemical Company
> and people whom he might interest in fabrication of
> magnesium would, from a patent standpoint, find
> heavy weather.[3]

In a later report it was acknowledged that:

> The patents of Dow, taken as a group, are the
> strongest group of patents on magnesium base alloys
> in this country. It appears that they will cover the
> newly developed alloys which will be important in
> future years. . . . We would state that of the three
> parties (AMC, I.G. and Dow), Dow has the alloy
> patent situation containing the best inherent future
> possibilities.
>
> *   *   *
>
> AMC and Dow together own valuable heat treat-
> ment patents which effectively prevent, under present
> practice, the successful heat treatment of magnesium
> base alloys in this country (by other parties). . . .
> I.G. has no heat treatment patents and is utterly with-

out status in this country in this connection but applications are on file. . . . The valuable heat treatment patents have now issued. It is doubtful whether any exceptionally broad heat treatment patents will issue in the future to any of the parties or to any other persons.[4]

As a result of Dow's capitulation to the constrictor tactics of Alcoa, Dow was assured of its own monopoly in the production of magnesium metal in the United States. It gave up, however, its freedom of action with respect to expanding the magnesium business, and in the formulation of price policies it was apparently understood that Dow would adhere at all times to two considerations. First of all, the general price relationship between magnesium and aluminum appeared in a ratio of 3-2. With only a few exceptions, the price record supports the contention that magnesium was artificially and arbitrarily valued until the advent of war. Secondly, A.M.C.'s position in the industry was safeguarded by what might be called a "more favored nation" policy, by which A.M.C. was granted not only a discount which might properly accrue to quantity purchases of the metal, but received preferential treatment equivalent to any reduction achieved by Dow in the latter's production costs. There was, of course, a further implication of such pricing: it prevented the sale of fabricated products either by Dow or any other manufacturer on a basis competitive with A.M.C.

The fact that Dow acted under duress in establishing a rapport with I.G. in the magnesium business might, perhaps, be excused in part on the ground that Dow, like many another enterprise, found itself faced with protracted litigation and the certainty of cutthroat competition and, following the law of self-preservation, bargained as well as it could.

Turning now to I.G.'s part in "developing" the magnesium industry, I.G. had, of course, attained its desired status in the American magnesium industry, and by reason of the Alig Agreement, could at any time veto expansion of production capacity by Alcoa. I.G. was not content with thus proscribing the size of the industry, but also sought to guard against any disturbance of the international magnesium market. In 1934, I.G. offered to purchase from Dow 350 tons of magnesium, to be followed in 1935 by purchases of 600 tons, with options for similar amounts in 1936 and 1937. The quantities of these orders represented a significant portion of Dow's capacity.

The specific clause which shows I.G.'s control of the world market reads as follows:

> Dow agrees to confine its sales in Europe solely to the I.G., with the exception that it reserves the right to sell the British Maxium or its successors not more than 300,000 pounds (150 tons) per annum at a price not lower than the price quoted to I.G. for the same quantities, plus an extra charge of not less

than 4 cents per pound for I.G.'s larger consumption. Dow further promises to use its best endeavor to keep British Maxium or its successors from reselling Magnesium in ingot form and will try to limit its purchases to its own use in fabricating.[5]

The price at which magnesium was sold to I.G. was to be at least four cents less than that to Great Britain. Magnesium sold in the American market for thirty cents per pound at that time. The price to I.G. was twenty cents per pound, or a discount of $33\frac{1}{3}\%$. I.G. thus strengthened its own position in the European magnesium market, and by cornering as much as 60% of Dow's current output, forestalled the latter's acceptance of any offers from other countries.

There is a significant corollary to this transaction. Great Britain was primarily dependent upon Germany for its magnesium during the years this contract was in operation. In 1934, Great Britain received 130 tons of magnesium from the United States and 861 from Germany; in 1937 it received 147 tons from the United States and 2,011 tons from Germany; in 1938 its imports from this country totalled 186 tons, and from Germany, 1,500 tons. In peace, I.G. was building its capacity for war. Because I.G. had employed the same methods in the magnesium industry in Great Britain as it did in the United States, Great Britain found itself cut off at a single stroke from the major part of its magnesium supply by the declaration of war. Great Britain had given a hostage by depending on I.G. Dow made its unwitting contribution to Britain's weakness because I.G. had once more fulfilled its role.

As might be expected, there was a European magnesium cartel in which I.G. was the dominant member. While no direct evidence is available concerning the extent to which I.G. retarded magnesium production in France or other future victims of conquest, it is certain that within Germany magnesium production expanded as rapidly as facilities could be increased. The comparative production figures of the United States and Germany for the years 1937-1940 are as follows:

	1937	*1938*	*1939*	*1940*
United States ...	2,059	2,918	3,039	5,680
Germany	12,080	14,100	16,500	19,000[6]

The frantic efforts which have been necessary to meet our war-time needs for magnesium are the most concrete comment that could be made as to the effect of Alcoa's partnership and Dow's consortium with I.G.

17. BERYLLIUM—THE MAGIC METAL

THERE is no tin in Germany. Neither is there tin in the United States. Its major source is in Asia, unavailable to either. Yet tin is an important metal to a country at war. Our Army and Navy Munitions Board includes it among the fourteen strategic materials necessary to national defense.*

Glass and paper can be used instead of tin-plated steel to preserve food. Germany, for instance, in 1938 alone used 133,000,000 cellulose containers. But tin has another use of great value to armies in the field for which a substitute or ersatz material has for many years eluded capture. This is in its use with copper to make bronze, a traditional war metal.

The laboratories of the great Siemens-Halske Company, an important factor in Germany's scheme for war, by 1929 mastered the problem. They discovered how to make bronze with beryllium instead of tin, and punched another gap in the United Nations' basic strategy—the blockading of Germany.

* Antimony, chromium, coconut shell char, manganese, manila fiber, mercury, mica, nickel, quartz crystal, quinine, rubber, silk, tin, tungsten.

The firm of Siemens & Halske is one of the world's great producers of light and heavy electrical machinery and equipment. Siemens & Halske was organized in 1847 by Ernst Werner von Siemens, a Prussian Army officer, a specialist in artillery, often credited with the invention of the dynamo, and certain military devices. The Encyclopedia of Social Sciences says of Werner von Siemens, "In his business activity Siemens stressed quality, not price [and], the supremacy of collective economic interests over private ones." Today Siemens & Halske, still in control of the Siemens family, is one of Germany's largest concerns, and a member of as many international cartels as I.G., with over 100,000 employees. A district in Berlin, the Siemensstadt, is the headquarters of the firm.

A qualified expert, in his testimony before the T.N.E.C., describes a Siemens & Halske enterprise as follows:

> Dr. Rohn [of Siemens] has the most wonderful metal-working plant I have ever seen in the world at Hanau, near Frankfort, the equivalent of many millions of dollars in this plant, and equipment that will produce alloys, that will produce results that I don't believe can be duplicated anywhere else in the world. I think most prominent metallurgists will bear me out in that statement.[1]

While it may be argued that Germany has to depend on outside sources for beryllium as well as tin, the conditions are somewhat different. Beryl ore which is found in large quantities in South America (where Germany, by the way, got most of its beryl ore), Africa and Asia, is more accessible to Germany than tin. Secondly and most important, beryllium bronze requires only 2% of beryllium instead of 12% tin used in ordinary bronze. For certain kinds of bronze, at least, a stock pile of beryllium is five to six times more effective than tin.

Tin, originally found in the Cornish mines of England by the Phoenicians, has been tied to England, no matter where it was located. The Cornish mines are no longer an important source of tin. The major deposits are now in Malaya and the Dutch East Indies, with Bolivia following far behind. Like rubber, tin is controlled by a British-dominated cartel known as the International Tin Committee, which has jealously guarded its position in the mining and smelting of this strategic metal. Not only the Malayan and Dutch East Indian tin, but also Bolivian tin is reported to be under the dominance of the cartel. For this reason, it is charged, until the Global War no tin smelters were constructed in the United States.[1]

Beryllium is the fourth lightest element known. Only hydrogen, helium, and lithium precede it on the periodic table. Standing alone, it is of little value, as yet, being used in minute quantities in certain precision equipment. When small amounts are alloyed with certain other metals, however, it takes on amazing qualities. For instance, two parts of beryllium added to 98 parts of copper result in an alloy harder than structural steel. Even more astonishing is its tensile strength, which measures 185,000 pounds per square inch. When the same quantities of beryllium are alloyed with nickel it forms one of the hardest metals, and has a tensile strength of 300,000 pounds per square inch.

Comparative figures with other metals will make the qualities of beryllium clearer:

	Tensile Strength	
Duralumin (5% copper, 95% aluminum)	53,000	lbs.
Structural Steel	60,000	"
Yellow Brass	70,000	"
Silicon Bronze	90,000	"
Stainless Steel	90,000	"
Phosphor Bronze	100,000	"
Monel Metal	125,000	"
Beryllium	110,000	"
Beryllium Copper	185,000	"
Beryllium Nickel	300,000	"

In other words, a bar one inch square of beryllium nickel would support a weight of 150 tons before giving way.

As a spring, beryllium copper's qualities are second to none. Where a phosphor bronze spring will break after 400,000 vibrations, the best steel spring, after two or three million, beryllium copper and beryllium nickel will go over *20 billion.*

Beryllium alloys were developed in Germany during the middle twenties; in the United States they were not in commercial production until 1934. In this disparity is found another story of Germany's preparation for war.

In 1929 a promoter, Andrew Gahagan, and a scientist, J. Kent Smith, began research in the beryllium field in the United States. After making considerable progress they learned by reading a technical journal that Siemens & Halske seemed to be far ahead. Thereupon Mr. Gahagan began a tour through the tortuous caverns of German deviousness.

First, he discovered that the Siemens & Halske patents in the beryllium field were owned by a New York company known as Metal and Thermit Company. Metal and Thermit referred Gahagan to Dr. Frank, Siemens & Halske's representative in the United States. No one seemed to know precisely whether Metal and Thermit or Siemens & Halske owned the rights. Gahagan described his difficulties as follows:

> For some 3 years, nearly, I had various conferences with the representative of Siemens & Halske. . . . I couldn't find out whether Metal and Thermit owned the patents or whether they didn't own them, or whether Siemens were going into the beryllium business in the United States or whether they were not going into the business.
>
> That left us in a rather precarious position, because if we continued our development, by this time we had

spent considerable money and a few years' work; if
we continued the development we might find after 5
or 10 years a lot of overhanging patents, owned by
Siemens, which would be held against us and we
would be told some day, "Well, you can't operate any
more," or "You can't make beryllium copper and
heat treat it, or you can't use beryllium copper alloys
for certain specific purposes, or you can't heat treat
beryllium nickel," and so forth, and the customers
we had, or hoped to have in the future, might also be
embarrassed.

You see, we had a situation with which I was familiar before the war; a number of patents in dyestuffs were taken out in this country and as a result
no dye businesses were started in this country. The
patents were held merely, as you are more familiar
with than I am, merely as a means of preventing
a business in this country.[2]

Mr. Gahagan's suspicions were by no means un-
founded. Investigation of the beryllium industry by the
Temporary National Economic Committee in 1939 disclosed that Metal and Thermit was acting as a dummy
for Siemens & Halske. Under an agreement Metal and
Thermit was to receive $10,000 for prosecuting the
patents in the United States, so that their German
identity could be concealed, then holding them for
Siemens in escrow until such time as the latter company
desired them back.

Siemens & Halske had not forgotten the activities of
the Alien Property Custodian during the war. If war

was to come again would these patents be subject to seizure? Who would know that the assignment of patents was spurious, subject to an escrow agreement? Siemens was also concerned lest beryllium develop in the United States under uncontrolled auspices. In this light the Siemens-Metal and Thermit relationship becomes clearer. The cover is lifted somewhat by the following portion of a letter sent to Metal and Thermit by Siemens & Halske in 1929:

> I would at once agree to have the application assigned to your firm, if thereby the matter could be better pursued, when it appears under American auspices before the Patent Office, in a new shape or form. Since you, as I was happy to learn from Dr. Frank, have decided to take up the Beryllium matter in America, I assume that you, too, are interested in the fight for that patent rights (sic), *so that outsiders, like the Beryllium Corporation (and) the General Electric Co., etc., cannot secure any ground in the realm of the Beryllium-Heavy-Metal industry.* [Italics supplied] [3]

Mr. Gahagan's difficulties were not accidental. It should be noted that during these years of procrastination and delay, patents stood guard at the entrance to the beryllium industry in the United States. Mr. Gahagan's statement indicates the power of this sentry. Despite the fact that all indications pointed to growing industry in Germany by 1934, not a pound of beryllium copper had been produced commercially in the United States.

In December 1933 Gahagan decided to deal directly with Siemens & Halske in Germany, after four years of fruitless negotiating in this country. Arriving at Siemens & Halske he learned that they did not desire to license Gahagan's Beryllium Corporation of America or exchange patent rights with him. Thereupon Gahagan left for Paris to try to make a similar deal with the French. This apparently was of great concern to the Germans, for upon learning of Gahagan's trip they wired him to return and resume negotiations.

The resulting contract followed the prescribed formula. The parties, the Beryllium Corporation of America and the Heraeus-Vacuumschmelze Co., which was the beryllium division of Siemens, agreed to exchange know-how and patent rights. The world was divided into certain exclusive areas with Siemens taking all of Europe including the British Isles, while the Beryllium Corporation received the continent of America. The rest of the world remained unallocated, probably due to the infant nature of the industry, although concerning these "other countries agreements will be made from year to year."

What Mr. Gahagan got into after the signing of the contract caused Leon Henderson, Executive Secretary of the T.N.E.C. during the investigation, to exclaim, "It certainly seems to me, Mr. Chairman, that he got into a series of things that out-Oppenheimed Oppenheim in reality and this whole question of international agreements and understandings ought to be gone into." The verbatim testimony is most eloquent, considering its date, May, 1939:

Mr. Cox: [Special assistant to the Attorney General, in charge of the examination] There is one modification (of the contract) I wanted to have Mr. Gahagan tell us about now; the modification to which I refer is the one which permitted you to exercise certain rights in England. Will you tell us about that, Mr. Gahagan?

Mr. Gahagan: Well, last year when I was going to Europe I was told that a Mr. Jamieson in England was one of my stockholders and that he wanted me to be sure to see him in England. As a matter of fact, he more or less gave me a command to look him up in London. Mr. Jamieson is the chairman of the board of the Vickers Co. The Vickers Co., as you all probably know, is the largest manufacturer of airplanes in England. I was rather surprised at this because I didn't know I had any such stockholder or any stockholder at all in England, so I called on Mr. Jamieson and asked him why he had such an interest in beryllium. *He told me he was very interested in beryllium because he considered that it would probably be a most important metal from a military point of view in the next world war, and I asked him why. He said, "We are entirely dependent upon the Malay Straits and Bolivia for tin, for the manufacture of bronze. The Malay States might be cut off. The few tin mines in Bolivia might be blown up* and beryllium copper would be the only thing we could use for certain purposes, and beryllium copper is much better than tin bronze. Therefore, I think beryllium copper is extremely important and I wanted to become one of your stockholders to follow your development." As a matter of fact, curiously enough, about every 6 months I have some representative of the British aviation, military attaché, or someone in Washington call on me to find out what we are doing and how we are getting along. They have been doing that for the past 10 years.

Well, Mr. Jamieson then said, "You have a contract with Siemens & Halske, and collateral agreements with other companies."

I said, "Yes, sir; we have."

He said, "You have a provision in that contract whereby you turn over everything to Siemens & Halske in Europe and you agree not to sell in Europe."

I said, "Yes, sir; we have. I am very surprised, however, that you know that because as far as I know there are only three copies of that. One is in my safe, one is in the safe of Siemens & Halske in Berlin, and the other is in Dr. Rohn's safe at Hanau."

He said, "I know it. How I found it out I can't tell you, but," he said, "you are going to modify that contract, because England will not be dependent upon Germany for any military needs."

He said, "We are doing a great deal of experimental work in Rolls-Royce, Vickers, and other companies in England on beryllium copper and beryllium nickel, and we are buying those materials for experimental purposes in Germany, but we are not going into production on any item unless we can secure our supplies from you entirely or from you as a second source of supply. We don't mind being dependent on you for a source of supply because we are dependent on the United States for a great many metals in any case, but we are not going to be dependent on any nation on the Continent."

He said, "I want you to modify that contract."

I told him, "Well, I have no way of modifying the contract. After all, I have signed it and I expect to live up to it."

He said, "Well, I'll take care of it. When are you going to Germany?" And I told him within a few days, that I would be there for some 3 or 4 weeks. So, after I had been there about 10 days, two unofficial representatives of the British Government came over and talked with Dr. Rohn, and we argued and discussed for about 3 days—I didn't do much discussing or arguing, but I listened to it. The British said, "If you don't modify that contract and permit importation from the United States we are going to confiscate all of your patents, and Mr. Gahagan's patents in England; we are not going to permit some international agreement whereby we are held up for military purposes."

I didn't know under what provisions or how they were going to be able to do that, apparently neither did Dr. Rohn, because he said, "You can't do that. After all, we are not in a war with England—Germany isn't and you can only expropriate patents in time of war."

He said, "Oh, yes; we can do that."

THE CHAIRMAN [Senator O'Mahoney]: Well, the British have a way of asserting what we would call public interest and they call it Empire's interest, over any private contract or private understanding.

MR. GAHAGAN: You can't take out a patent in England and just sit on it.

MR. COX: Was the contract modified then?

MR. GAHAGAN: Very curiously, the contract was modified, made effective the first of this year; under the terms of that we are permitted to sell to England. [Italics added] [4]

This by no means ends the story of beryllium. Once the agreement with the Beryllium Corporation was signed, the Germans were most anxious that the development of beryllium in the United States follow the cartel pattern. Any competitive exploitation might seriously disrupt their plans. For one thing, any new developments and patents or large scale production outside the compass of the cartel might seriously endanger the precise world division of territory. With this in mind, Dr. Rohn of Heraeus Vacuumschmelze came to talk to the P. R. Mallory Co. of Indianapolis. This company was interested in making beryllium copper electrodes. Dr. Rohn suggested to P. R. Mallory that their purchases of the beryllium copper alloy should be from Siemens if the Beryllium Corporation would give permission, or from the Beryllium Corporation itself. In any event, outsiders were not to be dealt with, lest P. R. Mallory's English subsidiary feel the economic power of Siemens & Halske. When questioned by James Wilson of the Department of Justice before the T.N.E.C.:

> "Have you any idea what would have happened to the English company if you had broken off negotiations with the Beryllium Corporation and started purchasing from competitors?"

Mallory's representative answered with a beautiful euphemism:

> "Well, I am quite sure our English company wouldn't have been able to sell very profitably." [5]

Hugh Cox's questioning of Mr. Gahagan about this clinched the point:

> MR. COX: Would it be accurate to say that you suggested to Dr. Rohn that no agreement should be made with the Mallory Co. with respect to the English situation or give it rights under the patent which Dr. Rohn's company controlled unless the Mallory Co. reached some kind of an agreement with you in this country?
>
> MR. GAHAGAN: That is right.
>
> MR. COX: And the agreement which you had in mind was an agreement under which the major company would purchase all of their requirements of the master alloy from your company?
>
> MR. GAHAGAN: That is right; or pay the royalty.

*　　*　　*

MR. Cox: And was it also a part of that understanding that you suggested to Dr. Rohn that the
Mallory Co. not go into any of the fields of fabrication in which your company was engaged?

MR. GAHAGAN: That is right.

MR. Cox: And Dr. Hensel was correct, was he not,
when he testified yesterday that as a matter of fact
Dr. Rohn did lay down those conditions before he
would reach any agreement with the Mallory Co.
either as to their English company or their use of any
patent rights which Dr. Rohn's company controlled?

MR. GAHAGAN: I didn't hear Dr. Hensel's testimony, but that is correct.

MR. Cox: You were so informed by Dr. Rohn?

MR. GAHAGAN: That is right.[6]

In 1935 Dr. Ferdinand Kertess, a representative of
the Deutsche Gold und Silber-Scheideanstalt, a German
corporation closely related to Siemens & Halske and
I.G., suggested to the one American producer outside
the cartel that "some cooperative basis" for the orderly
development be arranged.

> . . . It came to my mind whether it would be a
> good thing for all of us if you could consider some
> cooperative basis with beryllium products companies.
>
> *   *   *
>
> If you, for instance, could come to a compara-
> tively loose agreement with Beryllium Products Co.,
> your company handling the metal, Beryllium Prod-
> ucts handling the alloys, or whether you could even
> make up your mind to acquire shares in the Beryllium

Products Co. to make the tie a closer one, it would naturally be a matter you have to decide yourself.

Should such cooperation between you and Mr. Gahagan be possibly established, we would throw in our own experience and development. I feel that beryllium and its alloys could be made an object, giving extensive profits to all concerned, saving tremendous expense to each and everyone of us, and giving special benefit to all to make such thought worth while.[7]

It is significant to note that, on November 6, 1942, Dr. Kertess was indicted by a Federal Grand Jury in New York for smuggling metals to Germany.

Outsiders are dangerous to cartels. Nevertheless, Brush Beryllium Company turned down the proposal.

When the present war began in September of 1939, the Siemens & Halske Company demanded that the Beryllium Company refrain from selling to Great Britain, claiming they had the power to require this even under the amendment to the contract related above. The Beryllium Corporation disputed this interpretation and continued to supply Great Britain.

Beryllium is now part of our arsenal for war. Its future for peace is assured. Some day it may be used in its pure form to displace aluminum and magnesium especially in aviation. It is, after all, the lightest of all metals in a "Light Metals Age."

18. KRUPP

The Hammer of Thor

FOR more than a century the name of Krupp has been the symbol of martial industry and of German economic militarism. The history of this firm is a history of warfare. Since the era of Napoleon, Krupp's products have been present in every European struggle, more often than not used by both sides, but for the most part providing the artillery hammer of Prussian-German armies.

The firm of Krupp was founded in 1811 by Friedrich Krupp for the production of heavy iron and steel castings. In 1826, when Friedrich Krupp died, the management of the firm passed to Alfred Krupp, and it is because of his endeavors that the name of Krupp became inextricably linked with the production of armament and ordnance. It was Alfred Krupp who perfected the crucible steel used in producing the cannon which made Prussian artillery the master of the armies of Europe.

In 1867, Wilhelm the First became one of the largest shareholders in Krupp, and this relationship was boldly acknowledged. By the time Alfred Krupp died in 1887 he was known as the "Cannon King," and the products of Essen were rated as the best of their kind in the world.

Alfred Krupp's successor, Friedrich Alfred Krupp, combined in his person as in his name the abilities of his predecessors. Under his suzerainty the Krupp works further expanded to include iron mines, coal mines, blast furnaces, and similar sources of material required for the manufacture of arms. The Krupp laboratories, conducting research in metallurgy, especially the properties of steel and steel alloys, were comparable, although on a lesser scale, to those of I.G. When Friedrich Alfred Krupp died in 1902, the name of the firm was synonymous with German might.

In the following year, 1903, the Krupp works were formally incorporated with an authorized capital stock of some 160,000,000 gold marks. The corporate assets of Krupp included railroads, shipyards, coal and iron mines, massive foundries, blast furnaces, and all the appurtenances of the "heaviest" of industries. The plant at Essen measured nearly 300 acres, and Krupp's employees numbered 100,000.

During the decade from 1903 to 1913 Krupp arms, produced in ever-growing quantities, were sold to some extent outside of Germany, but it was to the minions of German imperialism that the bulk of Krupp's output was devoted. Of the estimated 53,000 cannon made by

Krupp up to 1912, some 26,000 were sold to Germany, and 27,000 to 52 different foreign countries. Krupp was "the matador of the international armament industry, preeminent in every department." Nor were the Krupp interests confined exclusively to heavy ordnance. They were represented in the international gunpowder cartel of 1897. Through the development of metallurgical processes and the procurement of patents, Krupp's associations with steel and arms makers outside Germany were firmly cemented. Although Krupp had not been, originally, a member of the German steel syndicate because of a disagreement over the proportionate output quota which it was to receive, it immediately joined when the 1904 cartel was formed, and obtained a much larger quota than that originally allotted. Thereafter, the behavior of the cartel was largely dominated by Krupp.

Since the possession of coal and iron is the prerequisite of industrial greatness, Germany was assured, once her economy passed from the handicraft to the machine age, of prominence in the concert of powers. Combination in the coal and iron industry began very early, and a succession of steel, coke, and coal cartels were formed during the second half of the nineteenth century. With the discovery of the Thomas process for the production of "basic steel" * the cartellization of the

---

* Sometimes called basic Bessemer.

steel industry went forward with increased vigor and intensity.

In the cartel in which Krupp held a controlling position, a central company, the Stahlwerksverband, became the legal personification through which the members effected their agreements. The objects of this cartel were the maintenance of the domestic market, the standardization of steel operations, and especially the elimination of any competition among its members in markets outside Germany. The thirty-one original members among them governed every branch of the steel industry. They were primarily concerned with the international market.

Through the medium of the International Steel Beam Pool, in which the steel makers of Belgium and France were included, and of which the United States Steel Corporation and the Pennsylvania, Maryland, and Cambria Steel companies were members, the world market was divided. The American producers received the United States, Central and South America, and the European producers, the rest of the world.

It is worth note that the American companies requested that the cartel keep secret the terms of the various agreements. The directors of the steel syndicate consequently refused to "discuss or divulge" agreements with American companies.

Already the manner has been pointed out in which German steel interests exercised patent control over

processes and products which this country later needed
when it entered the first World War. Krupp in particular held numerous patents on important steel and
ordnance techniques. The trailers for field guns which
the American Army used were covered by Krupp patents. Also, among the most valuable patents seized by
the Alien Property Custodian were those covering the
Krupp methods for making stainless steel.

Throughout the war, Krupp's factories and foundries
poured forth the torrent of cannons and other arms
which pounded the Allied lines for four long years.
It was not through any fault of Krupp that Germany
lost the war, and among the Allied Nations Kruppism
became the object of as much anathema as that which
attached to the imperial monarchy itself.

When the war ended, many of Krupp's machines
were dismantled, and Krupp was specifically forbidden
to engage in the further manufacture of arms. This
prohibition did not long stay its operations. The foundries and factories were turned over to the production
of locomotives, trucks, Diesel engines, cash registers,
and other ostensibly neutral articles of ordinary commerce.

Even before the war, Krupp had manufactured some
armaments outside of Germany proper. Thus, for example, the famous "Big Bertha," which was manufactured in 1911-12, was built in Hungary. After the
Treaty of Versailles, Krupp transferred many of its

operations to surrounding countries, and reestablished its connections with the major steel and metallurgical interests of the world, including the United States, England, and France. Although within Germany Krupp was supposed to be producing only peaceful articles of trade, the ink on the Treaty of Versailles was hardly dry before it had begun a refurbishing and reorganization of its armament industry. It is certain that Krupp was a factor during the 1920's in the international armament industry, as was shown by the abundance of testimony and evidence introduced in the Nye Committee hearings on the munitions industry in 1934.

The United States Army was acutely aware and made a conscientious study of Krupp's activities. The United States War Department on May 20, 1921, authorized the publication of the following:

> The Secretary of War has caused an investigation to be made of the patents and applications for patents recently announced as having been obtained by German citizens and assigned to Frederick Krupp. The investigation disclosed a rather striking circumstance in view of the conditions which Germany is supposed to observe as to disarmament and manufacture of war materials under her treaty obligations.

> Of the 228 patents and applications for patents assigned to Krupps, 26 were found to relate to artillery fire control devices, 18 to electric control apparatus, 9 to fuses and projectiles, 6 to gas engines and appurtenances, 17 to guns and their appurte-

nances, 3 to processes for the production of metals, 10 to naval fire control devices, 3 to projectiles and machines for handling same, 14 to railroad artillery, and the balance to varied uses, most of which might well relate to military use.

Incident to making this investigation, it was noted that a large number of patents and applications for patents had been assigned to numerous other German companies, and a casual examination indicates that a considerable number relate to aeroplanes and their accessories, chemicals, dyes, radio apparatus, and naval equipment.

One specific bit of evidence concerning the post-war activities of Krupp is given by Nicholas Snowden in his "Memoirs of a Spy." In 1921, he relates, while on a mission to Hungary, he visited Raab. He says:

> I learned there that the Krupps, although ostensibly devoting the plant to the making of agricultural implements, were actually and secretly manufacturing guns also. I learned through some of the workmen that whenever the Disarmament Control Commission of the Allies was to come for an inspection of the factory, the management was notified 48 hours in advance by the Hungarian military authorities. This gave time to stop the work in the departments where artillery and rifles were in the making, and to cover the machines and arrange things so that the Commission would find the place deserted.[1]

Krupp's relationships in the post-war era to other sectors of German industry provides an interesting commentary on the purposes and organization of the German cartel system during the years of the Weimar Republic. It is certain that Krupp is closely tied in with the Siemens-Halske interests and the other heavy industry groups in Germany. Even more startling is the relationship substantiated by a communication from H. E. Osann, a former officer with the American Army of Occupation in the Rhineland. In a letter dated January 19, 1929, from Osann to David Buckley, Jr., attorney for the Driggs Ordnance Company concerning certain projected negotiations with European ordnance companies, it is stated:

> I have made a little private investigation of my own regarding this interesting enterprise; I will not bother you with details, but can resume the result by stating that Bofors is Krupp and *Krupp is I. G. Dyeworks*. The frequency with which I refer to I. G. Dyeworks in my various reports to you is not due to the interest which I am taking in this concern with regard to a certain matter, but six weeks in Germany have convinced me that *I. G. Dyeworks is the real octopus embracing almost everything in the economic and a large part of the political, life of post-war Germany*. Whenever you mention the name of I. G. Dyeworks to anybody in Germany, he registers awe, fear, admiration, and the desire to be somehow involved in a transaction which might bring him closer to that giant organization.[2] [Italics added]

In support of this observation it may be pointed out that on purely technical grounds, Krupp and I.G. were bound to impinge on each other's orbit, not only through the activities of Krupp in the metallurgical field, but also through the increasing use of light metals in the production of plowshares and armaments. Krupp's interests in alloys and metallurgy and I.G.'s control of the light metal industry of Germany create a logical intercept joining their respective spheres of action. When Hitler came to power, the Krupp company developed the scheme whereby German industry contributed to the organization funds of the Nazi party.

It is significant that duPont's foreign representative was later informed of Krupp's action by representatives of I.G., as is indicated in a letter dated July 17, 1933, from Homer Ewing to W. R. Swint of duPont's Foreign Relations Department, which set forth results of his conferences during a trip to Germany, in which it is stated:

> . . . we called at the main offices of I. G. Farbenindustrie and spent some time with Dr. von Schnitzler and Dr. ter Meer, and were later joined at luncheon by Mr. Weber-Andreae. . . . The German gentlemen discussed the political situation in Germany, with particular reference to the positive position of the Government against the Jews. They also explained how Herr Krupp has developed a scheme whereby industry could contribute to the party organization funds.[3]

As the foremost German producer of steel and steel products, and as a member of several international car-

tels, Krupp tended constantly during the post-war era
as it had in the pre-war period to expand and reach
out into different branches of metallurgy. During that
signal year for the reconstitution of the German economy, 1926, a new international steel cartel came into
being. On April 1, 1926, Germany, France, Belgium,
and Luxembourg formed a cartel which was subse-
quently joined by the steel industries of Poland, Austria, Hungary, and Czechoslovakia. This reincarnation
was enthusiastically greeted by the public press in Germany and in France. As with similar agreements, the
main difficulties arose within a few years from the insistence by the German members, including Krupp, that
they be allowed to produce in excess of quota. Eventually German steel production, which rose from year to
year, far outstripped the other nations of Europe, including England, whose steel makers continued to observe the limits set in the various agreements.

When the blitz began in 1939 the Hammer of Thor
struck hard.

19. TUNGSTEN CARBIDE—
THE MARTIAL DIAMOND

THE steel forged by Krupp must be carved into tanks and cannons. To hew the fearful contours of howitzers and panzers from hardened steel is not an easy task. Only the toughest and sharpest edge can be pitted against its strength and resistance, to drill, thread, shape, and cut its adamantine mass.

Just as Siemens-Halske developed beryllium to harden copper, Krupp evolved the use of tungsten to harden steel.* To machine a steel so obdurate, tools with even greater cutting power were needed. Tungsten carbide was Krupp's solution to this dilemma.

In modern war, machine tools are the engineer battalion of industry. The machines which slash at the enemy must first be fashioned in factories behind the front. The place of machine tools in our mechanized civilization has been neatly depicted by Dr. Ernst Ammann, a director of Krupp:

* This is not to say that Krupp was first or alone in the making of tungsten steel. Krupp's laboratories, however, made long strides in tungsten's applications.

Tools and machine tools form the basis for any professional production of goods in a country generally. They serve the production of all other machines, expedients and devices for traffic, agriculture, power production and trade. Without highly developed tools and machine tool industry in no country is there a production of goods economical to the maximum.[1]

When a shortage of machine tools appears, the production lines slow down. In this country, the scarcity of machine tools is rated as the third most critical deficiency, preceded only by airplane engines and armor plate.

The essential part of these industrial scalpels is their cutting edge, which in America is largely made of stellite, a high speed tungsten steel.

Tungsten is mined chiefly in China, which possesses the most abundant sources, and provides the largest portion of the world's supply. The United States, India, South America, and Europe, in approximately that order, furnish the balance. While not produced in large amounts because of the scarcity of its occurrence and the difficulties surrounding its extraction, it is "one of the most essential metals of modern industry." Hugh Farrell says, "Tungsten would supplant copper tomorrow if there were enough of it, but there isn't. It might also supplant steel, but for the same handicap. *Tungsten is king of metals.*"[2]

The large reserves of tungsten were far away from Germany over the horizon of the oceans. The "sand-box" of Europe contained a pittance. A stock pile no matter how enormous was finite. If Germany could re-duce the use of tungsten in cutting tools, more would be available for ordnance. Tungsten carbide was the answer.*

By using it Germany could most efficiently husband the limited tungsten which it could draw from its re-serves once war began. The Germans were denied ac-cess to the rich sources of this metal in China, but the United States and Britain were also denied access once Japan became a warrior partner of Germany.

It is interesting to compare the estimates of an Amer-ican and a German expert on the utility of tungsten carbide. The contrast between the geopolitical acumen of the two statements, however, explains the difference between the quantities of the compound employed in the two countries.

The American writer, an official of the General Elec-tric Company, in a "sales letter" to the War Depart-ment, states:

Cemented carbide is, of course, a new material— at least from the standpoint of war. It was not avail-able at all during the World War and, in fact, it had its beginning in a search for a substitute for diamonds for wire-drawing dies. Even though the industry is

* Sometimes called cemented carbide.

only about 10 years old, Germany has taken advantage of the fact that a pound of tungsten will go much further in industrial production in the form of cemented carbide than in the form of high-speed steel; the same is true with reference to stellite, an alloy of chromium, cobalt, and tungsten. The extent of this superiority cannot be stated with accuracy, but in some cases it is at least 100 to 1.

For the last several years Germany has used probably three times as much of this material as all the rest of the world together.[3]

Dr. Ammann, of Krupp, in a general report on tungsten carbide, analyzed the position of the United States as follows:

. . . from the point of view of the interests of political economics . . . the United States too is lacking tungsten resources and has to import 75% of its requirements from foreign countries. . . . If cemented carbides were introduced generally the American domestic production of tungsten would be sufficient to cover the entire tungsten requirements of the American machining industry.[4]

Again the same old story—China's tungsten could be transported only on Britain's highway. Germany did not even try to cross this reef of the war. By combining the means at hand in their most efficient proportions, it was possible to stay within the British quarantine, and out of a bad situation make something better.

Tungsten carbide is second in hardness only to the

diamond. It is harder than sapphire. It is the best material discovered yet for machine cutting tools and wire-drawing dies. Qualified experts have stated that tungsten carbide is the key to a 20% increase in the total industrial production of the United States. In the January 1942 issue of *Fortune* magazine is made the following estimate:

> *How was impoverished Germany able to build her awesome war machine in . . . six short years . . . ?*
> The answers have been many. . . . All the popular explanations have overlooked the possibility that a few hundred tons of phenomenal steel-cutting material called tungsten carbide may have been a decisive factor in the building of the arsenal of Hitlerism. . . . Monstrous Big Bertha of World War I was tooled with tungsten carbide, and the new substance gave German industry a decided advantage over the Allies (who had developed nothing comparable) in armament production.
> . . . In many machining operations substitution of tungsten carbide for highspeed steel multiplies the rate of production at least 500 per cent. . . . *Britain, France, and the U. S. were sluggish about retooling, and it is estimated that in 1938 Germany had twenty times as much tungsten carbide in use as in the U. S.* This—according to many experts—is one of the great secrets of German rearmament. These experts also think that without tungsten carbide it would have taken the Reich twice as long to achieve half the results. Furthermore, fragments of shells picked up on

various battlefields indicate that Germany is using tungsten carbide for projectile tips and even may have developed a superior lightweight armor plate consisting of thin layers of carbide and steel.

In 1928 Krupp was selling small amounts of tungsten carbide in the United States at a price of fifty dollars per pound. The General Electric Company, at about the same time, had also made some discoveries concerning the amazing properties of this compound.

What followed is a syllogism in political economy. Krupp is a German cartel. General Electric is the chief proponent of "stabilization" of industry in the United States. From these corporate premises, only a cartel agreement could be deduced. They were drawn to each other by the polarity of conflicting patents.

The first agreement between Krupp and General Electric was dated November 5, 1928. This meeting of minds provided that G.E. prescribe and set prices and conditions of sale of all tungsten carbide sold in the United States. Krupp received in return "certain specified money," determined by the quantity which G.E. sold. Krupp was to refrain from production of tungsten carbide in this country. Technical knowledge and patents were pooled.

Because G.E. feared the possibilities of Krupp's competition in the United States, as Krupp had the right to sell here, and openly desired to engross the world market, the 1928 contract was unsatisfactory. Krupp, on

its part, did not like G.E.'s potential exports. Therefore, with mutual consent, the old agreement was modified in 1936.

Krupp promised neither to sell nor to ship tungsten
carbide in bulk or tools to the United States; G.E.
agreed not to export such products. G.E. was given
the United States market, and Krupp the world.

In addition, Krupp reserved significant control over
the future of tungsten carbide development in the
United States. G.E. could grant no one permission to
manufacture or sell tungsten carbide, other than those
licenses already granted, *without the approval of
Krupp*. Although Krupp agreed to stay out of the
United States market, it retained its grip on the right
of American producers to enter this important industry.
Krupp thus had power which the Supreme Court decided could not be exercised by the government of a
state of our Union:

> . . . it is beyond the power of a state, "under the
> guise of protecting the public, arbitrarily (to) inter-
> fere with private business or prohibit lawful occu-
> pations or impose unreasonable and unnecessary re-
> strictions upon them." [5]

Those few concerns operating under licenses from the
G.E.-Krupp entente were required to sell at prices in
accordance with General Electric's.

The extreme differential in the use of tungsten car-

bide in this country and in Germany springs directly
from these arrangements. Price fixing has as its aim the
receipt of optimum revenue for a minimum of output.
G.E. sold tungsten carbide for sums as high as four
hundred and fifty-three dollars a pound—nine times as
much as its selling price in Germany, even more than
the price of gold.

At no time during the General Electric-Krupp arrangement did the price in the United States drop below
two hundred and five dollars a pound. A comparison
of American and German prices on tungsten carbide reveals much in a few figures:

G. E. Price per Pound	*Krupp Price per Pound*
$407.70	$90.60
362.40	67.95
298.98	49.83
280.86	45.30
253.68	45.30
249.15	45.30
240.09	43.035
231.03	41.676
226.50	40.317
217.44	39.411
208.38	38.958
203.85	37.599
199.32	37.146

Meanwhile, Krupp sold ever larger amounts of tungsten carbide to German industry.

The same two officials quoted above emphasize the discrepancy in the use of tungsten carbide in their respective countries. The G.E. official states:

> Concerning the amount of business being done by the Germans and ourselves, a few figures and calculations may be of interest. By combining the information obtained from Drs. Oehake and Ammann it appears that together they are making about 8,000 pounds of hardmetal composition monthly; this is approximately the amount being sold in one year in the United States. We also got the amount of business in marks, which totals for both groups about 900,000 marks per month.[6]

Dr. Ammann cites in unmistakable terms the reason for Germany's extensive use of the compound:

> Under the pressure for *higher efficiency* and *shorter deliveries* [the opposite of too little and too late!] the use of cemented carbides in Germany has achieved a tremendous uplift, in comparison with which the American development is the less understandable, as America is generally known for its trend of grasping for the latest and most progressive manufacturing methods and developing them further. [Italics added][7]

The uncontaminated "instinct of workmanship" of a G.E. engineer rebelled at this "conscientious withdrawal of efficiency" which was reflected in the non-use of tungsten carbide by American industry. In a report addressed to the Employee's Suggestion Committee of G.E., this engineer pointed out the "absurdly fictitious prices" which G.E. was charging. Stating that the aura of intricacy in which G.E. shrouded tungsten carbide's manufacture was feigned, the technician says:

> *A great deal of mystery has surrounded the production of this material since its inception.* As a matter of fact, it is just about as complicated as making a good grade of concrete for a sidewalk: Grind up material, pass it through a mesh, put a certain percentage of binder with it, press it into a cake and bake it.
>
> We are equipped in Schenectady at the present time to manufacture 200 lbs. per week in various tip sizes ready to be ground for tools. This is based on an 8 hr. shift of one man and one boy. [Italics added]

To remedy this situation, the engineer suggested that the price be reduced to

> . . . $50.00 a pound which is a fair market price for these goods and is approximately the price that I found the Krupp Company were selling tip material for last year.[8]

G.E. turned down this proposal, for:

> . . . due to the contractual relations now existing between the General Company and the Carboloy Company on the one hand and the Krupp Company, the Firth-Sterling Company, and the Ludlum Steel Company, it would be impractical at the present time. . . .[9]

G.E.'s licensees in the United States champed at the bit which curbed their eagerness to produce and sell tungsten carbide on a much larger scale. They also understood the cause and effects of the cartel. As stated tersely by Gerald Firth, the principal sublicensee of G.E., and second largest producer in the United States, in a letter written in 1931:

> Please bear in mind that as I have said before, the price in this country is from ten to fifteen times the German price and that is a difficult thing to justify now that industry in general is recognizing the value of our product.[10]

A decade later Mr. Firth could render an even more damning verdict:

> The control of the tungsten carbide patents by the General Electric Company and the Krupp Company has resulted in keeping the prices at exorbitant levels. Now when the emergency has come, industry has not learned how to use tungsten carbide and has not the machines, the skilled men, or the technique which it would have had if the material had been available at the same low prices at which it was available to German industries.[11]

20. THE WIZARDS OF JENA

NOTHING has been more characteristic of German militarism than its exactness and love of detail. No branch of the German Kriegswirtschaft * is more pains-taking or precise than the Carl Zeiss factories of Jena, which make the precision optical goods that control the aiming and firing of bomb and shell.

Because of the function in Germany's preparations for war, the Zeiss-works have been for decades the special ward of the General Staff. Army officers are assigned to Zeiss at all times, to participate in research.

The wizards of Jena epitomize the perverted virtues of the Teuton mind. Their goal is scientific perfection— they approach the ultimate symmetry of art and science. Zeiss cameras have no peer, and their sale provides the profit which supports research in optics. But this research achieves its pinnacle in instruments of war. Figuratively, Zeiss makes the monocles which Krupp cannons and Stukas wear.

Among the 50,000 or so essential items required by the Army, Navy, and Air Force of a modern nation at

* War economy.

war, none are more necessary, with the exception of munitions, than the "eyes" and "automatic brains" which locate a target, calculate its position, and control the firing of the big guns or the "bracketing" of an objective by bombs. These duties are performed in the main, by precision instruments whose utility results from the use of high grade optical glass.

The position of strategic importance occupied by the optical glass industry derives from the absolute dependence of military, naval, and aeronautical operations on the optical precision instruments which they must employ. Precision instruments are as necessary in preliminary reconnaissance as they are in the successful execution of combat operations, but it is in the latter that their use is critical. Whether in an encounter between great battle fleets at sea, or in an artillery engagement on land, or a "dog-fight" in the air, accuracy and timing of fire are decisive in the outcome. Superiority, or at least equality, with respect to the precision instruments available to its fighting services is therefore vital to a nation at war.

In ordinary usage, the words "optical glass" are associated with spectacles. Actually, there is a great difference between the ophthalmic glass used for correcting poor vision and the optical glass used in precision instruments which serve as the eye-pieces of science, industry, and war. The names of the principal types of precision instruments indicate their respective functions.

The general class includes microscopes, telescopes, spectroscopes, and photographic lenses for scientic, industrial and military use. The specific group of military optical goods includes all manner of periscopes for submarines, torpedo directors, range-finders and height-finders (altimeters), bomb sights, bore sights for battleship guns, and all the other complicated mechanism employed in controlling the speed and accuracy of fire.

During the nineteenth century, the production of optical glass was carried on almost exclusively in Europe, especially in Germany, with France and Great Britain contributing minor amounts. Within Germany, the pioneer work in optics and the manufacture of optical glass and precision instruments was primarily carried forward by the researches of Carl Zeiss and Professor Ernst Abbe. Carl Zeiss (1816-1888) in 1846 established in Jena a workshop manufacturing scientific instruments, and acquired a reputation for the quality of his microscopes.

In 1866 Zeiss was joined by Dr. Abbe, a mathematician and physicist, whose talent for original research was amply displayed in the contributions he made to the theory and practice of optics. A third figure, Dr. Otto Schott, whose ability supplemented that of Zeiss and Abbe, is noted as one of the first makers of the kinds of optical glass which were called for by the "dream optics" with which Abbe was concerned.

Schott joined Zeiss and Abbe in Jena in 1882, and

although the Schott Glass Works were at first nominally separate from Zeiss, they became a working unit, and are directly merged in the Zeiss Foundation. This was formed in 1891, and is a type of "trustee foundation," a quasi-state-controlled and state-administered enterprise, supported by the original endowment and, at least partly by the government, but operating theoretically as a "guild." The board of directors are the controllers of its general policies.

Zeiss became not only the largest, but by all odds the leader of the world in the field of military optical equipment. From its laboratories and shops poured forth a stream of instruments and inventions which assured Zeiss world monopoly.

The Zeiss trademark became the "stamp of perfection" for all types of optical instruments, ranging from simple microscopes to the most complex aerial camera or range-finder.

The Zeiss Stiftung (Foundation) stipulated that the manufacturing plant might not be moved from Jena, but subsidiary factories have been built, both in other cities in Germany, and other countries in Europe. Branches exist in Vienna, Raab (Hungary), Riga (Latvia) and in Dresden (where Zeiss controls the Ica Co., the largest European makers of photographic apparatus), Göttingen, and Saalfeld, in Germany. Zeiss controls or licenses several lesser optical firms in Germany and France, and even before the World War

Zeiss distributing outlets covered "the entire globe." Before 1939 Zeiss plants were built in the "safe area," where Germany seeks to hide many of its war-plants from the eyes of enemy bombers.

Zeiss dominates the "interest-group" of German optical industries, in which the C. P. Goerz A.G., Ica, Contessa-Nettel A.G., and Ernemann A.G. are fused directly under the controlling interest which Zeiss has in each. An I.G. subsidiary, Rietschel G.m.b.H., does not enter directly into the Zeiss-Icon group, but serves I.G.'s own interests in this field.

During the World War, Zeiss alone employed more than 10,000 people. The period following the war did not affect Zeiss's business although at the war's end 90% of its products went to the Imperial German Government. Zeiss built new plants in surrounding countries, and soon was operating internationally much as it had before 1914. It is today the largest of all optical instrument manufacturers.[1]

German monopoly in the industry was reflected in the advantages enjoyed by German arms. The amazing accuracy of Admiral Hipper's battle cruisers in the engagement with Beatty during the Battle of Jutland, when half of Beatty's fleet was destroyed in a few minutes, is attributed to the superiority of the fire-control and range-finding equipment of the German ships. When Beatty said, "Chatfield, there seems to be something wrong with our —— ships today," he was unwittingly complimenting the skill of Zeiss in making optical equipment which Jutland proved to be the best in the world at that time.

The cutting off of imports from Germany to the United States created a deficiency in optical glass, such as that which existed in dyestuffs. In the U. S. Ordnance Department report on the problem of optical glass in the World War, it is stated, "In industries of a highly technical nature, such as—the optical glass and instrument industry, the Germans had established such effective control that at the beginning of the war we were seriously embarrassed because we did not manufacture these commodities, and did not know how to make them."

Geometrical optics is the basis of the military optical goods industry. This involves the investigation of the structure and function of all optical precision instruments and their application in scientific, industrial and military pursuits.

The productive factors of the military optical industry are deceptively simple. Pure sand, and common oxides of metals, such as potassium, sodium, barium, boron, and others, are the chief components of optical glass.

The manufacture of optical glass is intrinsically a secretive, jealously guarded craft. "Know-how" is much more important than any formal patent prescriptions, and this has been the basis of Germany's monopoly in the industry. Although the formulae of the different types of glass are generally known, it is in the esoteric, yet actually ultra-scientific judgment, patience, and attention by which a batch of sand is slowly smelted, annealed, tempered, and ground into a perfect optical lens that the clew resides.

Time, men and machines are the factors on which the industry depends. The initial step in making optical glass is the moulding of the clay-pot in which the sand is fused. This pot is the heart of the process, and requires months to season before it can be used, and then only once.

Once the "melt" of optical glass has been brought safely through the fusing and cooling periods, it must be carefully broken, and finished, both by machinery and by hand, before it is possible to achieve the perfect lenses and prisms which will go into a range-finder or a bomb-sight. The whole arduous task of manufacture can be made worthless if inexpert or inaccurate polishing ruins a high-powered lens.

The fine machinery used is difficult to design and construct. If there has been no preparation, it is impossible to make these machines in a short time, for they are the product of years of research.

The human element, however, is hardest of all the components to locate. The art of optical workers results from years of training, and is handed down from father to son.

Neither legislation nor money can by themselves call into being an optical glass industry. This is the reason that a monopoly in the industry is dangerous. If war comes to a nation that does not already have an optical industry, the seizure of patents means nothing. Because of the time required to train skilled workers, make precision tools, and painfully experiment with batch after batch of glass, it is next to impossible to correct overnight the failure to prepare.

In 1848-49 two gifted immigrants journeyed to the United States, economic refugees from the Germany of 1848. Henry Lomb and John Jacob Bausch established a small retail spectacle industry in Rochester, N. Y., in 1853. Time was kind, and the business prospered. In 1876, Bausch & Lomb undertook to produce such optical instruments as microscopes, but on a relatively small scale. In 1883 photographic lenses were added to their products, but since 1921 few have been made. At the present time the company is capitalized at $9,100,000, has a net worth of nearly fourteen millions, and an annual sales volume of some $18,500,000.

In 1888 Edward Bausch, son of the founder, went to Germany and obtained licenses from Zeiss for the manufacture of optical measuring devices, military optical goods, and similar products. This arrangement continued for a number of years, until 1907.

In 1904, Professor Siegfried Czapski, the successor to Abbe, visited the United States, intending to open a branch manufacturing plant for Zeiss military apparatus in this country. He visited Rochester for some time, conferring with Bausch & Lomb and with George Saegmuller, of the Fauth Instrument Co., which manufactured equipment for the Navy. Czapski returned to Germany, and as a result of his negotiations, Bausch & Lomb merged with Saegmuller's company.

In 1907 a contract was entered into between Bausch & Lomb and Zeiss, by which the former became the exclusive agent of Zeiss in the United States. Zeiss bought one-fifth of the capital stock of Bausch & Lomb, and this alliance continued in force until the United States entered the World War.

Throughout the entire period, until 1914, no optical glass was made in the United States. From the beginning of its operations in the instrument business, Bausch & Lomb purchased the glass it used in its products from Germany, entirely from Zeiss, whose monopoly with regard to the glass, without which any precision instrument is useless, was virtually complete. Even in England, where Chance Brothers produced optical glass, Zeiss was a major factor in the market. In France, as Hauser remarks, "—the country of Foucault" was a "payer of tribute to Zeiss." *

Even before the war, more than one-half of all Zeiss production in Germany went to the German Army and Navy. Consequently, when war began, those countries

* J. B. L. Foucault was a famous French physicist (1819-1868).

dependent on Zeiss for optical instruments, like those dependent on I.G., encountered a severe shortage of military optical apparatus which continued through the entire period of hostilities.

Bausch & Lomb had, most opportunely, begun experimenting in the production of optical glass in 1912, but when we joined the Allies, these efforts were still unsatisfactory. The Ordnance report quoted above states, "The quality of glass obtained (i.e., by B. & L., Pittsburgh Plate Glass, the Bureau of Standards, et al.) was not, however, entirely satisfactory, and by the time we entered the war the shortage of optical glass of high quality was so serious that unless something was done speedily to relieve the situation, the Army and Navy would not be equipped with the necessary optical instruments."

The strenuous efforts of the Government, and those of Bausch & Lomb and the other manufacturers, to learn the "know-how" were able to overcome the shortage, and to produce some 600,000 pounds of fairly good glass. "This was accomplished, however, under high pressure and at large expense—." Bausch & Lomb were later commended for their part in these efforts.

In 1914 the Allies had sought to place orders with Bausch & Lomb, as Zeiss no longer could be a source of supply. Zeiss objected, and it appears that Bausch & Lomb bought back the stock in their company which was owned up to that time by Zeiss. This cessation of

relationships continued until after the war. When the
United States came in, the Zeiss patents were seized by
the Alien Property Custodian and later sold to the
Chemical Foundation. But the effect of the pre-war
monopoly could not be readily escaped. The Navy issued appeals to the public to contribute field-glasses and
other usable optical devices. The Alien Property Custodian later uncovered sizable stores of telescopes, binoculars, and other optical instruments, which had been
placed in warehouses by German interests.

After the Armistice, the concerns other than Bausch
& Lomb which had made glass for war purposes left the
field largely to the Rochester firm, although the Bureau
of Standards continued to produce some. In 1921, after
trips to Germany by executives of Bausch & Lomb, relations with Zeiss were resumed. In a contract, written
in German, dated April 28, 1921, intended to endure
for twenty-one years, Bausch & Lomb and Zeiss demonstrated that, to quote a pamphlet issued by the former,
they had agreed to let "bygones be bygones."

This contract is a curious document, but corresponds
to the now-familiar form of an international cartel
agreement sponsored by a German concern. Under the
Versailles Treaty, Zeiss had been forbidden to make
military optical goods, but apparently anticipated the
resumption of its "forte," directly and indirectly.

The 1921 Agreement divided the world market for
optical goods, the United States to be the exclusive ter-

ritory of B&L, reserving the rest of the world to Zeiss in the manufacture and sale of military instruments. B&L received exclusive rights under Zeiss patents and "know-how," and in consideration Zeiss received a royalty of 7% on all military apparatus sold by B&L, regardless of its inclusion in the Zeiss patents. If either party received bids from a source outside its exclusive territory, it was to inform the other, and to quote a price 20% above the regular selling price. Even such marked-up bids could be submitted only with the consent of the other party.

The contract provided for the establishment of a "Military Department" in the Bausch & Lomb organization, to be solely responsible to the Board of Directors, and to be headed by personnel approved by Zeiss. Both were to have access to each other's workshops, and to receive the benefit of future developments made or acquired by either. The contract specifically stipulates that Bausch & Lomb is to make available to Zeiss any "independent" inventions or patents procured from other sources.

One or two paragraphs in this contract merit quotation as having peculiar connotations. First, it is stated that "The contracting parties agree to keep the foregoing agreement in strict confidence as regards a third party, and to guard silence concerning this agreement also with their own employees as far as this may be practical under the circumstances." [2]

This 1921 contract was modified in 1926, when it came to the attention of Bausch & Lomb's attorneys. At their insistence that the market-dividing clause overtly violated the Sherman Act, a new contract was drawn up on November 26, 1926, which altered the wording of the objectionable sections, and added the proviso that Bausch & Lomb were to communicate bids from commercial houses in Zeiss territory to the N. V. Nederlandsche Instrumenten Compagnie, the wholly owned Zeiss subsidiary located at the Hague.

Governmental and shipyard inquiries from outside the United States were to be communicated directly to Zeiss in Jena. The essential monopolies of Bausch & Lomb as the exclusive licensee in the United States, and of Zeiss in the rest of the world were not touched, and it is only in the phraseology that there is any alteration in the paragraphs which the attorneys questioned.

Some notable consequences ensued from these cartel agreements. In the first place, it is clear that by the medium of accounting on royalty payments, Zeiss was constantly aware of all the particular types of sales made by the American company. Thus, it became a simple matter for Zeiss to ascertain exactly what kinds of equipment the government of the United States was buying from Bausch & Lomb. That this flow of military information to Zeiss was fraught with grave questions is indicated in a letter of July 9, 1929, from Bausch & Lomb, Rochester, N. Y., to Mr. August Lomb of

Bausch & Lomb Optical Company, Frankfurt, Germany, concerning a statement of military transactions for April, May, and June of that year, including anti-aircraft range-finders, periscopes, and telescopes. The letter states:

> Heretofore the Government has merely been insistent that none of the details as regards the designs of these instruments be made public, but it seems as if the quantities, prices, etc., and the amount of the equipment purchased are also considered secret. Obviously, our agreement with Messrs. Carl Zeiss cannot work satisfactorily unless, at least the latter information, becomes common knowledge to both parties, but some arrangements must be made whereby we are assured this information will be kept in strictest confidence.[3]

In a later letter from Bausch & Lomb to Carl Zeiss, dated December 21, 1932, it is stated:

> It occurs to us that we were not sufficiently specific regarding the condition that must be exercised for our protection in keeping the loan of this pamphlet a secret, and particularly as regards the inspector. If any question should arise with regard to the pamphlet which you are preparing, please do not admit to anyone that this has been prepared analogous to our copy.
>
> By reason of the importance which we attach to the secrecy of this question, the copy has been sent via our Frankfurt Office, and please make sure that after it has served its purpose it is again safely returned to our Mr. August Lomb.[4]

Waiving any conjecture as to the possible underlying motivation of such statements, it is clear that the intimacy of the participants in this cartel could not avoid the conflict of political and military interest with commercial relationships. Assuming their conscious separation Bausch & Lomb is placed in a most ambiguous or equivocal position. It is certain that in at least fifty-four instances, some as recent as February 1940, when South American and European governments attempted to place orders with Bausch & Lomb, who in turn sought permission from Zeiss, the latter refused, even though the "protective price" differential would in all likelihood have discouraged the potential buyer.

In 1935, after Hitler had brought German rearmament into the open, Bausch & Lomb refused contracts with Great Britain and France for $1,500,000 worth of military instruments. This extraordinary forcbearance from ordinary profitable and business-like behavior is explicable only by the contract with Zeiss.

Bausch & Lomb, however, announced their abstinence publicly, and from a decidedly different point of view. As it was reported at the time in *The Literary Digest*, this altruistic perspective is described as follows:

> Millions of dollars of foreign Government orders for military optical instruments have been rejected by the Bausch & Lomb Co., of Rochester, New York, because they might conceivably be used against the United States or its interests in another War.

Proudly last week, vigorous, eighty-two-year-old Dr. Edward Bausch, founder and Chairman, declared that to be his company's settled policy, developed "Through a close understanding with the Departments of the Army and Navy of our Government." Officers of both services are stationed in the company's plant supervising the manufacture of such material, he disclosed, but under no circumstances will foreign Governments be supplied.

Chiefly, Bausch & Lomb's rejected orders have been offered by England and France, have been for range-finders, periscopes, gun-sights, binoculars, artillery fire-control instruments. Business from these two Governments would have exceeded $1,500,000. Various smaller nations have also sought to make contracts and have been refused. *Self-sufficient Germany, however, has shown no needs.*

—Promptly with the reappearance of the European war-scares several years ago, however, the policy of no supplies to potential combatants abroad was adopted. *"They are not prepared for war over there,"* a company officer gravely explained last week, "and if we refuse to help them prepare, it puts it off just that much." [5] [Italics added]

For this self-denial Dr. Edward Bausch was awarded the Laurel Wreath by the publication *Social Justice,* the organ of Father Coughlin. The award was announced in the issue of January 11, 1937.

There is an almost sibylline prescience in the words, "They [meaning France and England] are not prepared for war—," for the spokesman must have known that "self-sufficient Germany," by reason of the Zeiss Works, was under no such handicap. But aside from the oracular vision which time has proved true so far as England and France were concerned, what about the United States?

As with other American entrants into cartel agreements with German firms, once the German Government integrated its whole economy with its policy of conquest, Bausch & Lomb found that actual disclosures of information were no longer forthcoming from Zeiss. After 1938 royalties were paid only on military goods covered by Zeiss patents. When war began in 1939, such payments due to Zeiss were held in escrow by Bausch & Lomb, and relations between them governed by the "political contingency" clause of their agreement.

Since 1921 numerous Zeiss patents in the United States have been taken out in the name of Bausch & Lomb, but it is almost unnecessary to point out that they are still Zeiss patents. Neither Zeiss nor Bausch & Lomb has at any time been willing to license any applicant under these patents.

In 1940 the magazine *Fortune* stated that the Army Facilities Bureau rated the shortage in optical instruments as the fourth most serious bottle-neck in our preparedness program, ranking only after airplane engines, armor plate, and machine tools. Bausch & Lomb's capacity to produce optical glass was then estimated at about 200,000 pounds annually. In 1918, it had produced some 480,000 pounds, but in the intervening years it depended again primarily on Zeiss, importing lenses and instruments which it did not itself make, and following the cartel pattern of restricting output. That we still lack optical equipment is shown by the continuous requests made by the Navy Department to the public for high-powered binoculars and optical instruments.

How a monopoly in the manufacture of optical instruments can be used to exert pressure has been stated by Thurman Arnold. After Bausch & Lomb had been indicted by the Department of Justice, it exhibited—

. . . the typical reaction of a private cartel. The Navy Department was building two new cruisers. Bausch & Lomb was the sole bidder for optical equipment because it controlled the supply. It informed the Navy Department that it would have to delay furnishing the range-finders for these cruisers for six months because of the antitrust indictment. Bausch & Lomb thus threatened to tie up the construction of battleships while it contested its right to retain monopoly power. The threat, however, was unsuccessful. On May 21, 1940, the Bausch & Lomb Optical Company submitted to the maximum fine of $40,000 imposed on the company and its indicted officers and withdrew its suggestion to the Navy Department that the cruisers' equipment would have to be delayed six months.[6]

21. NEMESIS?—HUNGER BLOCKADE

THE Kaiser's armies in the World War held the Allies at bay for four long years. Not an inch of German soil was a battleground, and despite a two-front war the army was never routed or reduced to impotence. When the Armistice was signed, the German army withdrew from its lines inside of France. Neither brilliant Allied planning nor the velocity of Allied attack had actually broken or bent the German shield. What then accounted for the collapse?

Not the British blockade of raw materials from which the German might was fashioned, but the blockade on the home front was the most effective weapon in the hands of the Allies. The raw material shortage did weaken the German offensive, but could not make the army retreat. Germany cracked internally, surrendering to the most primitive urge of man. Hunger was the nemesis of German arms.

Germany is the "bare backbone of Europe." Despite all advances in science, the basic problem of Germany is still the struggle for food.

Since our ancient forebears first tilled a patch of

ground with the crude implements of the late Stone Age, the contest between man and nature has never gone far beyond the laborious effort required to wrest from the earth our daily bread. Man's customs, his beliefs, and his institutions, shaken as these have been by scientific change, still center largely about the relationship between humanity and the never-ceasing effort necessary to obtain the sustenance upon which his existence depends. For these reasons the painfully acquired knowledge by which the food supply, now so casually taken for granted by city dwellers, has been increased marks perhaps the most significant of all historical advances.

Germany knows that all of the ancient empires fell at least partly because centuries of ill-tutored cultivation stripped from the soil on which they rested its powers of regeneration. Egypt, Greece, and Rome reached the end of their dominance when the food supply could no longer sustain the structure of their civilization.

Not until the nineteenth century was any real progress made in the understanding and care necessary to prolong the fertility of the earth. It may be that even yet we have not learned enough, or how to apply what we do know. In the United States our Dustbowl is a monument to human stupidity. These reflections bear even more acutely at the present time on the destiny of nations. In Europe, in Asia, and in our own country, the common man first feels the bite of modern war in the rationing of foods. For the underlying populace, food scarcity is the penalty which wars and depressions inflict most cruelly.

In Germany, however, the rationing of food has been a national necessity long before the present war. The choice between "guns and butter" was really made at the end of the first World War. Iron rations sustained the German people for twenty years, training them to do without, and made them ravenous for the wealth of the outside world. When it is realized that even at the present time the world is never more than twelve or fourteen months ahead of starvation, the constant fear of famine caused by depletion of the soil and the threat of blockade which haunts the German people can be understood.

In 1840, Baron Justus von Liebig demonstrated for the first time that land is progressively exhausted by the removal of nitrates, phosphates, and potash salts, all of which are consumed in the growth of plants. Liebig's discoveries also pointed the way toward regenerating the nutritive properties of land by the addition of artificial fertilizers. In most of its compounds, potassium is so tightly locked that its extraction is a difficult and costly process. Consequently, search was instituted for natural sources of potassium salts, and it was as a result of this quest that the German potash industry came into being.

Nature has made few gifts to Germany. When it was

realized that the Stassfurt region contained beds of potash salts over five thousand feet thick, there was reason to believe that Germany might fill its own bread-basket. The importance of the·potash deposits to German national interests was recognized from the outset. In 1858 the Prussian Government opened the first mine, and from that day forward the German potash industry was under the heavy hand·of the Prussian regime. Several independent producers came into the market, and their increased production made prices fall. The government mines were forced to compete against the private producers. Such competition was not to Prussia's liking.

The Potash Syndicate, formed in 1888 under government auspices, has been called the classic cartel. It restricted output of potash salts, fixed prices, and enforced its will on the market. The Prussian Minister of Commerce and Industry retained the right to approve or veto prices set by the Syndicate. In the reorganization in 1903, the Potash Syndicate became the Kalisyndikat, which since that time has governed the German potash industry.

During the period from 1860 to 1905 the United States had become the largest consumer of Stassfurt potash, and this industry was entirely undeveloped here, since there were no readily accessible domestic sources. Several American chemical and fertilizer companies, in addition to the American representative of the cartel, imported the bulk of our needs. Some of the American importers had invested capital in previously independent mines in Stassfurt, and had also been able to obtain favorable contracts with some of the smaller producers.

It was the fixed policy of the cartel to charge a higher price for exported potash than for that sold within Germany. Since its monopoly was absolute in a geological sense, the cartel was able to enforce this practice. By 1909, when all of the potash producers were forced into the syndicate, a law was passed which imposed a super-tax on potash sold outside of Germany. American importers protested unavailingly against the incidence of a law which they held would be "clearly discriminatory against America."

The matter was brought to the attention of our State Department, which in June 1910 interceded with the German Government. Previously, President Taft had consulted the Cabinet on the matter, which had reached an "acute stage." The demand of the State Department for a reply was met, but the contents of the reply were not made public. Our Government took the position that the affair was a "private matter" to be settled by the parties immediately involved. In the following year a settlement, the terms of which are not entirely known, was made. All suits against the syndicate brought in the United States were dropped, and the syndicate took over those contracts which had been made with independent potash producers. In the opinion of one writer, the potash law was ". . . a tactical maneuver directed against American purchasers, and successful against them because of the unwillingness of the American Government to exercise vigorous influence in their behalf."

During the years following the one-sided settlement of the dispute between the American consumers and the German syndicate, practically no attempt was made to increase the domestic production of potash in the United States. With the beginning of the World War and the blockade of Germany, the United States was cut off from potash imports. In 1915 the total domestic production of pure potash was little more than 1,000 tons. As in the case of nitrogen, the shortage of potash threatened to cripple our farm production before we entered the war, and as the demand increased for food to supply to the Allies, and farmers were called upon to grow ever larger quantities of staples, it became evident that "potash hunger" rendered crops not only inferior in quality but made them far more susceptible to attack by plant diseases. Throughout the four years of the war, agriculture in the United States suffered from a famine of potash and, despite the enormous efforts made to overcome the potash shortage, by the end of 1918 our producing capacity was little more than 50,000 tons.

Again, as in the case of other chemicals and raw materials, German monopoly had been so exercised that her potential enemies were compelled, in addition to meeting the military challenge, to repair the loss of industrial initiative. In a report on potash made by the Department of Agriculture immediately after the World War, it was stated:

> It was the threat of the late German Empire that, because of the potash monopoly which it held, the world could be subjected at its will to potash starvation and be forced to yield to its dictation. This challenge was met in America by the prompt development of practically all the sources of potash already surveyed by governmental agencies and the establishment of potash manufactories which made America for the time being independent of all foreign potash.

When the war ended, this country was in a position to count upon an annual production of 100,000 tons of potash and, consequently, if the industry had continued to expand at a competitive rate, all of our domestic needs thereafter could have been met by our own production. As was the case in some of the other branches of industry, potash production declined with the cessation of war needs, so that a few years later one writer on fertilizer commented on "the swift fading of the war-born potash industry."

France recovered some of the potash-producing territory of Alsace, but Germany retained the major part of the deposits in the Stassfurt region, and did not find her position in the world potash industry affected by the Versailles Treaty. Following the general pattern of industry recovery in Germany, both her nitrogen and potash production were carried forward with no real handicap as a result of the war. In fact, by 1925 not only had the German potash cartel reestablished its own internal control, but it had succeeded in entering into an agreement with the French producers whereby the latter received a quota of 30% of the total annual output, with the Kalisyndikat receiving the remaining 70%.

Potash, nitrates, and starch-bearing plants were not enough to maintain Germany's food supply in the World War. The lack of proteins, of fats and oils, needed to provide energy and endurance proved to be the real Achilles' heel. The soldier at the front was fed much better than the civilian in the rear, but both were gradually weakened by the lack of the proteins which give the human body its heat and muscular power. In one of the official German histories of the World War, it is stated:

In the long run the food was not adequate to keep the soldier at the front capable of resistance amidst the terrible mental agitation, the feverish, nervous tension and the great physical exertions. Nor is there any doubt that if the food situation had been better the work of those boring worms who gnawed away from within would have been made considerably harder, perhaps impossible.

No one in Germany could forget in the post-war years that the lack of food had weakened German arms. The High Command took over the study of the food problem and for twenty years endeavored to find a way to prevent a repetition of the "turnip winter" of 1917-18. The nutrition problem became a central focus in German plans for the Global War.

The man to whom the study of Germany's war food economy was assigned was Ernst Pieszczek, the Privy Councillor or Permanent Under-Secretary of the Ministry of War. It was his task to analyze the causes which had brought Germany to her knees in 1918 and, if possible, to find a way to overcome such shortages in the future. In his attack on this problem Pieszczek had the cooperation of the Department of Agriculture, the German High Command, I. G. Farben, and all other agencies concerned. In an article in the official journal of the German War Ministry, *Wissen und Wehr* (Science and Defense), in 1932, Pieszczek summed up his findings of the causes of the food shortage in the first World War.[1]

Bread was available throughout the war in Germany, and presented no problem. While potatoes were plentiful, transportation made their distribution difficult. Meat had to be rationed, and the supply throughout the war was inadequate. The people seldom received the minimum rations which had been promised.

The most important factor in the breakdown of the German food supply was protein, contained in meat, milk, cheese, and eggs. Pieszczek states:

> The fat supply was always most critical. Soon after the outbreak of the war, considerable difficulties arose because, as already mentioned, more than two-fifths of the total consumption was imported. . . .
>
> *   *   *
>
> *The lack of foreign cattle feed was the principal problem of the whole war food program.* By far too much cattle was bred considering the amount of feed produced in Germany. This brought about a vicious circle. If the breeding of cattle was reduced because of the lack of feed, the meat, fat and milk supply suffered. If, on the other hand, the number of cattle was maintained, then the breeder was apt to feed the cattle bread grains in order not to let his cattle starve, instead of leaving the grain for direct human consumption.
>
> *   *   *
>
> . . . *The German economy was unable to improve this negative balance and that meant that as far as the food economy was concerned, the war was already lost at the beginning of the third war year. What followed after that was merely a futile pulling to stretch the German food blanket which had become too short.* [Italics added]

In this same article Pieszczek strikes the warning note that Germany could now aspire to protein self-sufficiency:

Today, the German economy is able to point new ways which might make it possible to avoid at least partly, if not entirely, the scarcity of animal feed. [Italics added]

During the first World War a process had been partially developed by which albuminous feed for cattle could be made from carbohydrates with the use of so-called mineral yeast. There were, however, insufficient quantities of carbohydrates to permit the application of this process on a large scale. In 1926, Dr. Scholler, of the Torncsch Wood Sugar Development and Research Corporation, worked out a process by which wood cellulose could be turned into wood sugar without loss. This was the crux of the matter, for previous efforts to make sugar from wood had been unsuccessful because of the tendency of such wood sugar to decompose before it could be taken out of the manufacturing process.

Because the problem of protein had such importance in her plans, all of Germany's skill in science was concentrated on its solution. Germany became interested in the development of soyabeans. As much as two and one-half million tons of soyabeans were imported annually from Manchuria by a special company set up for that purpose. The planting and cultivation of soyabeans in Roumania and other Balkan states was promoted by German interests, because these latter countries could not be cut off by a British blockade. Soyabeans would not grow in Germany's own harsh climate. An insufficient number of hours of sunshine prevented the crops from maturing. I. G. Farben experimented with soyas, and when it was found that this was not practical, turned to another source.

The lupine beans, which grow abundantly in Germany, contained the essential ingredients of protein cattle feed. There was, however, a major drawback. Lupine beans are bitter, and cattle will not eat them. The German Government's scientists applied themselves to the task of removing the bitter taste, and actually succeeded in making the lupines more palatable. After twelve years of very costly study, a carefully nurtured crop was fed to cattle with excellent results. The milk, the butter, and the meat were richer. Germany's problem apparently was solved.

The next year an enormous acreage of lupine beans was planted. The sweetened lupine bean became a form of nectar on which German cows would fatten. When the new crop was ripe and harvested, much to the consternation of the German Ministry of War, the cows and pigs and other livestock turned up their noses and refused to eat the beans.

What had happened is reminiscent of the cackling of the geese on the walls of Rome. Bees have no geopolitical sense, although they exist in the most totalitarian of all animal kingdoms. When the sweetened lupines bloomed, the bees swarmed onto the fields. Unable to distinguish between the bitter wild plant and the sweet cultivated variety, the bees carried pollen from one plant to the other. The pure sweetened lupines and the wild bitter ones were mixed in an interracial orgy. When the beans ripened, they were once more bitter. The coach turned out to be a pumpkin.

Defeated by forces of nature which even the Nazis could not control, the War Ministry redoubled its efforts to develop the potentialities of wood. Germany produced approximately 285,000,000 cubic meters of wood, the waste from which could serve as raw material for wood sugar.

In 1942 the British Broadcasting Company circulated a humorous anecdote. They reported that the German Propaganda Ministry had announced that air blockade of Britain was proving hugely successful: the British people had been reduced to eating garbage. The German spokesman went on to assure the German listeners that they themselves had no cause to fear. I. G. Farben was successfully preparing a substitute for garbage.

This would be truly humorous if it were not so grim, for Germany actually is putting its waste to effective use as food.

Pieszczek visited the Tornesch wood-sugar plant. So impressed was the War Minister that he undertook to use his own influence to obtain government funds for further research. Finally, Pieszczek proposed that the German government monopoly buy 50% of the stock of the Tornesch company. Leading members of the

German General Staff were conducted on tours of Tornesch and were elated at what they saw. It was determined by the War Department that future plants for the production of wood sugar from waste should be built as rapidly as possible.

Meanwhile, the Nazis had come to power, and accelerated the program. The agreement between the Economics Ministry and the Scholler-Tornesch company indicates the value placed on wood sugar:

> The Scholler-Tornesch method is for the Reich, so far as the afore-mentioned wood sugar for fodder will be further developed, in the framework of interest of the Four Year Plan. The projected taking over of the enterprise serves thereby in the foremost line of the "Volk's" interest.

These plants were located in what is known as the "safe area" of Germany between the Elbe and the Oder Rivers. Dr. Keppler, Hitler's own economic adviser, supervised the location of the plants.

The government acquired all rights to the manufacturing of "feeding yeast" from wood waste. It was arranged with the Air Ministry that an airdrome with a complete fighter squadron attached should be built for the exclusive protection of the principal plant at Tornesch.

The possible shortage of protein is the one most dangerous weakness in Germany's entire war economy. The loot of Denmark, Holland, and the Balkans can only postpone the day when Germany will once more be faced with the need of "killing little pigs."

From the long-range point of view, therefore, the strength of blockade by the United Nations may be the stumbling block in German plans.

German airpower could dent the blockade and make the capital ship a hunted thing, but only within the range of land-based planes. There are still vast stretches of the ocean which cannot be commanded from the air. British and American ships still control the sea, and Germany can get nothing from outside. The final test of blockade is yet to come. In the meantime, the vicious circle begins once more to close. Reports have been forthcoming that cattle and hogs have been slaughtered en masse. Veal is a large item of diet in Germany today. This means that meat, milk, and butter will be even more scarce next year. Veal is the meat of young calves. When these are killed, they cannot grow up and reproduce.

Wishful thinkers are inclined to see in these facts the signs of Germany's downfall. If the wood sugar plants were enlarged enough to supply German needs the last thread in the garrote around Germany would snap.

The Germans found in their forests a universal raw material from which an increasing variety of products are made. Fodder, textiles, explosives, lubricants, plastics, and other military essentials all can be cheaply produced. Aircraft made of plywood are lighter and inexpensive, and may someday replace metal planes. In this country, over 74% of our wood is wasted. Germany wastes almost none, even recovering part of the wood normally lost through fire and disease. The trees of the occupied countries are treasure groves which Germany can convert into war matériel.

There is another chapter in this sylvan tale. In the two remaining Axis countries, Italy and Japan, wood sugar plants were built under license and supervision from Germany by 1939. The United Nations as yet have not even tried to undertake comparable development of the wood sugar industry, which might enormously augment their nutritive resources.

22. THE SORCERER'S APPRENTICE

IT would be a tragic blunder for the United Nations to elevate Hitler and the Nazis to the dignity of the principal enemy. Hitler is the embodiment of all that is demonic—all the mephitic mists of the German martial ego assembled in corporal form. That is why it is dangerously easy to mistake the form for the substance —for Hitler is only one incarnation of the ruthless Teutonic vanity that finds release in war. *Germany is still a feudal nation;* Nazism is cameralism rampant.

The warrior caste of Prussian Junkers were not overthrown in Germany by an industrial middle class. The former serfs were drilled into factories, instead of on farms, and the whole industrial plant run, not as competitive enterprise, but as a regiment of cartels. The land-poor Junkers became cartel magnates, and the whole economy a more efficient service of supply.

Nazis were chosen jointly by the generals and industrial barons at a time when the framework of war economy had been completed. The Junkers put Hitler in office when his star was already waning. For the real rulers the Nazis possessed an entirely functional value.

305

The Nazis could unite dissident "splinter" parties by force, and forge into a single sword the energies of the people.

The Junkers saw in Hitler the psychological magnet with which to align the fears, unreasoning resentments, and the need of the German people for a common purpose. Hitler sang in crescendo the monotone of Versailles—that only by force could the scales of justice be balanced.

Hitler focussed the national will while protecting cartel interests. He provided the philosophy and the excuse to set in motion the sleek, streamlined metallic monster so circumspectly contrived. Hitler had the dynamic touch which ignited giant motors. The Rhineland, Austria, and Spain gave the machine its trial run.

The Junkers erred in making Hitler the Fuehrer. Along with his canting theories went his intuition, which they could not control. Hitler became the State, enforcing his nightmare orders with the sadism of the Gestapo. Neither wealth nor station could protect the man who dared to question the Fuehrer's wisdom. The mortality rate of German generals increases with every schism.

Hitler consulted clairvoyance more than maps and graphs. He is the sorcerer's apprentice, wielding the warlock's powers he cannot fathom.* Not able to think

* After this book had been printed in galleys, *The Self-Betrayed, the Glory and Doom of the German Generals,* a brilliant study of German militarists by Curt Riess, was published. In a different context, Mr. Riess employed the figure

with the same icy logic that devised the Master Plan, Hitler wildly careened into war.

Flushed with the initial triumphs of Munich and the fall of France, Hitler's military judgment was to be weighed and found wanting. The attempt to achieve a second Munich failed, for no strategy of terror could conceal the inability of the Wehrmacht to cross the Channel. Hitler had badly underestimated the stoutness of England, and his planes still could not scuttle enough of the Fleet.

Balked at Dunkirk, Hitler could not stop moving. The Panzers and Stukas had to be used while fresh. He had no other choice than to turn to the East. The malignant sequence of error once started, Hitler could not halt the flood of the war he had loosed too soon.

Hitler's intuition reduced the High Command to fearful silence. The Generals had read the thermometer of Russia's preparation, and were not warmed by the thought of a two-front war. Russia, too, was a realist nation, armed and willing to fight. Russia had seized the Baltic States, warred with Finland, met the Reichswehr half-way in Poland, and stirred the Balkan Kettle against Germany.

What was Hitler's excuse? He stated, to quell all doubts, that the German High Command "could no longer vouch" for a "radical conclusion of the war in

of the Sorcerer's Apprentice. The authors willingly concede priority in the use of this symbol to Mr. Riess.

the west, particularly as regards aircraft." According
to this convenient theory, however true it was, the presence of Russian armies on German borders kept too
many planes in the east. Actually, Hitler could neither
admit that he had been wrong, nor stay the tempo of
fighting. His intuition again was called forth to justify
the deed.

Such miscalculations have a cumulating effect. The
attack on Moscow was prolonged until the last moment,
to bolster German morale. Whether the political victory achieved by encouraging Japan to assault the
United States was worth the military cost, only time can
tell. The immediate results were disastrous to the striking efficiency of the German army.

Mistakes of our enemy are mortal only if we exploit
them. As 1942 drew to a close Germany had not won its
Lightning War. The bravery and skill of the R.A.F.
and the "red badge of courage" which Russia wore bore
witness that the first phase of the Master Plan had
failed.

The flaws were not all in the plan itself, but in the
instant of their execution. All of that terrible energy
assembled in German technology had not grown to its
fullest stature.

The gap of technology narrowed; the Global War
had become a massive trial of endurance. The inexorable
force of attrition began to take its toll. As American
troops swarmed into Africa, and the Russian Winter

froze the Wehrmacht in the East, Germany was once more faced, as in 1918, with the fearful quadrennial of War—that "fourth year" which every German general viewed aghast, and which brought back nightmare memories to the German people.

The war is not yet over, and the point must be driven home. Germany perceives the meaning of the race that is being run. Neither bombings nor the demands of the Russian front stayed the German retooling of the aircraft industry. The Focke-Wulfs and sub-stratosphere bombers which make their appearance over the Channel and Iceland are forerunners of what is to come.

Lightning War may return, and in this consideration lies both the hope and the peril of the United Nations. As the quality of technology changes, the contest is transferred to another plane. The sprawling mills and factories and the volume of their output can be pinioned like clumsy giants by a single flash of genius.

Since the beginning of "civilized" warfare, military philosophers have sought a key to enduring world-rule. Usually some spot on the map has been chosen as the control-point from which the rest of the world might be held. In turn, Egypt, Gibraltar, Alaska, and the so-called Heartland of European Russia and Turkey have been selected by those who ponder the question of world empire. But the cult of Mackinder and Haushofer is rendered meaningless by the contemplation of the power of technology. The continents, mountains, and seas have military value only so long as invention does not shrink their importance and make all lands equally accessible.

Against a foe so resourceful—such a master of science and war—the United Nations can ill afford to falter. Airpower is only one instrument—the next one may be a ray which grounds all planes or directs a lethal beam along an electrical path. It may be an old lance resharpened—I.G. can still make gas.

In the rules of war the only bar to the use of any destructive weapon is the threat of retaliation. This diminishes as technological disparity becomes greater, and the ability to strike back is lessened.

Or, as the rope grows tighter around the belly of our adversary, it will approach the desperation of a starving man. What is there to stop Germany from the use of bacteria?

23. REVEILLE

GERMANY lost the World War, but I.G. gained the peace. Stronger in 1919 than five years before, I.G. and its cartel-brethren in German industry took back control of crucial fields despite all the laws enacted here to prevent their doing so. The Versailles Treaty stripped Germany of its foreign possessions, but the cartels acquired more colonies than the Empire contained at its height. These conquests were made by contracts, which allowed German firms to "divide and rule" world markets.

Territorial control, however, was only the means to military ends. Given freedom from our competition, the German cartels engaged in calculated over-production, thereby sustaining their capacities in peace at war-time levels. By the very same agreements which gave the Germans markets, democratic cartellists were bound to restrict production. To Germany, cartel understandings were stimulants; to her enemies, they were opiates, lulling them into false delusions of peace and prosperity.

The consequences of the next peace are now in the blueprint stage. In all the United Nations post-war reconstruction programs are being drawn. They are based

311

on the noble precepts of freedom and abundance. For these we are fighting.

The post-war planners should view with alarm and perceive with understanding the reconstruction plans of German industry. Hitler will pass in time, more rapidly if the war is lost. But win, lose, or draw, the Junker-cartels are prepared. Before Hitler was ever thought of, cartel agreements provided for the coming war.

The sum of the evidence could be documented at length. Consider some excellent examples; the Bausch & Lomb-Carl Zeiss agreement:

> . . . *if, by reason of unforeseen political events,* the execution of this contract shall be made impossible, temporarily or permanently, or the firm of Carl Zeiss limited in the enjoyment of its full license claim, this agreement shall be suspended for that time, and upon an appeal, the board of arbitrators shall make such dispositions as seem necessary in order to carry out the will of the parties to this agreement under the changed conditions, if possible.[1]

and the Standard Oil-I. G. Farben agreement:

> . . . it is our understanding . . . that each party proposes to hold itself willing to take care of any future eventualities in a spirit of mutual helpfulness, particularly along the following lines:
>
> In the event of the performance of these agreements . . . by either party should be hereafter restrained or prevented by operation of any existing or future law, or the beneficial interest of either party

be alienated to substantial degree by operation of law or governmental authority, the parties should enter into new negotiations in the spirit of the present agreements and endeavor to adapt their relations to the changed conditions which have so arisen.

*   *   *

Both parties agree that in the event of an attack by a third party brought against either of them directly or indirectly, in attempted derogation of the title to patent rights transferred hereunder, they will cooperate loyally in defense of such attack.[2]

One ruse of the Germans has confused our legal minds. Both before and after conquests, the Germans have observed the form of lawful "purchase" of resources, plants, and property. The architects of the master plan are objective realists, and do not preclude the possibility of defeat or negotiated peace. Dr. Egon Glesinger, a shrewd observer of German plans for conquest, says of the designers, "They assume . . . that while the law-abiding democracies will be sticklers for the return of confiscated property, purchases made in outward legality will be blessed." Here is the reason that the forests, mines, factories, patents, and processes have been "bought" by Germans from their owners in conquered countries, when they could have been taken without ado.

The economic feudalists in the United States, Great Britain, and the other United Nations know that tech-

nology goes on, war or no war, but they can view this
truth only from the perspective of their own invest-
ments. Democratic industrialists are not traitors. They
will fight for their country, or send their sons to die.
But by identifying their loyalty to stockholders with
their duty to the nation, they fail to see the difference
between public interest and private trust. This cartel
attitude is propounded by the frank and brilliant expression of a representative of the world's largest combine:

> Upon completion of that agreement, the war inter-
> vened because our grouping of interested parties in-
> cluded Americans, British, Dutch, Germans, and the
> war introduced quite a number of complications. *How
> we are going to make these belligerent parties lie
> down in the same bed isn't quite clear as yet.* We are
> now addressing ourselves to that phase of the prob-
> lem and I hope we will find some solution. *Technol-
> ogy has to carry on—war or no war—*so we must find
> some solution to these last problems. [Italics added] [3]

The enormous expansion of productive facilities in
the steel, aluminum, magnesium, plastics, synthetic rubber, and chemical industries in Germany will be a threat
to the cartel-minded producers in this country, whether
Germany wins or goes down to military defeat. In the
United States, the imperious necessity of war has forced
a parallel increase in our productive facilities. The fear
of post-war over-production has had a stifling effect on

our own war output. Industrial courage must take the place of fear.

When the war is over, the pressure of national interest will relax. Vigilance will cease. Will new cartels flourish and old ones revive?

The fear of German technology should be met not by agreements to halt or regulate progress; such agreements restrict only ourselves. Germany knows the value of an unimpeded technology. *Twice* we should have learned in Ordeal by Battle. Will the second lesson prove as futile as the first? Technology is the final judge of history.

America need not stand in awe of Teutonic science. It was we who invented the airplane and submarine, which our enemies have merely copied and improved. Mass production systems and most modern arms are results of American invention. With our resources and ingenuity there are few accomplishments of Germany which we cannot entirely dwarf. To release the vitality inherent in democracy and its free institutions we must cast off the industrial lethargy caused by monopolies which enervate our production.

The principles of democracy are its strength. Desertion from these principles are its danger. People dedicated to peace and freedom must be strong. To be strong they must have access to technology; to have access to technology they must be free. We want no private planners nor do we need a paternal bureaucracy. The weakness of democracy lies not in its lack of planning, but in its tolerance of industrial oligarchy, the economic twin of Fascism.

The battles of rubber, quinine, magnesium, aluminum, and all the others must not have been fought in vain. The resurgence of German power must be the book of revelation from which we draw the text of our future national policy. The violence of war is ephemeral; the conditions of war endure. Peace gestates the elements of strife. "Disastrous wars are the failures of peace."

BIBLIOGRAPHY

Arnold, Lieut. Gen. H. H., and Maj. Gen. Ira C. Eaker, *Winged Warfare.* Harper & Bros., 1941.

Artucio, H. F., *The Nazi Underground in South America.* Farrar and Rinehart, 1942.

Beals, Carleton, *The Coming Struggle for Latin America.* Lippincott, 1938.

Bliven, Bruce, *The Men Who Make the Future.* Duell, Sloan and Pearce, 1942.

British Air Ministry, *The Battle of Britain.* Garden City Publishing Co., 1940.

Bruck, Dr. Werner F., *Social and Economic History of Germany 1888-1938.* Oxford Univ. Press, 1938.

Burlingame, R., *The March of the Iron Men.* Scribner's, 1938.

Churchill, Rt. Hon. Winston S., *The World Crisis.* Scribner's, 1931.

Churchill, Rt. Hon. Winston S., *While England Slept.* Putnam, 1937.

Crowther, Samuel, *America Self-Contained.* Doubleday, Doran, 1933.

Davis, Watson, *The Advance of Science.* Doubleday, Doran, 1934.

Dupuy, R. E., and G. F. Eliot, *If War Comes.* Macmillan, 1937.

Emeny, Brooks, *The Strategy of Raw Materials.* Macmillan, 1937.

Englebrecht, H. C., *Johann Gottlieb Fichte.* Columbia University Press, 1933.

Englebrecht, H. C., *One Hell of a Business.* McBride, 1934.

Englebrecht, H. C., *Revolt Against War.* Dodd, Mead & Co., N. Y., 1937.

Englebrecht, H. C., and F. C. Hanighen, *Merchants of Death.* Dodd, Mead & Co., N. Y., 1934.

Farrell, Hugh, *What Price Progress.* Putnam, N. Y., 1926.

Fay, S. B., *The Origins of the World War,* Vols. I & II. Macmillan, 1928.

Flynn, John T., *God's Gold.* Chautauqua, 1932.

Folk, G. E., *Patents and Industrial Progress.* Harper, 1942.

Foster, Dr. Wm., *The Romance of Chemistry.* Century Co., 1927.

Gilfillan, S. C., *The Sociology of Invention.* Follet Publishing Co., 1935.

Hale, Dr. Harrison, *American Chemistry.* D. Van Nostrand, N. Y., 1928.

Hale, W., *The Farm Chemurgic.* Stratford, 1934.

Hamilton, W. H., *The Pattern of Competition.* Columbia University Press, 1940.

Hammond, J. W., *Men and Volts,* Lippincott, 1941.

Handbuch der Deutschen Industrie.

Hart, Liddell, *The War in Outline.* Random House, 1936.

Hauser, Henri, *Germany's Commercial Grip on the World.* Scribner's, N. Y., 1918.

Haynes, William, *This Chemical Age*. Knopf, N. Y., 1942.

Haynes, William, *Men, Money and Molecules*. Doubleday, Doran, 1936.

Heiser, Dr. V., *An American Doctor's Odyssey*. Norton, 1936.

Irwin, Will, *The Next War*. Dutton, 1921.

Johnston, S. P., *Horizons Unlimited*. Duell, Sloan and Pearce, 1941.

Kaempffert, W., *Modern Wonder Workers*. Blue Ribbon Books, 1924.

Lea, Homer, *The Day of the Saxons*. Harper, 1912 (1942).

Lea, Homer, *The Valor of Ignorance*. Harper, 1909 (1942).

Liefmann, Dr. R., *Cartels, Concerns, and Trusts*. Dutton, 1932.

MacLiesh, F., and C. Reynolds, *Strategy of the Americas*. Duell, Sloan and Pearce, 1941.

Moody, Blair, *Boom or Bust*, Duell, Sloan and Pearce, 1942.

National Resources Committee, *Technological Trends and National Policy.* U. S. Gov. Printing Office, 1937.

Neumann, Franz L., *Behemoth: The Structure and Practice of National Socialism*. Oxford Univ. Press, 1942.

Noel-Baker, P., *The Private Manufacture of Armaments*. Oxford, 1931.

Olden, Rudolf, *Hitler*. Covici-Friede, 1936.

Report of the U. S. Alien Property Custodian, 1918-1922.

Riess, Curt, *The Self-Betrayed*. Putnam, 1942.

Rickard, T. A., *Man and Metals*, Vols. I & II. Whittlesey House, 1932.

Seldes, George, *Iron, Blood, and Profits*. Harper, N. Y., 1934.

Slosson, E. E., *Creative Chemistry*. Century Co., N. Y.

Spykman, N. J., *America's Strategy in World Politics*. Harcourt, Brace & Co., 1942.

Strausz-Hupé, Robert, *Geopolitics*. G. P. Putnam's Sons, N. Y., 1942.

Taylor, E., *The Strategy of Terror*. Houghton Mifflin, N. Y., 1940.

Vagts, Alfred, *A History of Militarism*. Norton, N. Y., 1937.

Vanderlip, F. A., *What Happened to Europe*. Macmillan, 1919.

Veblen, Thorstein, B., *The Place of Science in Modern Civilization*. Huebsch, 1919.

Veblen, Thorstein, B., *Imperial Germany and the Industrial Revolution*. Huebsch, 1919.

Young, A. Morgan, *Imperial Japan*. 1926-1938, Morrow, 1938.

Ziff, W. B., *The Coming Battle of Germany*. Duell, Sloan and Pearce, 1942.

Zimmerman, E., *World Resources and Industries*. Harper, 1933.

CHAPTER NOTES

CHAPTER 1
1. Arnold, Lieut. Gen. H. H., and Maj. Gen. Ira C. Eaker, *Winged Warfare*. Harper (1941), p. 155.

CHAPTER 2
1. Ziff, W. B., *The Coming Battle of Germany*. Duell, Sloan and Pearce (1942), p. 90.

CHAPTER 3
1. Pellew, C. E., *Dyes and Dyeing*. McBride, Nast & Co. (1918), pp. 260 ff.
2. Ibid., p. 261-2.
3. Hearings, Temporary National Economic Committee, 75th Cong. (hereinafter "T.N.E.C. Hearings"), Vol. II, p. 1023.
4. Ibid., p. 1023.
5. Ibid., p. 1024.
6. Lefebure, V., *The Riddle of the Rhine*. Chemical Foundation (1923), p. 35.
7. Ibid., p. 147.
8. Ibid., p. 188.
9. Ibid., p. 206.
10. Report of the British Chemical Mission, March 1920, p. 24.
11. Lefebure, op. cit., p. 208.
12. Hearings, Special Committee Investigating the Munitions Industry, U. S. Senate, 73rd Cong. Report #944 (hereinafter "Munitions Hearings"), Part 3, p. 270.
13. Bruck, W. F., *Social and Economic History of Germany, 1888-1938*. Oxford University Press (1938), pp. 189-190.
14. Literary Digest, December 2, 1922, p. 27.

CHAPTER 4
1. Bruck, op. cit., p. xv.
2. Ibid., p. 39.
3. Ibid., p. 41.
4. Ibid., p. 144.
5. Ibid., p. 162.
6. Neumann, F., *Behemoth: The Structure and Practice of National Socialism*. Oxford University Press (1942), p. 14.

7. Munitions Hearings, Final Report, p. 247.
8. Ibid., p. 250.
9. Ibid., p. 231.
10. Strausz-Hupé, R., *Geopolitics*. Putnam (1942), p. 93.
11. Munitions Hearings, Part 12, pp. 2723-2724.
12. Englebrecht, H. C., and F. C. Hanighen, *Merchants of Death*. Dodd, Mead & Co. (1934), p. 241-2.
13. Munitions Hearings, Part 12, p. 2783.
14. Lea, Homer, *The Day of the Saxons*. Harper (1942), p. 134.

CHAPTER 5

1. Hearings, Sub-committee of Committee on Judiciary, U. S. Senate, S. R. 77, March 1922, p. 255, 262 (hereinafter Hearings, SR77).
2. Seward, A. C., *Science and the Nation*. Cambridge University Press (1917), p. 18.
3. Hearings, SR77, March 1922, p. 224.
4. Ibid., p. 226.
5. Ibid., p. 226.
6. Ibid., p. 223.

CHAPTER 6

1. Munitions Hearings, Report No. 944, Part 3, p. 21.
2. Stevens, W., Quarterly Journal of Economics, *The Powder Trust* (1912), pp. 444-481.

CHAPTER 7

1. Hearings before the Committee on Patents, U. S. Senate, 77th Cong. 2nd Session, on S-2303 and S-2491 (hereinafter referred to as Bone Committee). Part 5, p. 2071 (1942).
2. Ibid., p. 2072.
3. Ibid., p. 2074.
4. Ibid., p. 2102.
5. Ibid., p. 2089.
6. Ibid., p. 2090.
7. Testimony of Assistant Attorney General Thurman Arnold before the U. S. Senate Special Committee Investigating the National Defense Program (1942). Part 11, p. 4819.
8. Bone Committee, Part 5, p. 2118.
9. Ibid.

CHAPTER 8

1. Bone Committee, Part 2, p. 671.
2. Ibid., p. 672.
3. Ibid., p. 685.
4. Ibid., p. 686.

CHAPTER NOTES   321

5. Ibid., p. 689.
6. Ibid., p. 689.
7. Ibid., p. 690.
8. Ibid., p. 691.
9. Ibid., p. 691.
10. Ibid., p. 838.
11. Ibid., p. 876.
12. Ibid., p. 877.

CHAPTER 9

1. *U. S.* v. *Alba Pharmaceutical Company, Inc., et al.* Information filed
September 5, 1941.
2. Ibid.
3. Ibid.
4. *U. S.* v. *Schering Corporation, et al.* Information filed Dec. 17, 1941.

CHAPTER 10

1. Arnold, Lieut. Gen. H. H., and Maj. Gen. Ira C. Eaker, op. cit., p. 155.

CHAPTER 12

1. Heiser, Dr. Victor, *An American Doctor's Odyssey.* Norton (1936), p.
440.

CHAPTER 13

1. Munitions Hearings, Part 12, p. 2884.
2. Liefmann, R., *Cartels, Concerns and Trusts.* Dutton (1933), p. 5 et seq.
3. Hearings, Special Committee Investigating the National Defense Program, U. S. Senate, 77th Cong. 2nd Sess. 1942 (hereinafter referred to as
Truman Committee), Part 11, p. 4312.
4. Ibid., Part 11, p. 4561 et seq. (exhibits 360-364A).
5. Churchill, Rt. Hon. Winston, *The World Crisis.* Scribner's (1931), p. 77.

CHAPTER 14

1. Truman Committee, Part 11, p. 4313.
2. Ibid., p. 4313.
3. Ibid., p. 4313.
4. Ibid., p. 4814.
5. Ibid., p. 4314.
6. Ibid., p. 4314.
7. Ibid., p. 4311.
8. Ibid., p. 4315.
9. Ibid., p. 4315-6.

CHAPTER 15

1. The documentary evidence on which this chapter is based is to be found
in the briefs, record, and exhibits of *U. S.* v. *Aluminum Company of America
et al.,* in the District Court of the United States for the Southern District of
New York. filed 1938.

2. Ibid., 1931, 1932, 1933.

3. Minerals Year Books for 1938, 1939, 1940, 1941; Dept of Interior.

CHAPTER 16

1. Bone Committee, Part 2, p. 961.

2. Ibid., p. 963.

3. Ibid., p. 975.

4. Ibid., p. 975-6.

5. Ibid., p. 1112.

6. Minerals Year Book for 1941; Dept. of Interior.

CHAPTER 17

1. T.N.E.C. Hearings, Vol. 5, p. 2039.

2. MacLiesh, Fleming, and Cushman Reynolds, *Strategy of the Americas.* Duell, Sloan and Pearce (1941), p. 28-9.

3. T.N.E.C. Hearings, Vol. 5, p. 2038.

4. Ibid., p. 2278.

5. Ibid., p. 2042-2044.

6. Ibid., p. 2059-2067.

7. Ibid., p. 2070-1.

CHAPTER 18

1. Snowden, N., *Memoirs of a Spy.* Scribner's (1933), p. 249.

2. Munitions Hearings, Vol. 2, p. 542.

3. Ibid., Part 12, p. 2889.

CHAPTER 19

1. Bone Committee, Vol. 1, p. 90.

2. Farrell, Hugh, *What Price Progress.* Putnam's (1926), p. 92.

3. Bone Committee, Vol. 1, p. 261.

4. Ibid., p. 92.

5. *New State Ice Co.* v. *Liebmann,* 285 U. S. 271.

6. Bone Committee, Vol. 1, p. 380.

7. Ibid., p. 92.

8. Ibid., p. 92-93.

9. Ibid., p. 96.

10. Ibid., p. 98.

11. Detroit News, January 1, 1941.

CHAPTER 20

1. Auerbach, F., *The Zeiss Works.* W. & G. Foyle, London (1927), p. 183.

2. *U. S.* v. *Bausch & Lomb Optical Co., et al.* Complaint and consent decree, July 8-9, 1940.

3. Bone Committee, Part 2, p. 643.

4. Ibid., p. 644.

5. Literary Digest, Vol. 122, No. 24, Dec. 12, 1936, pp. 41-2.

6. Arnold, Thurman, *Bottlenecks of Business.* Reynal & Hitchcock (1940), p. 71.

CHAPTER 21

1. Wissen und Wehr Monetschefte, 1932, p. 444.

CHAPTER 23

1. *U. S.* v. *Bausch & Lomb Optical Co., et al.,* op. cit.
2. Truman Committee, Vol. 11, p. 4572.
3. Bone Committee, Vol. 7, p. 3410.

APPENDIX

I. G. Farbenindustrie, A. G.

ON December 9, 1925, the Badische Anilin und Soda-fabrik, Ludwigshafen a. Rhein, the largest of the member firms of the Interessengemeinschaft (Combine of Interests) of the German Dyestuffs industry, changed its own name to I. G. Farbenindustrie Aktiengesellschaft. Five other firms were merged with Badische. These were:

> Farbenfabriken vorm. Friedr. Bayer & Co., Lever-kusen,
> Farbwerke vorm. Meister Lucius & Bruening, Hoechst,
> Aktiengesellschaft für Anilinfabrikaten, Berlin,
> Chemische Fabriken vorm. Weiler-ter Meer, Uer-dingen, and
> Chemische Fabrik Griesheim-Elektron, Frankfurt a.M.

Two further firms which had also belonged to the former Combine of Interests (Trust), namely, Leopold Cassela & Co. G.m.b.H., Frankfurt a.M. and Kalle &

Co., Aktiengesellschaft, Biebrich, were not included in the merger inasmuch as their shares were already held to their greater part by the other I.G. firms. They were, however, included in the organization and further development of the I. G. Farbenindustrie. The names of the merged firms were retained by registering them as branches. All the said enterprises were organized at brief intervals at the beginning of the '60's of the last Century as a consequence of the revolutionizing inventions in the field of coal tar dyes.

In 1904 the first Trust, or I.G., as it was called, was formed by the Bayer Company of Elberfeld, the Badische Company of Ludwigshafen, and the Aktiengesellschaft für Anilinfabrikaten, Berlin. In addition to this I.G., the firms of Hoechst, Cassela, and Kalle entered into a combine which was brought under the financial control of I.G.

The I.G. group has undergone since its formation in 1904 a series of reorganizations. The first of these, in 1916, added to the scope of I.G.'s interests, and integrated its wartime functions. The reorganization in 1919 further augmented the sphere of I.G.'s operations. Early in 1926, after the formal incorporation of I.G., a number of important concerns were added to the eight firms which formed the nucleus for the Trust. These were:

Dynamit-Actien-Gesellschaft vorm. Alfred Nobel & Co., Hamburg;

Rheinisch-Westfaelische Sprengstoff-A. G. Koeln;
Aktiengesellschaft Siegener Dynamitfabrik, Koeln;
Deutsche Celluloidfabrik, Eilenburg; and
A. Riebeck'sche Montanwerke A.-G., Halle.

A list of I.G.'s subsidiaries is not easy to decipher.
Some subsidiaries are wholly owned and controlled.
Some are partially owned or divided between one or
more of the nuclear corporations in I.G. In the case of
some subsidiaries, their corporate identities have been
maintained, while their assets and facilities have been
entirely merged with others. The following list is not
complete. It is based upon the Handbook of German
Industries, upon Moody's, upon the lists given by Dr.
Liefmann in "Cartels, Concerns, and Trusts," on the
Enquete-Ausschuss III on the German chemical industry, upon a booklet entitled "I. G. Farbenindustrie,
A. G." published in German by I.G., and upon annual
reports of I. G. Farbenindustrie.

The components of I. G. Farbenindustrie A. G. and
its principal subsidiaries are:

Badische Anilin und Sodafabrik
Ammoniakwerke Merseburg-Oppau G.m.b.H.
Farbefabriken vorm. Friedr. Bayer und Co.
Farbwerke vorm. Meister Lucius und Bruening
Leopold Cassela und Co.
Chemische Fabrik Griesheim-Elektron
Akt.-Ges. fuer Anilin-fabrikaten
Chemische Fabriken vorm. Weiler-ter-Meer

Kalle und Co.
Koeln-Rottweil A.-G.
Dynamit A.-G. vorm. Nobel
Rheinisch-Westfaelische Sprengstoff A.-G.
Wuelfing, Dahl und Co. A.-G.
Karl Jaeger G.m.b.H.
Oehler
Chemikalien-Werke Griesheim G.m.b.H.
A.-G. fuer Stickstoffduenger Knapsack
Stickstoff-Kredit G.m.b.H.
A.-G. fuer Landeskultur
Koliner Kunstduenger und Chemische Fabrik
Zuckerfabrik Koerbisdorf
Chemische Werke Schuster und Wilhelmy A.-G.
Wolff-Werke Chemische Fabriken
Chemische Werke Lothringen
Delvendahl und Kuentzel G.m.b.H.
Chemische Werke Durand und Huguenin A.-G.
Alexander Wacker A.-G.
Elektrochemische Werke A.-G.
Elektrochemische Werke G.m.b.H.
Aluminium-Werke G.m.b.H.
Elekto-Nitrum A.-G.
Soc. Electroquimica de Flix
Ampère G.m.b.H.
Deutsche Edelsteingesellschaft vorm. Herm. Wild
    A.-G.
Duisburger Kupferhuette A.-G.
Deutsche Molybdaenwerke
Auguste Viktoria mine
Rheinische Stahlwerke
Riebecksche Montanwerke A.-G.

Erdoel- und Kohleverwertungs A.-G.

Bergin Kohle A.-G.

Chemische Fabriken und Asphaltwerke A.-G.

Doerstewitz-Rattmannsdorfer Braunkohlenindustrie A.-G.

Gewerkschaft Elise II

Frechen Lignite Mine

Jacob's Mine at Preussisch-Boernecke

Theodor I and II mines at Bitterfeld

Hermine Mine

Deutsche Grube A.-G. (lignite works)

Marie and Antonie mines

Deutsche Braunkohlengesellschaft A.-G.

Deutsche Gasolin A.-G.

Olea Mineraloelwerke A.-G.

Sueddeutsche Oel und Melanolwerke G.m.b.H.

Ford Motor Co. A.-G. (part)

Metallgesellschaft (part)

Griesheimer Autogen-Verkaufsgesellschaft m.b.H.

Deutsche Oxyhydric A.-G.

Gesellschaft fuer Lindes Eismaschinen A.-G.

Karl Neuhaus G.m.b.H.

Verwollungs A.-G.

Hoelkenseide G.m.b.H.

Textilosewerke und Kunstweberei Claviez A.-G.

Philana A.-G.

China-Export-, Import- und Bank-Compagnie

Chimica, Industrial Bayer and Westkott & Cia.

Teer-farben-Industrie A.-G.

Oestliche Handelsgesellschaft and Bayer Products, Ltd.

Productos Quimicos Meister Lucius Bruening, S.-A.

Kalk- und Emmailierwerke Gebr. Wandesleben, m.g.H.

Heggener Kalkwerke G.m.b.H.

A. H. Rietschel G.m.b.H.

Kremer-Klaergesellschaft m.b.H.

Deutsche Laenderbank A.-G.

Riebecksche Montanwerke

Gustav Genschow & Co. A.-G.

Wachtberg Group of brown coal mines in West Germany

Koerbisdorf sugar factory's brown coal mine

Dr. Albert Wacker G.m.b.H.

Chemische Werke Lothringen G.m.b.H.

Aceta artificial silk factory

Sachtleben A.-G.

Behring-Werke A.-G.

Norsk Hydro Elektrisk Kvaelstof A.-G.

Leuna-Werke Ammoniak-Werk Merseburg

Internationale Gesellschaft für Chemische Unternehmungen

General Aniline & Film Company

Agfa-Ansco Corporation

General Aniline Works

A. G. für Chemische Industrie, Gelsenkirchen-Schalke

Buna-Werke G.m.b.H.

Braunkohle-Benzin, A.-G.

Chemische-Werke Aussig-Falkenau G.m.b.H.

Ch. W. Huls, G.m.b.H

Deutsche Celluloid-Fabrik, A.G.

Hydrierwerke Politz A.G.

Pulverfabrik Skodawerke-Wetzler A.G.

Titangesellschaft m.b.H.
Aziende Colori Nazionali Affini (ACNA), S. A.
Societa Chimica Lombarda A. E. Bianchi

With the same reservation as to completeness, the following list of fields of production of I.G. is given:

Coal tar dyestuffs, including crudes, intermediates, and finished dyes;

Auxiliary products which are used in connection with dyestuffs to obtain desired effects or to improve the dyeing process;

Innumerable organic and inorganic chemicals;

Solvents such as those for paints, lacquers, and varnishes;

Accelerators and anti-oxydents;

Preservatives;

Tanning agents;

Mineral colors;

Synthetic building materials;

Compressed and rare gases;

Light and heavy metals, including aluminum, magnesium, and the rare and precious metals;

Machinery and equipment used in the chemical industry and in other branches of scientific production and research;

Pharmaceutical operations comprised of veritable legions of compounds derived from coal tar, sulphur, and other bases;

Synthetic gems;

Synthetic perfumes;

Insecticides and fungicides;

Photographic products and equipment;

Cell wool;
Rayon;
Celluloid;
Plastics;
Synthetic gasoline;
Synthetic rubber;
Explosives;
Nitrates and fertilizers; and
Vistra (synthetic textiles).

I.G.'s own operating units are situated in the following areas within Germany: Ludwigshafen am Rhein, Oppau, Zweckel, Leuna, Gipswerk Niedersachswerfen, Schkopau, Frankfurt am Main-Hochst, Gersthofen, Frankfurt a-M-Mainkur, Fr. a-M-Griesheim, Offenbach a.M., Bremen, Dortmund, Duisberg, Essen-Steele, Gleuvitz, Heilbrom A-N., Herrenwyk, Karlsruhe, Kassel, Kraftborn b. Breslau, Krefeld, Leipzig, Saarbrucken, Stuttgart, Weidenau, Wuppertal-Elberfeld, Knapsack, Marburg a.d. Lahn, Marbach, Eystrup, Neuhausen (Ost Preuss), Leverkusen, Dormagen, Uerdingen, Wolfen, Bitterfeld, Aken, Stassfurt, Teutschenthal, Dobertiz, Rheinfelden i.B., Berlin-Lichtenburg, Munchen, Bobingen, Premnitz, Rottweil, Weisbaden-Biebrich.

INDEX